WOMEN WORKING THE NAFTA FOOD CHAIN

WOMEN, FOOD & GLOBALIZATION

D0746921

WOMEN'S ISSUES PUBLISHING PROGRAM

WOMEN WORKING THE NAFTA FOOD CHAIN

WOMEN, FOOD & GLOBALIZATION

EDITED BY

Deborah Barndt

SUMACH
PRESS

WOMEN'S ISSUES PUBLISHING PROGRAM

SERIES EDITOR: BETH MCAULEY

NATIONAL LIBRARY OF CANADA CATALOGUING IN PUBLICATION

Women working the NAFTA food chain:
women, food and globalization/edited by Deborah Barndt.

Includes bibliographical references.
ISBN 1-894549-35-X

1. Women in the food industry – North America. 2. Women agricultural
laborers – North America. 3. Foreign trade and employment —
North America. I. Barndt, Deborah.

HD6073.F72N67 2004   331.4'81338197   C2004-900450-6

Edited by Beth McAuley

*Sumach Press acknowledges the support of the
Ontario Arts Council and the Canada Council for the Arts
for our publishing program. We acknowledge the financial support of the
Government of Canada through the Book Publishing Industry Development
Program (BPIDP) for our publishing activities.*

Published by
SUMACH PRESS
*1415 Bathurst Street #202
Toronto, ON, Canada
M5R 3H8*

*sumachpress@on.aibn.com
www.sumachpress.com*

For all women workers in the global food system,
whose labour — at work and at home,
paid and unpaid — feeds us,
and especially for Teresa, Isabel and Wendy,
whose hands and hearts have inspired this book.

CONTENTS

PERHAPS THE WORLD ENDS HERE

Joy Harjo

The world begins at a kitchen table. No matter what,
we must eat to live.

The gifts of earth are brought and prepared, set on the table.
So it has been since creation, and it will go on.

We chase chickens or dogs away from it. Babies teethe at the
corners. They scrape their knees under it.

It is here that children are given instructions on what it means
to be human. We make men at it, we make women.

At this table we gossip, recall enemies and the ghosts of lovers.

Our dreams drink coffee with us as they put their arms around
our children.
They laugh with us at our poor falling-down selves and as we put
ourselves back together once again at this table.

This table has been a house in the rain, an umbrella in the sun.

Wars have begun and ended at this table. It is a place to hide
in the shadow of terror. A place to celebrate the terrible victory.

We have given birth on this table, and have prepared
our parents for burial here.

At this table we sing with joy, with sorrow. We pray of
suffering and remorse. We give thanks.

Perhaps the world will end at the kitchen table, while we are
laughing and crying, eating of the last sweet bite.

IN THE BELLY OF THE BEAST:

A MOVEABLE FEAST

IN THE BELLY OF THE BEAST:

A MOVEABLE FEAST

Deborah Barndt

THIS BOOK IS ABOUT food. But food is not just food, and this book is not just a book. Both are codes for much broader and deeper social processes, both carry stories behind stories. We all connect with food. It is a great catalyst, a starting point for exploring many kinds of issues — from changing agricultural practices to shifting patterns of consumption. Food is the "intimate commodity"[1] that we not only grow, make and buy but also imbibe; it shapes us — physically, personally, culturally.

There is a special connection between women and food: in most cultures, women have played major roles in growing and preparing food. In the continental food system, which is the focus of this book, women are central to its production and consumption — from those who cultivate, pick and pack fresh produce in agribusinesses to those who work in assembly lines processing food into cans and bottles; from the cashiers who scan and weigh, price and package our purchases to the cooks and waitresses in restaurants who chop and cook and serve us meals. The experiences of women in the food system offer a window on the restructuring of work in the new global economy. And it is also women who are leading their communities in creating local alternatives to the increasingly globalized food system.

Food is not only the subject of the essays you read here, it has also been a part of this book's process — what I call a "moveable feast."[2] The table for this feast was set, so to speak, in 1995, when I began a three-year cross-border research project. Called the Tomasita Project, the research traced the journey of a tomato from the Mexican field to a

Canadian fast-food restaurant. The project evolved into several different mediums: a cartoon booklet, a video and two books, of which this is one.[3] I chose the tomato as a code for globalization and as a device for exploring the shifting role of women (as both producers and consumers) in this long and twisting journey, and called her Tomasita. Using a Spanish name and a female character emphasizes the fact that the continental food system similarly exploits Mexicans, women workers and the environment. In other words, the continental food system deepens inequalities between North and South as well as between men and women (with class and race complicating the picture); at the same time, it perpetuates human domination of the environment.

With funding secured,[4] I began to gather collaborators for this book from Canada, Mexico and the US: women academics, activists and popular educators[5] who were concerned with understanding the relationship between women, food, work and globalization. All of the contributors to this book have sat at Tomasita's table and have, in some way or the other, participated in the Tomasita Project. There has been, however, a central contradiction in our process. The key subjects of this cross-border study, women workers in the NAFTA food chain, did not participate in the writing and publishing stages of the project. We remain, for the most part, middle-class (some with working-class roots and links) activists and academics, framing their stories with our own analyses. But these chapters do reflect ongoing collaboration with these women workers and a commitment that their stories be known.

A Feast Over Time and Space

The Tomasita Project has given us opportunities to make bread and break bread together across borders (of class and culture). Those of us who have had the privilege to travel have shared good meals and have enjoyed our "moveable feast," which has nourished the growth of this book. It has been a progressive feast: appetizers in one country, the first course in another, the table becoming fuller and the conversation richer as our project progressed. The working hands in the photograph at the beginning of this introduction represent our connections to one another and to those who have taught us and nourished us: Teresa, a salaried worker for a Mexican agribusiness in Sayula, Jalisco, making tortillas for her extended family working in the tomato fields; Mary Lou, a Canadian contributor, barbecuing salmon at our book retreat; my mother, Laura, teaching me how to make her traditional dinner rolls at her home in Ohio; and Antonieta, a Mexican academic and contributor to this project, making tortillas for the authors at our book retreat. The connections among the project's contributors were shaped and strengthened as the research project itself took shape.

October 1996: After exploratory trips to Mexico, the research team for the Tomasita Project convened for the first time in Toronto, Canada. Economists Antonieta Barrón and Kirsten Appendini came from Mexico to attend a panel at the conference of the Canadian Association for Latin American and Caribbean Studies (CALACS). Following the panel, Ester Reiter, York University sociologist, and Ann Eyerman, Stephanie Conway and Lauren Baker, graduate students and research assistants from the Faculty of Environmental Studies, joined us for our first project meeting. Over a lunch of spinach lasagna and caesar salad, we charted our path into this new kind of collaborative work. At a Thai restaurant over dinner, we had our first meal with Beth McAuley, the editor of this series, and envisioned this collection as a way to integrate our different and unique contributions.

December 1996: Antonieta, Kirsten and I met over *huevos rancheros* at a Mexico City restaurant to exchange notes about fieldwork with Mexican rural labour. Lauren joined me in the state of Jalisco to gather stories of women fieldworkers.

April 1997: Fran Ansley, a law professor and the sole US member of the research team, connected with Antonieta and me at the Latin American Studies Association Congress in Guadalajara, Mexico. Over chicken *enchiladas*, we sketched our respective chapters for this book.

July 1997: A brunch (of fresh salad from our garden) in Toronto brought to the table and to the book project Harriet Friedmann, University of Toronto sociologist, and Debbie Field, executive director of FoodShare. Their decades of experience studying global food regimes and of creating local food alternatives, respectively, complemented and broadened the focus of the project.

August 1997 (and later, August 1998): Mexican team member Antonieta created a new meaning for cross-border research by reversing the usual pattern of Northern researchers going South. Instead, she came North to interview Mexican women migrant workers brought to Ontario every summer to pick our local produce. After speaking together on a panel at the Rural Sociology Association meeting, we organized a pot-luck dinner with our Toronto-based collaborators and welcomed Jan Kainer to the project. A recent PhD graduate of York University, Jan's work on supermarket cashiers informed our own research in this area.

September 1997: A brunch in my garden (with corn and tomatoes, home-grown by housemate Sandy Gillians) welcomed Fran to Toronto and Egla Martinez-Salazar to the team as a graduate research assistant. We visited Mexican women migrant workers on Ontario farms, who invited us for an outdoor feast of *pozole*,[6] a typical Mexican corn-based meal.

December 1997: Funded by the North American Mobility Program for a consortium on Sustainable Community Development and Planning, York University colleagues and I met in Guadalajara, Mexico, with faculty from eight other universities in Canada, the US and Mexico. Ofelia Perez Peña, of the University of Guadalajara, co-ordinated the Mexican end of the exchange. It was over Ofelia's stove, as she taught me how to make *chilaquiles*,[7] that her contribution to this project was born.

During this same visit to Mexico, Antonieta and I made the journey to Miacatlán, in the state of Morelos, to visit Isabel Gomez, one of the migrant farmworkers we had met in Ontario six months earlier. Over dinner in Miacatlán, Isabel shared her life story with us.

March 1998: A six-month collaborative project between the Faculty of Environmental Studies at York University and FoodShare culminated in "Roots and Routes: Nourishing Connections from Land to Table," an Eco Art and Media Festival in Toronto. FoodShare runs the Focus on Food program, which is co-ordinated by contributor Mary Lou Morgan and Zahra Parvinian. As part of the Festival, eight women participants of the program prepared food from their diverse cultures and shared stories in oral and visual form of their own "roots and routes."[8] This process of "telling food and eating stories" deepened our belief in the potential of food to catalyze profound reflection, critical analysis and personal and collective transformation.

Friday noons, 1995–1998: Food is a daily sustenance, and besides these special meals and meetings over the three years of this project, there have been innumerable small gatherings around tables of various sizes and shapes. Sometimes we interviewed supermarket cashiers and fast-food women workers in our own dining rooms or in their lunchrooms. Sometimes there were lunch meetings at my house with graduate research assistants Karen Serwonka, Melissa Tkachyk, Anuja Mendiratta, Deborah Moffett, Emily Levitt, Lauren Baker, Ann Eyerman, Stephanie Conway and Egla Martinez-Salazar. Meeting over meals kept us conscious of the important connections between nourishing our bodies, our minds and our hearts.

A FEAST IN THE COUNTRY

May 1998: All paths led to Kimbercote Farm in northern Ontario, and it was there for three days in May, with the Canadian earth in full rebirth, that we met to put together the pieces of our collective puzzle, to start stirring the big pot. Twelve of the fifteen contributors were able to gather round the large table in the farmhouse, feasting on Mary Lou's Canadian salmon[9] one night and Antonieta's Mexican chicken *mole rojo*[10] the next. The kitchen was a gathering space where thinking, feeling and doing merged; while chopping or steaming, setting the table or washing the dishes, we chewed on ideas, digested each other's stories and deepened our own connections among ourselves.

It was a simple idea, really: a place in the country, three days away from work and family demands, good food and time to savour it, walks along the Bruce Trail, and hours to read, write and talk. We read one another's draft essays and offered collective feedback. It was an intense seminar; the kind we would hope this book might stimulate for its readers. Debbie Field told us about the practice of dipping a wooden spoon in one pot and then another, picking up the flavours from each, while leaving a bit of all the tastes in each pot. This seems to be a good way of thinking about our process and our book; while each chapter maintains its own character, it has been enriched by the content and comments of others. There is a chemistry in cooking, too, a process of mixing that creates something new, that is more than any single ingredient. We hope you can savour this book as a whole as well, and enjoy the juxtaposition and combination of tastes that it offers.

One night by candlelight we shared our own personal food stories, both humorous and painful, but always heart-warming, accentuating both our differences and our commonalities, embodying the strong personal-political connection that food engenders. We also made some collective decisions about the book, brainstorming titles, suggesting distribution networks, and agreeing to donate all royalties to a group of popular health promoters in Sayula, Mexico, who endeavour to improve the working and living conditions of Indigenous migrant women in the tomato fields.

Contributors took home the collective feedback and rewrote their individual chapters, integrating conversations from our book retreat. Harriet Friedmann joined me for another moveable feast in late May, our version of an in-town retreat, café hopping across Toronto over three days (from Kensington Kitchen to Mitzi's, our neighbourhood café) as we discussed the direction of the pieces and the whole. Both Harriet and Egla Martinez-Salazar have served as consulting editors for this book. Harriet has analyzed the politics and policies of food and agriculture from both a global and local perspective. Egla was especially helpful with the editing and development of the three chapters originally written in Spanish. Though I take responsibility for the translations of these pieces into English (those by Barrón, Peña and Villagomez), her deeper understanding of the context and language made feedback to the authors both more relevant and pointed.

Through the various stages of research, writing and rewriting, I have felt the essays here grow in spirit and broaden in analysis. In the endnotes of each chapter you will find the references that authors make to one another's work, reflecting this cross-fertilization. We hope the result is less like a juxtaposition of isolated chapters and more an ongoing dialogue, which has involved the writers in face-to-face discussions and now proposes to engage you, the reader, in a similar process. To emphasize this spirit of dialogue, we scatter throughout the book photographs of our own conversations taken throughout our collective process, our moveable feast. Now it's time for you to put yourself into the picture.

IN THE BELLY OF THE BEAST

It is important to contextualize our moveable feast. A metaphor we have found useful is the biblical reference from the story of Jonah and the whale, "the belly of the beast." It can be used to emphasize both the broader process of globalization, framing the issues discussed here, as well as the particular way that women engage with issues of food and globalization.

The "beast" is really a many-faced monster: it refers, in the broadest sense, to a continually globalizing economy that is built on centuries of colonization, imperialism and western-style development. The food system of the North American continent is one slice of this global economy, and it bears particular contradictions since the United States, the headquarters of most "global" corporations, is in the centre or in the belly of the continent. The book's essays use the latest development in the process of globalization, free trade, as a geopolitical and historical backdrop and, in particular, NAFTA, or the North American Free Trade Agreement. Since its implementation in January of 1994, citizens (or, as the corporations would have it, consumers) in Canada and the US have become much more aware of their Mexican neighbours and vice versa. NAFTA has had multiple ramifications — on land rights, on workers, on the environment — and this book explores some of those.

For all the marginal peoples, including the workers, women and Indigenous peoples who are featured in this book, surviving within the "belly of the beast" also means living within the contradictions of that location. These essays explore what it means to be both victim and agent (and, most often, a complex combination of these) within a global food system, both depending on it and resisting it. While the larger system and process may indeed seem at times overwhelming, we all end up grappling daily with many small beasts that make up the monster: the commodification of food, the distance between production and consumption, the restructuring of work, the alienation of shifting eating practices. These issues are discussed in these chapters, as the authors engage the contradictions of living within a system that has gone awry, while trying to transform it. Understanding how this system came to be and uncovering its many layers is part of a process of moving towards change; exploring alternatives to the global food system or attempting to humanize it also empowers us to act. Critical analysis as well as creative and collective action are outcomes that we hope will result from this book. We hope that the book will connect to people working in communities as well as students exploring these issues. We hope it will feed thought, and that the thought will feed action.

The "belly" referred to in the metaphor is not only the part of our bodies most associated with food, it is also a site of knowledge, resistance and change. As feminist activists and academics, we draw upon the daily visceral experiences of women as producers and consumers of food. What we know about the food system and its impact on us, we know in our guts. Our bellies are sources of knowledge that are both physical and emotional. Feminist and pedagogical theories have been developing around notions of "embodied knowing," reclaiming the body and its intuitive knowledge as a powerful source of a deeper and more integrated understanding. Environmental philosophers suggest that the historical schisms between nature and culture, and consequently, the way we have learned to see our bodies and our minds as separate, have contributed to the current environmental crisis. The chapters in this book honour women's knowledge that re-integrates thought and feeling, visceral and rational ways of knowing. They ground abstract notions of globalization in the belly, and offer more wholistic analyses of both the roots of the problems of the global food system and the creative responses of communities to these problems.

WORKING THE NAFTA FOOD CHAIN

NAFTA is the particular geopolitical context for the essays in this book, representing an ever-deepening hemispheric economic integration. We see NAFTA as an integral part of the global processes shaping the food system and, often, threatening human and environmental health, the livelihood and dignity of workers, and the diversity and sustainability of communities. Women workers in Mexico, the US and Canada are linked by this NAFTA food chain — whether they work at the production- or consumption-end. Their increasing role, for example, as the majority of flexible part-time labour in agribusiness, food processing, supermarkets and restaurants binds them to this chain and to the new definitions of work reflected in its links and their interconnections. In their efforts to survive, women workers learn to "work the chain," both adapting to as well as finding ways to resist its more oppressive dimensions.

The chain is, in fact, an ambiguous metaphor: it can be associated with exploitation (as in the "chain gang"), but it can also be associated with the linking of people with common interests and experiences. In that sense, women working the NAFTA food chain are connected and can connect — across borders and companies, across age, race and class — to share their stories and to organize for better working conditions. While global links have often been motivated by corporate interests, workers, academics and activists are also connecting through this very chain to challenge those interests. The chapters in this book thus explore the nuances and the multiple meanings of this chain.

The first section, *The Bigger Picture: Gender and Global Restructuring*, provides the historical, structural and analytical groundwork. In the opening chapter, Harriet Friedmann brings her work of over two decades to "Remaking 'Traditions': How We Eat, What We Eat and the Changing Political Economy of Food." She offers us a map into the territory by tracing the effects colonial processes, trade agreements and government (particularly US) policies have had on the movement of food and the structuring (and restructuring) of "traditions" around production and consumption. Harriet also takes us to the roots of the family wage system and the shaping of gender inequities in both workplaces and homes in North America and Europe. And finally, she opens the door to the many ways communities across the hemisphere are challenging these inequities. Her essay offers the historical and global backdrop for the other chapters.

In chapter 2, "Whose 'Choice'? 'Flexible' Women Workers in the Tomato Food Chain," I compare how corporate strategies of "flexibilization" — an aspect of the more recent global restructuring of the economy and work — affect the daily lives of women, both as consumers and as producers in four different sectors of the food system, from Mexican agribusiness to the Canadian fast-food restaurant. In chapter 3, "Serving the McCustomer: Fast Food Is Not About Food," Ester Reiter shows how multinational corporations such as McDonald's have turned citizens into customers, part of a deeper social process eroding both the public sphere and democracy. McDonald's serves as the model for employment based on part-time work, low wages, company loyalty and individualized, unorganized labour. This first section, then, weaves several strands into the chain: an overview of historical and contemporary food regimes, a critique of agricultural production and consumption in Mexico and Canada, and women's particular and shifting roles in the continental food system.

The main body of the book, *Women Workers in the Food System: Stories from Mexico to Canada*, offers case studies of women workers in the field and in the expanding service sector. In these chapters, the authors reveal deteriorating working conditions and the workers' organized struggles to improve them. In chapter 4, "The 'Poisoning' of Indigenous Migrant Women Workers and Children: From Deadly Colonialism to Toxic Globalization," Egla Martinez-Salazar reminds us that the most marginalized workers in this system are not only women, they are also Indigenous workers. Offering a historical analysis (originating in colonialism) of the racial, class-based and gendered nature of agricultural migrant labour, she shows how Indigenous women workers continue to take the greatest risks on the front line in agribusinesses that use highly toxic agrochemicals without providing adequate protection or information. This physical exploitation is only one aspect of Indigenous women's multiple oppression, which is deeply rooted and systemic.

Migrant labour is also the focus of chapter 5, "Mexican Women on the Move: Migrant Workers in Mexico and Canada." Antonieta Barrón analyzes original data on the shifting composition of the labour force in Mexican agribusinesses since NAFTA, particularly in the more internationally competitive fruit and vegetable industry. She also offers a unique perspective on a little-known story of Mexican migrant labour brought annually to Ontario to harvest local produce and compares the working and living conditions of Mexican women workers in both contexts.

Chapter 6 focuses on another process in the NAFTA food system — the packing of fresh produce. In "'From Where Have All the Flowers Come?' Women Workers in Mexico's Non-Traditional Markets," Kirsten Appendini analyzes the introduction of new work practices and the impact of neoliberal policies on the lives of women working in non-traditional markets, burgeoning with Northern consumer demand. We learn through the lives of three women, packers in the flower, avocado and mango industries, how restructured workplaces are built on entrenched gender ideologies.

The only reflection on how global restructuring has affected US workers in this food chain is provided in chapter 7. Fran Ansley, in "Putting the Pieces Together: Tennessee Women Find the Global Economy in Their Own Backyards," exposes the struggles of Appalachian workers who have also suffered with NAFTA, as US plants have moved South to take advantage of the cheaper labour in Mexico. Through a case study of an unemployed woman forced to enter the poultry business to survive, Fran unveils the complexities and interconnections of the changes as they affect daily lives in the North as well as in the South. Her chapter challenges any simplistic analyses that fail to take into account the multiple and contradictory ways that global processes impede upon local survival strategies. In chapter 8, "Serving Up Service: Fast-Food and Office Women Workers Doing It with A Smile," Ann Eyerman examines the way that global restructuring and corporate flexible labour strategies are affecting women workers in Canada, revealing the similarities between the shifting conditions of fast-food workers and office workers. Ann's oral histories of these women, informed by her own years of office work experience, bring their stories to life as they describe how the ideology behind McJobs affects their daily work practices and their very sense of self.

How women workers respond to the changing definition of work and deteriorating working conditions is critical. One of the consequences of free trade and accompanying neoliberal policies is the erosion of unionization, as part-time work, for example, makes it harder to organize the workforce to act collectively. In most of the food system, in fact, workers are not unionized. The focus of chapter 9, "Not Quite What They Bargained For: Female Labour in Canadian Supermarkets," considers the gendered nature of supermarket work and the deterioration of wages and working conditions of women workers. Jan Kainer reveals that in fighting corporate strategies, such as lean production, wage tiers and employee buyouts, historically rooted gender ideologies are often reinforced, sometimes even by union bargaining units.

Unveiling the NAFTA food chain and uncovering the stories of women workers within it can be quite sobering. As indicated earlier, we did not want to limit our analysis to how things are within those increasingly corporate spaces. Our intention is to encourage both critical thinking and creative acting; that is, to integrate tales of resistance into these stories. The third section of the book, *Signs of Hope: Women Creating Food Alternatives*, offers a sense of possibility through examples of local communities, in Mexico and in Canada, where women are involved in creating local alternatives to the global food system, of which the NAFTA food chain is a part. All of the authors of these essays bring years of experience in community-based work, and so they offer us a hope that is grounded in the reality of daily struggle, of people on the front line doing it, not just talking about it. Debbie Field starts off this section with chapter 10, "Putting Food First: Women's Role in Creating a Grassroots System outside the Marketplace." Debbie offers a daring and positive proposal for a cross-sectoral alliance to fight for policies that would assure wholesale healthy food for everyone.

Chapter 11 takes us to the Mexican context. In "Grassroots Responses to Globalization: Mexican Rural and Urban Women's Collective Alternatives," Maria Dolores Villagomez offers two examples of how Mexican women are resisting and recreating the food system. We learn of peasant women organizing their own savings club while urban women set up community kitchens for collective buying, cooking and eating. Similar projects in Canada are the subject of chapter 12, Deborah Moffett and Mary Lou Morgan's "Women as Organizers: Building Confidence and Community through Food." Moffett and Morgan focus on two Toronto-based projects they've participated in — the Good Food Box (neighbourhood-based distribution of fresh produce) and the Focus on Food training program, which engaged immigrant women in telling their own food stories. They reflect on these experiences in terms of their potential for empowering women, both personally and collectively.

An ecological perspective is offered by Ofelia Perez Peña in chapter 13, "A Day in the Life of Maria: Women, Food, Ecology and the Will to Live." Through the story of Maria, a Mexican rural widow, Ofelia suggests that peasant communities have rich ecological knowledge and more sustainable practices to draw upon as they confront the current changes in their lives. The closing chapter by Lauren Baker, "A Different Tomato: Creating Vernacular Foodscapes," provides a synthesis of the tensions running through the book. As a key researcher in the Tomasita

Project, and now a founder and manager of community-based food alternatives, Lauren juxtaposes the stories of two different tomatoes: the commodified and imported fruit compared with the diverse varieties she grows on a rooftop garden in downtown Toronto. She embodies the critical understanding of the global system and the creative initiative of women in communities everywhere in the tale of these two tomatoes.

CONNECTING ACROSS BOUNDARIES

Both the content of the last section and the process of putting the book together represent another side of the globalization picture, the "other globalization." Sometimes called "globalization from below," it refers to a process of connecting across boundaries that is not limited to corporate strategies, but rather is a part of a globalizing of social movements. This book project itself is an attempt to work in more collaborative ways — between women academics and activists in Mexico, the US and Canada. NAFTA became both an excuse and a challenge for us to carve out new ways of working together; that is, just as we question how NAFTA's neoliberal policies affect women's daily lives, we also strive to create more equitable societies and practices.

In our work together, we have crossed geographic and geopolitical borders as well as challenged boundaries between academics and activists. While some of the contributors to this volume might identify themselves more as academics and others more as activists, we all share a common commitment to critical analysis and to social movement-building. The interchange among us, sometimes reflecting the tensions of our different locations, is an important part of building a movement that honours diversity, reflection and action. The chapters that describe community-based alternatives help ground those pieces that offer a more macro-structural analysis, while our experiences of writing and sharing our pieces helped deepen the reflection and analysis of activists as well as academics. The processes that led to this volume also have helped build bridges between the university and the community. In the Tomasita Project, students from York University's Faculty of Environmental Studies became involved with community-based programs such as FoodShare, modelling an approach to learning and acting that enriches both sides. In yet another sense, we challenged the boundaries between teachers and students sometimes rigidly defined in academic contexts. The "students" involved in this project have also been "teachers" to those of us working as professors, and so they have helped counter hierarchies of knowledge and power and have contributed substantially to an alternative and collective learning process.

Other boundaries we confronted were the differences among us based on class, race, age and occupation. We must acknowledge a certain lack of diversity, which reflects and reinforces inequalities. While some pieces speak to Native women's experiences, for example, none of us is Aboriginal, except Joy Harjo, whose poem opens the book. The text remains heavily dominated by Canadian experiences. The Mexican pieces represent the beginning of growing relationships that we hope will shape more collaborative work in the future. The challenge of working across languages is a major one. Three of the chapters had to be translated from Spanish, and our conversations mediated by translators (though many contributors are bilingual, and thus are bridge-builders in the linguistic sense as well). The same excuse does not hold, however, for the lack of involvement of women from the US or of US cases. Because the book grew quite directly out of the Tomasita Project, it is shaped by the project's limitations. The initial project focused on production in Mexico and consumption in Canada. Future projects will need to become more trinational.

We also attempted in this process to cross disciplinary boundaries. While we feel that this is essential for moving towards any kind of understanding of women and the food system, it is not always easy for economists to speak with ecologists, for example, or for quantitative researchers to communicate with participatory researchers. At least we shared a feminist perspective on issues, even though we surely ascribe to a diverse range of feminisms, as will be evident in the chapters.

And while we are both educators and activists, none of us is actually a worker in the NAFTA food chain (except as women working in our own kitchens and with alternative food projects); yet, we are bringing to these pages the experiences of women who are. Our deepest gratitude goes to them: the Mexican fieldworkers and packers who welcomed us into their workplaces and homes; the unemployed women struggling to survive in the post-NAFTA US; and, in Canada, office workers, fast-food workers, supermarket cashiers, caterers and gardeners. We hope that we have done justice to their stories and to their cause, which we believe is our cause — and ultimately and intimately related to the future of us all. There is an urgency, we feel, in the issues we are discussing, that has to do with the survival of our bodies and of our souls, indeed of the Earth herself. We believe the challenge of creating alternatives to the current food system requires the imagination, energy and hard work of all of us bringing diverse skills to a common project — to create a world where equitable and sustainable food practices not only fill our bellies but build communities that are healthier, in every sense of the word.

SHARING THE FEAST

The production of this book has involved, then, crossing many kinds of boundaries. And it has been nurtured along the way by our moveable feast. I want to acknowledge the generosity and support of my dear friends, Valerie Miller and Harriet Friedmann, who offered me beautiful and peaceful spaces (in Vermont and Ontario), supportive feedback and great food during the editing of this book. The research has been funded for three years by the Social Science and Humanities Research Council of Canada and has been strengthened by the collaboration of the Mexican Institute for Community Development (IMDEC) in Guadalajara, Mexico, and of FoodShare in Toronto, Canada. The Faculty of Environmental Studies at York University has been a wonderful base for the inter-disciplinary work reflected here. Thanks to Carina Hernandez, who helped prepare the manuscript, and to graduate research assistants Anuja Mendiratta and Melissa Tkachyk, who helped with the glossary. Second Story Press, too, nurtured the vision of this book project from the start. Beth McAuley worked with each of us over recent months to make our discussions clearer and our essays more accessible. Her skillful editing and Liz Martin's artistic design helped turn our dream into reality.

My own family has provided the most constant nourishment for me and for this work. My parents, Laura and Bill Barndt, remain my greatest inspiration as both nurturers (of body, mind and spirit) and activists. And my teenaged son, Joshua, whose health and happiness has been a deep motivation for this project, has tested both food and ideas with me — in the fields, markets and restaurants of Mexico, the US and Canada. While he wonders why it takes so long to unravel this NAFTA food chain, he has become a very articulate critic of the global food system and an advocate of local alternatives. Our conversations continue around the dinner table, as we struggle to maintain and cherish the fading ritual of the family meal, which nurtures bodies, minds and relationships.

And now the feast that is this book moves into your community centres and schools, kitchens and classrooms, challenging the beast while nourishing the belly. Savour it and digest it, question it and engage it ... as you craft your own visions and take your own action ...

Contributors toast the collective book project at our May 1998 retreat.

NOTES

1. Anthony Winson, *The Intimate Commodity: Food and Development of the Agro-Industrial Complex in Canada* (Toronto: Garamond Press, 1993).

2. While Ernest Hemingway wrote a book by the same title, this story is much more a women's version of a "moveable feast."

3. See note 5 for more information about the project's publications and productions.

4. I am deeply grateful to the Social Science and Humanities Research Council for their generous support of the three-year cross-border research project that led to this book. The more direct results of the research of the Tomasita Project will appear in published form in *Tomasita's Trail: Women, Work and the World Through a Tomato* (forthcoming).

5. The popular education centres initially involved in the Tomasita Project included the Mexican Institute for Community Development (IMDEC) in Guadalajara, the Highlander Research and Education Center in Tennessee, and the Doris Marshall Institute for Education and Action (DMI) in Toronto. Since the DMI closed in 1997, FoodShare MetroToronto has been the site for the local, educational and activist aspects of the project. While this book draws more from the research itself, the above centres have been involved in the collaborative production of popular education materials: a cartoon booklet, "Tomasita Tells All: The True Story of the Abused Tomato," co-produced in English and Spanish with the Mexican Institute for Community Development (IMDEC); a video entitled "The Global Food Puzzle," produced in collaboration with FoodShare; and two photo-stories of a Mexican tomato worker and a Canadian supermarket cashier, to be published in *Tomasita's Trail* (see note 4 above). For more information about these materials, contact The Tomasita Project, Faculty of Environmental Studies, York University, 4700 Keele Street, Toronto, Ontario M3J 1P3.

6. Isabel Gomez, a Mexican migrant worker picking tomatoes in southern Ontario, invited us for a *pozole* prepared in this way: Soak 3 pounds (1.4 kg) of corn kernels (large white corn) overnight, then boil them for about thirty minutes with a small amount of limestone powder to soften the skin. Rinse thoroughly, remove the skin, kernel by kernel, then rinse carefully again (to remove limestone residue). Boil in fresh water with a few onions, jalapeño chiles and a potpourri of herbs (cumin, laurel, rosemary and oregano) for another thirty minutes, then add meat (pork and chicken) along with some chicken broth, and cook for another thirty minutes. Garnish with diced onions, oregano and fresh lime juice. Eat with toasted tortillas.

7. Ofelia's recipe for *chilaquiles* is for four people. It uses twelve fried tortillas, three medium-sized tomatoes, an onion, a clove of garlic, oregano, salt and soft white cheese. Break the tortillas into small pieces and fry until golden. Roast the tomatoes so they can be easily peeled; blend them with the garlic and a dash of salt. Bits of chile peppers can also be added for colour. Boil the sauce in a saucepan, add chicken broth. When the sauce is well-seasoned, add the tortilla pieces and continue boiling for a few minutes. Separately, dice the onion, crumble the cheese

into small pieces, and chop oregano and marjoram. Blend this mixture together. Spoon on top of the dish or on each individual serving.

8. See Deborah Barndt and Anuja Mendiratta, "Embracing the Contradictions: Women Resisting/Revisioning the Food System," paper presented at the World Congress of Sociology, Montreal, Quebec, August 1998.

9. Mary Lou Morgan prepared the salmon by cooking it whole and directly on the barbecue (no filet, no foil, no sauce). It was garnished with fresh lemon for those who wanted it and served with wild rice and fresh asparagus. The most important step is finding good fresh salmon. See also Kathryn MacDonald and Mary Lou Morgan, *The Farm and City Cookbook* (Toronto: Second Story Press, 1994).

10. *Mole rojo*, or red mole, is a powdered form of ground chili peppers and chocolate. Antonieta boils chicken (all parts of the chicken, for greater flavour) with onions, garlic and a dash of pepper and salt. She fries the *mole rojo* in vegetable oil, stirring constantly, at low heat for five to ten minutes; then she adds the chicken broth to the pot until the sauce is the desired thickness. The chicken pieces are added to the sauce and cooked for a few more minutes. It is served with rice. We should note that the *mole rojo* tastes better if it has been smuggled in — direct from Mexico!

Part I

THE BIGGER PICTURE:
GENDER AND
GLOBAL RESTRUCTURING

Chapter One

REMAKING "TRADITIONS":

HOW WE EAT, WHAT WE EAT AND THE

CHANGING POLITICAL ECONOMY OF FOOD

Young women sort, select and pack the tomatoes that we eat in winter.

REMAKING "TRADITIONS":

HOW WE EAT, WHAT WE EAT AND THE

CHANGING POLITICAL ECONOMY OF FOOD

Harriet Friedmann

FOOD FLOWS CONSTANTLY through our bodies. It flows steadily, too, through the arteries of highways, railways, waterways and airways. Money flows in a reverse network through the veins of finance. Food, therefore, can reveal changes in the world economy. The most intimate daily practices of people around the world who are unknown to one another are connected — and disconnected — through growing, processing, transporting, selling, buying, cooking and eating food. Many chapters in this book explore the intimacy — and alienation — of working with food and living from food, and many connect the experience with larger social, political and economic processes. In this chapter, I offer an overview of historical changes in the structures and practices that shape our lives as workers, shoppers, preparers and consumers of food. Two key practices and structures now considered to be "traditional," and which I examine in this chapter, are international patterns of food production and trade, and family relations that facilitate acquiring and sharing food.

People use the word "traditional" to name what they are used to. This word allows us to avoid thinking about how, when and why our patterns of work, trade and family life came to be. When we think of something as "traditional," we make it seem natural or divine rather than historical. But everything has origins and causes. In this chapter, I use quotation marks around the word "tradition" because I want to encourage the reader never to use the word again as if she knows what it means. Every "tradition" was once constructed. Today we are experiencing rapid and comprehensive change. If we simply use the word "non-traditional" to name changes, we miss the opportunity to ask questions about the history of "traditions" that are changing. Many practices and relations are being (re)constructed, and they will eventually seem "traditional." That will give us a historical perspective for understanding the present construction of new practices and relations.

Our connections are deepening across the continent and the globe. As we shall see, the most important connections now, supported by new government policies and by international agreements, empower corporations to link workers and consumers in distant places. This chapter identifies changes in international trade and personal life, which are linked to one another, in the hope that we may better choose those practices that suit our needs.

CHANGES IN THE POLITICAL ECONOMY OF FOOD

Changes in many "traditions" of food production and trade are rapidly unfolding in all parts of the world. "Non-traditional" exports have been, or promise to be, intensified through the unfolding of international political and economic events. In 1982, the international debt crisis officially began, and in 1994 the North American Free Trade Agreement came into effect, hard on the heels of the new World Trade Organization (WTO). After many difficult years of negotiations, the WTO replaced the 1947 General Agreement on Tariffs and Trade (GATT). The GATT was one of several sets of international rules that supported national economic development. In that framework, some types of food production were encouraged, such as maize in Zimbabwe, and also some patterns of trade, such as bananas from Honduras. Both now seem "traditional" even though maize and bananas had been introduced to those countries by colonial rulers. What is changing now is the national basis of food consumption and production. That national framework was in its time constructed, too. For that perpsective, we must turn to the history of colonial production and trade.

"TRADITIONS" ROOTED IN THE COLONIAL WORLD ORDER

Let us begin with the local side of the global–local relationship. "Traditional" agricultures and cuisines often refer to two distinct patterns, dating from two earlier periods of colonial integration. One is called peasant. In the 1500s, some ancient peasant societies were transformed and some new ones created. Whether in France, the Punjab, Zaire, Japan or Mexico, peasant societies integrated their farm systems and food cultures[1] and grew their food locally. Even though linked by world markets, they continued the old peasant features. The mix of cultivated and wild ingredients supported a reasonably healthy population, barring any disasters in the local ecosystems. (Overpopulation could culminate in sudden crisis as it put extreme pressure on the ecosystem to produce enough food.) Most of what was grown was eaten locally by people or their dependent animals. Wastes were absorbed locally, usually entering as decayed vegetation or manure to renew the soil. When crises prevented continued evolution of "tradition," communities died out, changed or moved on. If they relocated successfully, they adapted to a new social and ecological environment, creating new "traditions" of farming and cooking. Peasant societies were at the bottom of agrarian hierarchies,[2] which played a role in colonial conquest and changes in production. Local landlords usually demanded extra crops and animals, or special ones, and usually had a separate, elite cuisine. These landlords could be incorporated or replaced by colonial rulers, who often required peasants to produce export crops, sometimes introduced from other parts of the world, such as coffee from North Africa (via the Middle East) produced in Java (Indonesia). By the 1800s, in many parts of the world, this led to specialization in a single crop (called monoculture) that was sent away from the community to the colonial country.

Monocultures were introduced from the outset in the second pattern of "traditional" agriculture — plantations, which were created by colonial rule. Less extreme forms of plantation agriculture used indentured workers or locally hired workers, who also produced their own food in small plots. The most extreme cases were slave plantations, which introduced new plants and people to replace local social and ecological systems. For example, sugar from Asia and people from Africa were put at the service of English, French or Dutch plantation owners, who seized the land from Indigenous peoples. The sugar was sent back to Europe, and luxury goods for the plantation owner and often food for the slaves were imported. This was the beginning of a now familiar state of affairs: what was grown became disconnected from what was eaten, and for the first time in history, money determined what people ate and even if they ate.

This shift, which is now over five hundred years old and which still exists today, finally broke the patterns of diet and cultivation that had been in place in many parts of the world for thousands of years.[3] The production of specialized exports came to be experienced as "traditional." By the 1800s, Ghana specialized in cocoa; Honduras in bananas; Martinique in sugar; Java (Indonesia) in coffee; and Saskatchewan (Canada) in wheat. These export monocultures were the result of colonialism. For example, Ghana, an African colony of Britain, began to specialize in cocoa, a plant native to Central America and which English colonizers introduced. Spanish colonial rulers brought Asian plants to the "new world" — bananas to Central America and Mexico and sugar to Cuba. Coffee, introduced by European merchants and planters to Latin America, originated in Ethiopia. European settlers brought wheat to Canada, a crop long familiar in Europe, but adapted over many centuries from its origins in the region now contained by Iraq and Iran.

These patterns of food production we now call "traditional," then, resulted from massive movements of people, plants and animals, which began in the 1500s with colonization. In the many "new worlds" initiated by these massive colonial movements, foods were exchanged from one country to another and people adapted what they grew and how they prepared it, melding the knowledges of newcomers and native peoples into "creole" farming and food systems. As "traditional" foods began to change, so did diets and cultivation. Mexico contributed tomatoes for sauces and corn for polenta to Italian "traditional" cuisine and farming. Mexico also gave Spanish and Portuguese cuisine capsicum (hot pepper), which Columbus introduced as a replacement for black pepper. It wasn't long before Mexican capsicum reached India via the Portuguese colony of Goa and became a "traditional" spice there. Potatoes, which originated in Peru, became "traditional" (after long resistance) not only to South Asians, but also to Irish and Poles.[4] Mexican corn became the staple of peasant communities in Zambia and other parts of Africa. As African-Caribbeans were freed from generations of slavery, they formed communities of peasant cultivators in the Caribbean and sent the corn back to their home country. Jamaican gardens and prepared dishes came to include mangos, carried by indentured workers from India who replaced freed slaves on sugar plantations.

At the same time, diets in non-producing countries began to depend on foods grown in producing countries and stimulated the growth of export monoculture. Merchants not only carried plants from one place to another to sell for profit, but also encouraged plantation owners to export exotic goods in order to build up trade. Europeans and North Americans, for example, came to consider coffee, tea, chocolate (from cocoa), sugar and bananas "traditional" to their diets. To meet this need, peasant communities over generations built "traditions" around earning money from these monoculture crops.

In this context, Mexico has an unusual history of self-reliant peasant communities, growing and eating native plants, and enduring until the late twentieth century. Spanish America gained independence from Spain between 1810 and 1820. Spanish elites in each new country set themselves up as landlords and governors, building on the estates of forced labour created during colonial rule. But Mexico had another series of revolutions beginning in 1910, parallel to the Russian Revolution. The outcome was to create (or to recreate) legal communal landholdings called *ejidos*. On these lands, peasant cultivation and cuisine, both based on maize, beans and squash, were protected from pressures to grow export crops.

The impetus behind the Mexican revolutions was the redistribution of land and culminated in the organization of large areas of land for collective agriculture in the 1930s. Unlike Soviet collective farms under Stalin, however, the Mexican *ejidos*[5] removed land from the market not to serve the state's central plan but to provide the economic basis for self-governing communities of Indigenous peoples. Plantations, supermarkets and other aspects of a "modern" food system had to operate around the edges of a national agrofood system centred on self-governing Indigenous communities. Over time, however, the population outstripped self-provisioning, and many people, especially men, departed for seasonal migrant labour in other parts of Mexico or the United

States. Eventually women also left the *ejido* to find work in cities, in export processing zones called maquiladores on the US border, or in the US.

UNMAKING AND REMAKING "TRADITION":
THE US AND DEVELOPMENT

The unmaking of "traditions" rooted in the colonial world order began with decolonization in the 1950s and 1960s. Not only food but the whole political and economic system of the world had been dominated by British power during most of the 1800s and even into the early 1900s. But the First and Second World Wars hastened the relative decline of British power and the ascendancy of the United States, Germany, Japan and eventually the Soviet Union. During and after the Second World War, the United States finally took military and political leadership of the world economy and filled the vacuum left by the decline of British power. By the 1950s, however, the Soviet Union emerged as a rival power and the world was reorganized into two massive competing blocs led or dominated by either the US or the Soviet Union — the "superpowers." These superpowers competed for political legitimacy, which came to be understood as which economic system could offer the most rapid development. Since development in practice meant industrialization,[6] peasants and farmers who still produced food for themselves and local markets were pushed from centre stage.

Two American initiatives restructured the world food economy during this period. In its first initiative during the 1930s Depression, the US government established a policy in which it promised to buy wheat from American farmers at a higher than market price, if the price fell below a level set by Congress, to keep farmers from going bankrupt. After the Second World War, American farmers were having a difficult time exporting their wheat because their customers in Europe could not afford to buy it after all the destruction. The government imposed import restrictions to prevent farmers in other countries from selling to the US. The US policy thus separated the American market, where it offered high prices to its own farmers, from the rest of the world.

As a result, the US government wound up with a surplus of wheat, which it couldn't sell at home. If it tried to do so, the "market" price would go ever lower, and the gap between the falling "market" price and the government price would ever widen. The solution was to dispose of it abroad. Of course, markets were limited abroad for three reasons: 1) in Europe and Japan, both devastated by the Second World War, hungry people and their governments lacked dollars to pay for wheat; 2) the two superpowers would not trade with each other; and 3) in countries outside the superpowers most people still lived in agrarian communities, so that in most years they were able to provide themselves with enough food. These countries came to be known as Third World nations (countries not part of the US or Soviet systems), Less Developed Countries (LDCs), or the South (countries not part of the "rich" industrial North, either capitalist or socialist). However, with the development of food aid policies, these independent countries soon became dependent on food imports subsidized by the US.

The second initiative of the US government was as innovative as its farm program — the invention of a particular type of "foreign aid" designed to overcome obstacles to trade. It began in 1948 with the Foreign Assistance Act to Aid European Recovery, also known as the Marshall Plan. Through this scheme, the US would send goods to European countries (and Japan) to help them rebuild their war-torn industries and to make their agriculture more industrial, or "modern." Since the receiving countries had little to trade in return (except for raw materials from "their" colonies), they couldn't earn dollars to pay. Instead the US would accept payment in local currencies. These were called "counterpart funds" and were only good in the countries that issued them, but the US could spend that money on helping refugees, paying for military expenses and the like. Between 1948 and 1951, some US$13.5 billion was distributed through the Marshall Plan, helping to rebuild European economies so that they could export again in return for US imports. It achieved its purpose in restoring trade by rebuilding trading partners' economies.

The law that created aid to Third World countries was modelled on the Marshall Plan, but it did not have the same effects. Public Law (PL) 480, called "Food for Peace," was passed by the US in 1954. Like the Marshall Plan, it was also designed to create markets abroad for US wheat, and was also part of the US competition with the Soviet Union for allies. But unlike the Marshall Plan, it did not end by creating self-sufficient trading partners. Instead, the US chose Third World recipients for a variety of reasons, both humanitarian and strategic. It helped receiving governments, which were able to distribute cheap food, and industries in Third World cities, which were able to pay lower wages than if workers had to buy more expensive food. The US disposed of its surplus wheat abroad, but farm programs kept the supplies and the surpluses growing.

As a result of these foreign aid initiatives, the US outstripped other large export countries and became the dominant "breadbasket" of the world. Because the US dominated world food markets, adopted national protection and subsidized its own food exports, competing export countries such as Canada, Argentina, Australia and Brazil slipped behind. Because the governments of emerging Third World nations wanted to "develop," many accepted American food aid. These subsidized imports, produced by highly mechanized American farmers, often made it impossible for their own farmers to sell similar food products in local markets. Very soon many Third World countries moved from a situation of food self-sufficiency to one of food dependency. Peasants who could no longer farm were encouraged to move to cities where they were available to work for low wages to encourage industrialization. Food aid often kept food prices and wages lower than they would have been otherwise. While farming for local food markets became more and more difficult, export monoculture of sugar, pineapples and the like continued to be encouraged. The pattern of trade changed, then, from the old pattern of foods going to colonial powers from colonies, to a new one of food coming to the former European colonies, now called the Third World, from the hegemonic power (the US).[7] (An important exception was Mexico, where corn produced on *ejido* land was not in competition with US corn or wheat.)

During the period from 1954 to 1973, "Food for Peace" helped the US dominate the world wheat market and helped keep world prices low. The US, at the centre of the network, subsidized its farmers and exports and refused to allow agriculture to be part of international negotiations to reduce tariffs. Other countries adopted similar policies, changing them according to their place in the world economy. The European Community (now the European Union or EU), for example, which integrated agriculture long before its other industrial sectors, greatly subsidized its farmers, as did Japan. By the 1970s, the European Community subsidized exports, too, bringing itself into direct competition with the US.

Third World governments combined the defensive imitation of the European Community and the acceptance of foreign aid to "modernize" peasant farms. Under the rubric of the "Green Revolution," which offered hybrid seeds bred in special international research institutes, farmers were encouraged to switch from mixed farming to monocultures of wheat (Mexico), rice (Philippines, India) and a variety of other staple food crops. The goal was to increase productivity by using machines and especially chemicals (fertilizers and pesticides). When the goal was successful, farmers were able to produce more per unit of land. However, they had to import equipment and chemicals from the US instead of importing grain. The Green Revolution also created greater inequalities among farmers — some farms grew at the expense of others — and it simplified agriculture so that rural communities lost many long-standing sources of food, medicine, fuel and natural fertilizers.[8]

Oddly, since wheat is native to the old world, the international Green Revolution research centre located in Mexico was devoted to wheat. The corn-based food system of Mexico was difficult to "modernize" as long a farmers were protected by the *ejido*. Indeed, the whole Mexican food system moved towards ever greater national self-sufficiency under the direction of its own government policies. The Mexican government offered price supports and marketing assistance to its farmers, much like those of the US, Europe and Japan. This protection allowed a vast network of small *masa* (wet corn flour) and tortilla (corn flatbread) makers to supply consumers even in the largest cities. The Mexican government also owned factories to process and sell basic foods such as sugar and cooking oil. In the final stage of this integration, undertaken in the 1970s, just prior to the debt crisis of 1982, the Mexican government introduced CONASUPO, a system of local shops in areas too poor to support private merchants. It was a food system organized by the government to subsidize, and keep alive, small farmers and low-income consumers.

THE DEBT CRISIS AND GLOBALIZATION

Contradictions in international relations of food began to emerge in the early 1970s. Just as competition between US and European export subsidies was beginning, and as Green Revolution agriculture was reducing demand for imports in some Third World markets, a new factor appeared: economic ties between the US and the Soviet Union, countries which had not traded during the Cold War. The main feature was a mammoth grain deal, which removed so much wheat, corn and soy from world markets that prices tripled between 1972 and 1974. This stimulated what was then called a "food crisis." (When food surpluses returned to the markets in the 1980s, however, the crisis faded from the front pages of the press.) This food crisis coincided with the tripling of oil prices. For Third World nations dependent on importing both oil and grain, these food shortages and escalating prices put greater strain on their economies and made the possibility of borrowing money to feed their countries very attractive. At the same time, oil exporting states, which had little room to invest at home, deposited their increasing profits in the private banks of the West. The private banks, in turn, found it difficult to lend all this extra cash at a time when oil prices put western factories into recession. The banks pressed Third World (as well as socialist) governments to borrow money, without caring how it would be used or how likely it was that the governments would repay the loans. Governing elites of these borrowing nations took the money as a way to avoid dealing with the deeper problems of solving their import dependence. In 1982, less than ten years later, after the food and energy crises, Mexico defaulted on its loan payment and the debt crisis was officially on.

Another key factor came to the fore in the 1980s: the growth of transnational corporations (TNCs), which had grown up within the framework of the national, and international, structure of the food system. They began to push the new US agenda of including agriculture in free trade instead of protecting US farmers and pursued this new agenda in the GATT negotiations of 1986–1993 (often referred to in the press as the Uruguay Round). The agrofood corporations, which were TNCs, promoted an agenda of trade and financial liberalization. After growing for three decades within the elaborate framework of government subsidies, these corporations now found government support for farmers, consumers and national markets to be an obstacle to further profit.[9] Their new project was to dismantle subsidies to farmers and consumers in all countries.[10] Now that farmers and consumers were linked into food markets, the corporations no longer needed the trade subsidies designed to create those markets. TNCs anticipated a world free of national restrictions on their power to relocate production wherever they wished and to reshape consumption, especially of Third World consumers. The new rules were to be made and enforced by *international* institutions.

The leading institution forcing a shift from national to international rule-making was the International Monetary Fund (IMF). The IMF, created in 1944, was not a very powerful institution until the 1980s. Banks and Northern states, which did not want to accept the losses, searched for a way to co-ordinate responses to the impending default of many Third World and socialist governments. They decided to empower the IMF for this purpose. Since the beginning of the debt crisis in 1982, the IMF has gone into one country after another on the verge of default and presented an increasingly standard list of "conditions" the country has to meet if it is to receive more loans or extensions of payment dates. Since the point is to earn foreign currency to pay the debt, one goal is to increase exports, including agricultural exports. Another is to cut subsidies to farmers and consumers, including food, both as a way to reduce government spending (which can go to pay foreign debt) and as a way to force a shift of land and labour from protected food production into export production.

The changes demanded by the IMF are called "conditionalities," and the set of conditionalities imposed by the IMF and its sister organization, the World Bank, are called "structural adjustment programs" (SAPs). They are also often called "austerity measures" because they have such dire effects (believed by the IMF to be short-term) on the majority of poor in these indebted nations.[11]

In order to comply with the IMF's conditionalities or SAP requirements, governments must devalue their currencies, which reduces the spending power of everyone in the country and makes it easier for foreigners to buy up local properties. They must privatize public industries and marketing agencies, which makes it harder for governments to support national farmers. They must reduce or abolish subsidies to consumers and farmers, which drives out local farmers and makes it easier for locals or foreigners to produce agriculture for export. Abolishing subsidies also makes it difficult for people to obtain basic foods that were previously subsidized and often leads to a new form of food riots, which sociologists call "IMF riots."[12] Similar constraints are felt by other countries with budget deficits, such as Canada, mainly through the flight of capital and the fall of the country's currency, or if investors do not approve of government policies. In Northern countries, trade agreements will soon make it difficult to continue with marketing boards and other institutions that have supported farm sectors in wheat, dairy and other foods. Governments will then be forced to encourage exports, including converting local agriculture to grow crops to sell abroad, to earn dollars to repay debt. And so "structural adjustment" and its effects are not limited to the South, but can be seen in the erosion of the public sector in the North, including in agriculture.

Under both NAFTA and World Trade Organization agreements, Canada has begun to convert its supply management structures. The first stage is "tarification" — converting import controls to tariffs. The next is to reduce tariffs in the direction of free trade. As elsewhere, the move to remove national (and provincial) regulations coincides with concentration of production, particularly of animals, into larger and larger units. Farmers are either driven out by giant factories that are able to supply produce on a nearly continental scale or are incorporated into these giant production systems. Both trade rules and corporate concentration, along with shrinking consumer incomes and other factors, have contributed to growing distress among farmers in Canada.

Mexicans suffer in two ways. The abolition of the *ejido*, which came with the implementation of the SAPs and in anticipation of NAFTA, opened peasant farmers to competition from American corn farmers (who had industrialized their production under the protection of US farm subsidies). And the increasing impoverishment of Mexican farmers and workers/consumers makes them accept employment at very low wages in the growing export industries, including industrial export agriculture. Some export agriculture is farmed on areas of land that once grew food for local consumption; some is being farmed on land not previously farmed before, such as the dry northwestern regions of Sonora and Sinaloa.

As the commodification of food is intensified nearly everywhere, more and more people in Mexico and in other countries around the world, many of them from peasant communities, work to produce food that they may not ever eat themselves. Instead, they are supplying world markets and often eat what comes back to them from world markets. For example, tomato workers in Mexico cannot afford to buy the fruit they pick and pack for US and Canadian markets. They cannot produce their own food either. They will use their meagre wages to buy food. As cheaper US corn moves into the Mexican market, they will likely buy it, even though it tastes different and makes a different type of tortilla from what they have eaten in the past. As tastes change, by desire or necessity, corporations target new consumers in the Third World with whatever product they can afford, from cola drinks to hamburgers. Taco Bell has opened branches in Mexico to serve industrial tortillas to Mexicans uprooted from their village and urban networks through which they are made the old way(s). The "non-traditional" export of tomatoes and the "non-traditional" diet of purchased foods are created out of large-scale transformations in the political economy of food. The old links between local agriculture and local cuisines are being replaced by a new dependence on distant buyers and sellers. Abundance comes to mean not what rich people in a local or national culture eat, but what is best for transnational corporations to manufacture and sell.[13] The lives of the workers the TNCs employ and the customers they entice are changed in the most intimate ways.

CHANGES IN INTIMATE RELATIONS
BETWEEN FAMILIES AND FOOD

These profound changes that have taken place in the international political economy of food have affected how people work and how they live their daily lives outside of work. What people do to get food, how they prepare and share food, what food they eat, when and with whom are all influenced by shifts in the food chain. These in turn are intimately connected to the shape of family life. How people work and eat involves gender relations and family relations. Changes in women's and men's roles and in the family are a local counterpart to the global changes in the political economy of food. Of course, family structure is one of the most specific aspects of local cultures. Still, certain ideas of what is "traditional" link many parts of the world, especially in urban areas which now account for the majority of the world's population.

The type of family we name "traditional" in North America and Europe is some variant of the "breadwinner-homemaker" model that emerged in the nineteenth century.[14] Before money came to be the main means of securing food, most people in the western world lived in simple, extended or joint family households dominated by a male "head" or "master." (Many peasant and immigrant communities today still organize family life and subsistence in this way.) The growth of industrial capitalist relations changed this food production — as we have seen — and introduced the practice of using money to buy food. Money entered the household and became central to people's lives. To gain food, one now had to work for wages rather than farm one's own land or trade one's crafts or services for food in the local markets. The workers who spent their wages became consumers, customers of commercial farmers. Commercial farmers, in turn, were part of a new (eventually industrial) system of agriculture, the ones who could survive the competition to sell food for profit.

The need to have money to buy food brought other changes to the family. Family members had to go outside the home to work. In addition, thousands of people had to leave the countryside because they could not continue to have the kinds of families they had had as small farmers or villagers. They fled to cities where new industries were flourishing. In England, during the Industrial Revolution (1700s to 1800s), these new industries hired whomever they could for the lowest possible wages. Industries and other employers (such as those hiring private servants) hired people as individuals (and not family units) to work for long hours at low wages. Employers found they could hire women more cheaply than men, and children more cheaply than women. Child labour was common, as was illness and early death. It was difficult for many people to form families at all in these new urban contexts. Children were born outside of marriage in large numbers and many were abandoned by parents who could not care for them because they were too poor, too overworked or unemployed. With the spread of industrialization to North America, these conditions afflicted working families in the US and Canada, though not to the same degree. Similar conditions accompany displacement from the countryside in Third World countries today, as severe as those of early industrial England.

In the face of such suffering and inability to settle into stable lives and create stable families, working people (largely working men) in England, the US and Canada demanded changes to regulate working hours and wages. Landowning members of Parliament, who understood that capitalism could not continue if it slowly killed off its workers, supported the passage of laws restricting hours of work. The hours of work for men were limited to ten a day, six and a half days a week. Hours as well as types of work were greatly restricted for women and children. These laws drastically reduced the competition for jobs by women and children, and men, therefore, were able to demand higher wages, usually through unions.

The result was the idea of a "family wage," earned by a man and sufficient to support a dependent wife and children. As men formed unions and bargained for higher wages, women were relegated to the home where they performed domestic labour for no pay. Even when women did work for wages, they were much lower. In a situation of social breakdown, then, the family wage allowed the formation of a particular type of family in an economy in which individuals earned not "bread" but the wages to buy it.[15] And it was the breadwinner — usually the male head — who earned the wage.

This breadwinner-homemaker family of the working classes modelled itself after the bourgeois family of the capitalist class, whose traditions differed from those of the aristocracy, or landowners. The bourgeois family created a division between men, who went out to work in the new public sphere, and women, who stayed home in what remained the private sphere. The home was no longer recognized as a workplace but became idealized as a "haven" to which the husband could return. Women were considered too frail for the vicious worlds of commerce and politics (something different from the aristocratic or villager view of women), and they were seen best suited for "motherhood" (also a departure from the aristocratic and village "traditions" of the times). Of course, the bourgeois family was supported by servants, sometimes an army of servants. This part of the family structure could not be modelled by the working classes, who were themselves either servants or factory employees of bourgeois families. But the male (the husband) did go out to work and the woman (the wife) stayed home. In the working-class version, the woman shopped, cooked and cared for children without servants. In some sense, she was the servant, except she was not paid for her domestic work.

In actuality, the family wage never really provided an adequate income to the breadwinner. Only a minority of men actually achieved wages high enough to support their families. Many women had to work for wages even if they were married. A married woman's wages were considered "pin money," something extra to contribute to a family whose main income came from a husband (even if she didn't have one!). Single, separated or widowed women, with or without children, also had to work to support themselves, and always at lower wages than men — usually one-third of a man's wage. Rather than insist that women be paid as much as men, trade unions usually excluded women.[16] Quite apart from the injustice to women, who were forced into various combinations of dependence and poverty, this was a fatal flaw in the family wage system, because women were always potentially available to employers at lower wages.

The family wage was a very partial and unequal "solution" to early capitalist poverty and instability. It was also a trap that set men against women at home and in the labour market. Logically, it would have made sense for men to support equal wages for women; this would have reduced the temptation for employers to hire women more cheaply. Instead, men often found ways to exclude women from unions and collaborated in keeping them out of high-paid jobs. Low pay made it less desirable for women to work for wages and more desirable for them to stay home and care for the family. Women, therefore, became an unpaid support system for employed men — whether they also worked for wages or not. As long as certain industries remained stable enough to support exclusive contracts between unionized men and employers, those men could aspire to, and even achieve, a family wage. The family wage system deepened and spread to many countries, in one way or another, with the spread of industrialization and stayed in place well into the 1960s. It became "traditional."

By the 1950s, the family wage had become the standard in many of the main industries of North America and Europe, such as the automobile and steel industries. By this time there was also a formality about it. Key jobs were negotiated by unions and employers or regulated by minimum wages and other government policies. Different rates still existed for men and women. (This wage gap fuelled a major goal of feminism in the 1970s — pay equity.) The family wage was also based on the existence of a "core" of relatively stable workers. In Canada, the US and Mexico, these workers were native-born males of European descent. Immigrants, Indigenous people and women were largely absent from key industrial sectors. Thus both sexism and racism were structurally entrenched in the work practices and wage systems of this period. In the 1970s, 1980s and 1990s, when employers faced falling profits and became serious about reducing wages, they undercut the family wage system by hiring women or men of colour. They could do this by "restructuring" or relocating their industry.

In the 1970s, work began to be "restructured" in the food sector, and here, too, restructuring exploited the flaw in the family wage system. Women and young people, the marginal labour force, were assumed to work "flexibly" and more cheaply than men. This "flexibilization" changed the nature of work and conditions of employment and shifted gender relations in the workplace and family relations in private life. The hiring of women and young people to work in the fields for export crops and in fast-food outlets (what Deborah Barndt refers to as "maquilization" and "McDonaldization") contributed to undermining the "traditional" family/work nexus. It reversed the process by which the tradition of breadwinner-homemaker family and the family wage were constructed: today, people are once again facing the world as individual competitors for jobs, women can be hired more cheaply than men, and teenagers and even children more cheaply than women. The effect is to undermine unions, reduce men's wages and men's employment, and ultimately undermine everyone's economic well-being.

Food remained at home as part of women's roles in the "traditional" family. Expansion of food industries and especially services, penetrated this non-market domain in two stages. First, two economic growth sectors in the 1950s and 1960s — "durable" goods such as refrigerators and freezers and "durable" food commodities such as frozen ingredients and meals — deepened the market penetration of food practices within the home. The post-war reaffirmation of women's domestic roles included a new definition of housewife as consumer of domestic goods. This saved time for women who, paradoxically, were entering the paid labour force in greater numbers. Second, food services grew in the 1970s and after, both employing women and young people outside the home and offering individually prepared meals to replace home cooking. Cooking for wages instead of at home and buying meals that used to be made at home led to deeper market relations in food. Thus "traditional family values" — symbolized by the family meal — are giving way to individual life trajectories. Family members work long and odd shifts, especially in food retail and services, and buy meals.

Family and trade "traditions" are linked, in both origin and decline. The breadwinner–homemaker family grew up together with the divide between markets that organize production and families that organize consumption. Now they are changing together. This historical view helps us to see through an important illusion, which has run like a thread through both the stories of trade and families. The idea of "development" sounds very positive, but it hides complex changes which have negative features. In practice, "development" means deepening market transactions. From an economic accounting, this always sounds positive: more jobs, more goods, therefore better off.

But consider the situation concretely. If a hamburger is cooked at home, only the ingredients count in economic production. If the person who used to cook it at home now works instead at McDonald's, where it is sold, then both the making and the receiving count as "productive" contributions to the national economy. Yet the same human work is done, and the same number of meals are created.[17] The backward-looking question is, Are the work and the meals more life-enhancing when organized by McDonald's than by unpaid mothers at home? The forward-looking question is, Are the meals more life-enhancing when organized by McDonald's than by other ways of organizing our making and eating of meals?

Considered in this light, it is possible to ask whether making all work and all goods into market transactions is the best way to achieve a better life. The corporations that employ people to create food at all links in the chain from field to table are destroying old "traditions" of trade, work and family structure. Many aspects of these old ways are not to be regretted. Indeed, the creation of low-paid work at long and odd hours in the food sector and the breaking down of nationally organized food sectors were possible because of flaws in the family system, which kept women working for free at home, and in the international system, which kept people poor, especially in Third World countries. Corporations understandably seized opportunities to sell products never before sold and then found ways to produce them more cheaply and sell them more widely. In pursuit of cheaper labour and larger markets, corporations pressed for changes in international rules that favoured their mobility and expansion. As a result, we have become more dependent on corporations for our food, both as workers and as consumers.

WHAT FUTURE WILL WE CONSTRUCT — GLOBAL OR LOCAL?

Today, the ideal global meal may be the hamburger.[18] Although it is often assumed to be "traditionally" American, the hamburger has permeated US culture more recently than Mickey Mouse has. Its ancestry includes the sort of ground beef patty eaten in part of Germany, and variations appeared in county fairs in parts of the US settled by northern Europeans.[19] In general bread and beef derive mainly from European agronomy and cuisine, itself a descendent of larger Mediterranean cultures. The widespread use of the hamburger, however, accompanied the rise of fast-food industries. These marked a change of life from family to individual meals.

A recent magazine advertisement exemplifies the combined effects of corporate-guided changes in food practices. A young girl is offered a doll to help her learn to be a mother, a way girls have learned in many human societies. What exactly is she learning from this doll? To feed her baby, who is wearing a "Happy Meal" bib, a McDonald's burger, fries and shake! Another doll might teach her to breastfeed her baby or to mash bananas. But the food she is learning to serve her baby is bought from McDonald's. And the girl herself is not the blond child, typical of ads until quite recently. In the context of this book, her dark hair and eyes could easily be those of a Mexican child, who might otherwise be expected to think of food as tortillas and beans (and from the village rather than from Taco Bell). A toy company uses McDonald's to sell its product to children, which in turn advertises the corporate meals. Parents who buy this toy are paying for advertising that encourages their children to buy meals from the corporation! And as we will see in the chapters in this book, corporate meals are increasingly made and sold internationally, spanning the continent and even the globe.

As suggested by the "Happy Meals" doll, the hamburger is more a corporate food than an American one. It is part of the project of globalization pushed by corporations to replace the "traditional" project of "development" once regulated by national states, with the United States at the centre. The corporate hamburger marks a shift from what had by the 1970s become a "tradition" of regulated (male) employment and unpaid (female) preparation of home meals. The fast-food hamburger also marks a shift from US-centred food production to a world where ingredients are contracted from farmers and outlets are created by corporations which have escaped controls by governments. The corporate hamburger is prepared by casual, part-time workers for people who are eating out in deregulated markets. The new workers and the new customers are often the same people and they now spend less time with their families. "Industrial" prepared food is served hot and ready to eat immediately, and individuals "graze" meals — eat when they can, often from ubiquitous fast-food outlets. Corporations are trying to create a new global "tradition" for a culturally diverse world.

New patterns of production and trade accompany the eating changes creating new inequalities. Year-round fresh fruits and vegetables are now the fastest growing "non-traditional" exports. The new markets in exotic fruits, which include apples in Mexico as much as mangos in Canada, have been global from the outset. New workers, especially women, are hired to tend and process monocultures of tomatoes or strawberries in areas once devoted to peasant farming for local foods. These workers have less time and fewer ingredients to prepare "traditional" foods. They have little money to buy either corporate versions of their cuisines, such as Taco Bell in Mexico, or imported corporate foods such as hamburgers. A new pattern emerges in which local companies contract to transnational corporations and hire different workers; this in turn reconfigures family life, changes diets and, with it, cultures. This is what Vandana Shiva calls the globalization of western local knowledge. A truly cosmopolitan world culture would consist of many local cultures existing together, mutually and respectfully exchanging and learning from one another.[20]

The new patterns of work, trade and home life on offer are not the only ones possible. Indeed, they create such problems of exploitation, environmental damage, ill health and destruction of community life and local cultures, that sources of opposition and survival strategies are emerging everywhere. The alternatives to corporatization are necessarily local and particular to that area of the world, but they are not isolated from the alternatives in other areas of the world. Their success depends on individuals linking strategies and building mutual support across localities. These efforts require different rules of the game internationally than the deregulation of trade and investment presently rampaging across the globe, which only serves to "free" corporations at the expense of democratic institutions, communities, workers and consumers of food. New coalitions of groups concerned with food security, environmental degradation, labour rights, women and health are forming to propose new sets of rules that are more equitable and democratic.

Many local, regional and national alternatives still remain to be identified and connected. As a beginning, each of us can become aware of what is changing, where "traditions" came from, and what is possible — learning from the past and from others. The shift over time from an agriculture-centred to a food-centred system, with most people hired for wages and buying food, opens possibilities. For instance, community shared agriculture (CSA) is a new way to link farmers with eaters. In one model, eaters buy the crop in advance, help out on the farm and learn to eat what is good for the land to grow. Supported by their customers, Canadian farmers threatened with the loss of government protection can be more attentive to what is good for the soil, making a new science of ecological agriculture and developing a new source of employment on the land. They can also experiment with crops appropriate to immigrant cuisines. Similarly, community kitchens are not only a survival strategy for self-provisioning communities in Mexico which are losing their protections, but also a model for multicultural communities in Canada.

In both agriculture and eating practices, we have much to learn from places such as Mexico. Ironically, just as Canadians are becoming aware of the need to relocalize our food systems, trade liberalization and related changes in land and labour laws are threatening self-provisioning communities long in tune with local ecosystems in Mexico. We are learning from the experiences of community kitchens in Latin America. But we need also to learn about laws and practices that support farmers and farming communities, and to learn how to use the land wisely and sustainably.[21] In a time of growing unemployment and urban distress, particularly among young people, it seems wise to look to more labour-intensive — but also more knowledge-intensive — agriculture to support life and provide food. Mexican land and labour practices may well have needed change, but the wholesale adoption of problematic practices of industrial agrofood systems seems ill-advised. It also deprives us of an example to consider in Canada.

Conscious buying is another place to start. Food co-operatives and even local governments can try to support local, environmentally sound farming through food purchases (buying supplies for schools and hospitals, for example). Individuals can participate in "fair trade," organized by organizations such as OXFAM, to buy directly from co-operatives in other countries. Organizing and supporting local initiatives (such as the Good Food Box, farmers' markets, local food processors using local ingredients) helps ensure access for all to healthy food, grown in a sustainable way. International rules to support local empowerment rather than undermine it could allow communities at all levels of scale to use their organized powers to manage their own affairs to the maximum. Co-ordination among self-governing communities, including respect for the effects of one region on another, is more reflective of democracy, justice and sustainability than the present rush to corporate freedom.

It is worth remembering how and when changing "traditions" began. History helps us to track changes, to identify forks in the road, to grasp the interconnections among aspects of social life from the very small to the very large, and to know how our small choices, even the unconscious ones, contribute to this or that direction as the present unfolds into the future. If we make our choices conscious ones, each of us can do our part to take the path we want for everyone.

Harriet (right) engages co-author Fran Ansley in discussion and dish drying.

NOTES

This chapter also refers to ideas more fully discussed elsewhere in this volume. See Kirsten Appendini, "From Where Have All the Flowers Come?"; Deborah Barndt, "Whose 'Choice'?"; Antonieta Barrón, "Mexican Women on the Move"; Jan Kainer, "Not Quite What They Bargained For"; Ester Reiter, "Serving the McCustomer"; and the chapters in Part III.

1. T. P. Bayliss-Smith, *The Ecology of Agricultural Systems* (Cambridge: The University Press, 1982), 69–82. See also, Sidney Mintz, "Eating and Being: What Food Means," in Barbara Harriss-White and Sir Raymond Hoffenberg, eds., *Food: Multidisciplinary Perspectives* (Oxford: Blackwell, 1994), 102–115.

2. Eric Wolf, *Peasants* (Englewood Cliffs, NJ: Prentice-Hall, 1966).

3. See Vandana Shiva, *Monocultures of the Mind: Perspectives on Biodiversity and Biotechnology* (London: Zed Books, 1993); Mintz, "Eating and Being"; Harriet Friedmann, "Going in Circles: The Political Ecology of Food and Agriculture," in Raymond Grew, ed., *Food in Global History* (Boulder, CO: Westview, forthcoming).

4. Richard Schweid, *Hot Peppers: Cajuns and Capsicum in New Iberia, Louisiana* (Seattle, WA: Madrona Publishers, 1980), 12–16.

5. The *ejido* was a Mexican form of collective ownership by self-governing communities, understood as a way of recreating Indigenous ways of life in conjunction with modern forms of collective property. *Ejidos* developed differently from one another, with various combinations of common and individual rights to use and dispose of land. In general, *ejido* members were able to remain on the land and farm, buffered from national and international markets.

6. Philip McMichael, *Development and Social Change: A Global Analysis* (Thousand Oaks, CA: Pine Forge, 1996), 35–36.

7. Harriet Friedmann, "The Political Economy of Food: The Rise and Fall of the Postwar International Food Order," *American Journal of Sociology* 88 (1982), special supplement.

8. See Shiva, *Monocultures of the Mind*.

9. Harriet Friedmann, "International Relations of Food," in Harriss-White and Hoffenberg, eds., *Food*, 174–204. This article also appears in *New Left Review* 197 (1993), 29–57.

10. McMichael, *Development and Social Change*, 145–178.

11. See Michel Chossudovsky, *The Globalisation of Poverty: Impacts of IMF and World Bank Reforms* (London: Zed Books and Penang, Malaysia: Third World Network, 1997).

12. John Walton and David Seddon, *Free Markets and Food Riots: The Politics of Global Adjustment* (Oxford: Blackwell, 1994), 37–50.

13. Marvin Harris, *Sacred Cow, Abominable Pig: Riddles of Food and Culture* (New York: Simon and Schuster, 1985), 120–129.

14. Bonnie J. Fox, "The Rise and Fall of the Breadwinner-Homemaker Family," in Bonnie J. Fox, ed., *Family Patterns and Gender Relations* (Toronto: Oxford University Press, 1993), 147–158.

15. Jane Humphries, "The Working-Class Family, Women's Liberation and Class Struggle: The Case of Nineteenth-Century British History," *Review of Radical Political Economics* 9 (1977), 25–42.

16. Martha May, "Bread Before Roses: American Workingmen, Labor Unions and the Family Wage," in Fox, ed., *Family Patterns and Gender Relations*, 135–145.

17. This is the reasoning developed by Marilyn Waring, *If Women Counted: A New Feminist Economics* (San Francisco: HarperCollins, 1990).

18. George Ritzer, in *The McDonaldization of Society* (Thousand Oaks, CA: Pine Forge Press, 1993), uses the McDonald's hamburger as a way to understand a vast array of

changes in work and daily life.

19. Harris, *Sacred Cow*, 121–122.

20. Shiva, *Monocultures of the Mind*, 61–62.

21. See Colin Duncan, *The Centrality of Agriculture: Between Humankind and the Rest of Nature* (Montreal: McGill-Queens, 1996); David Ehrenfeld, *Beginning Again: People and Nature in the New Millennium* (New York: Oxford University Press, 1993).

Chapter Two

WHOSE "CHOICE"?

"FLEXIBLE" WOMEN WORKERS IN THE

TOMATO FOOD CHAIN

Female labour is central to all stages of food production and consumption: from picking and packing to working in supermarkets and restaurants.

WHOSE "CHOICE"?

"FLEXIBLE" WOMEN WORKERS IN THE

TOMATO FOOD CHAIN

Deborah Barndt

My whole family [works] at McDonald's: my mother, my sisters, my boyfriend, often at different times. And my dad, a police officer, works from eleven in the night 'til six in the morning. So there's no time we can eat together. We just grab something and put it in the microwave.[1]

THIS NARRATIVE, BY TANIA, a York University student working at McDonald's, may resonate with many young women in the North. At the Southern end of the NAFTA food chain, Tomasa, a Mexican fieldworker for Santa Anita Packers, one of the biggest domestic producers of tomatoes, describes her daily food preparations during the harvest season: "I get up at three a.m. to make tortillas for our lunch, then the truck comes at six to take us to the fields to start working by seven a.m."[2] An hour away at a Santa Anita greenhouse, Sara, a young tomato packer, tells us that the foreign management of Eco-Cultivos has just eliminated the two-hour lunch break, so workers no longer go home for the traditional noontime meal.[3]

These changes in the eating practices of women workers in the continental food system reflect several dimensions of the global economic restructuring that has reshaped the nature of their labour. Shifts in family eating practices have not been the "choice" of the women whose stories are told here, nor have they "chosen" the work shifts that involve them around the clock in growing and preparing food for other people.

"McDonaldization," initiated in the North and spreading to the South, and "maquilization," initiated in the South and now appearing in the North, are interrelated processes in the new global economy. McDonaldization, as George Ritzer[4] describes it, is the model that the fast-food restaurant has offered as a way to reorganize work in all other sectors. This model is based on efficiency, predictability, calculability or quantifiability, substitution of non-human technology, control and the irrationality of rationality. Central to this model is "flexible" part-time labour.

"Maquilization," originating in the maquila free trade zones of northern Mexico, now refers to a more generalized work process characterized by 1) the feminization of the labour force, 2) extreme segmentation of skill categories, 3) the lowering of real wages and 4) a non-union orientation.[5] In the traditional maquila sectors, such as the garment and electronic industries, there is full-time (though not necessarily stable) employment. However, the trade liberalization epitomized by NAFTA has opened the door for the development of maquilas throughout Mexico. "Agromaquilas," in particular, depend on more temporary, part-time and primarily female labour.

Central to both the McDonaldization of the retail and service sectors and the maquilization of the agro-industrial and manufacturing sectors in the continental food chain are the interrelated processes of the "feminization of poverty"[6] and the "flexibilization of labour."[7] Since the 1960s when export processing zones such as the Mexican maquilas began to employ primarily young women in low-skilled and low-wage jobs,[8] women have been key players in this new global formula.[9] In the reorganization of work by global capital, women workers have also become key players in new flexible labour strategies, building on an already established sexual division of labour and institutionalized sexism and racism in the societies where transnational corporations set up shop. In these sectors of the global food system, women bring their own meaning to flexible labour as they juggle their lives as both producers and consumers of food, as both part-time salaried workers and full-time domestic workers in managing households.

TOMASITA COMES NORTH WHILE
BIG MAC GOES SOUTH[10]

In the Tomasita Project, the journey of the tomato from the Mexican field through the United States to the Canadian fast-food restaurant reveals the dynamics of globalization. While food production and consumption takes place in all three countries, deep inequities, upon which NAFTA was based, remain among them.

The basic North–South contradiction of this continental (and increasingly hemispheric) system is that Mexico produces fresh fruit and vegetables (in this case, the tomato) for North American consumers, while Northern retail supermarkets[11] and fast-food restaurants, such as McDonald's, are moving South at record speed to market new foods, work and food practices, particularly as a result of NAFTA's trade liberalization. This contradiction is revealed in retail advertising, such as the Loblaws' billboard below. In its promotion of President's Choice products, Loblaws proclaims "Food Means the World to Us." We are seduced by such images into consuming an increasing "diversity" and seemingly endless array of fresh, "exotic"[12] and non-traditional foods. Meanwhile, there are hidden costs under which these foods were produced — the appropriation of Indigenous lands; the degradation of the environment

A Loblaws' billboard declares "Food Means the World To Us." Toronto 1998.

An "adbusted" version of the Loblaws' billboard reveals the hands and labour behind the "world food" we eat.

and the health and dignity of workers; increasing poverty; deepening sexist and racist employment practices[13] — which are kept (carefully and consciously) from our view.

The Tomasita Project aims to uncover these costs, particularly by exposing the living and working conditions of the women workers whose labour (not by choice) brings the "world of food" to us. A deconstruction of the Loblaws' ad would reveal these women workers as the producers behind the food product, and show that they, too, are part of a global system that links agro-export economies (such as Mexico) with the increasing consumer demand in the North for fresh produce all year round.

Tomasita is a both a material and symbolic "ecofeminist"[14] tomato within globalized food production — from biogenetic engineering to intensive use of agrochemicals, from long journeys in refrigerated trucks to shorter journeys across supermarket counters where their internationally standardized "product look up" numbers are punched in. Its fate is paralleled by the intertwining fates of women workers in the different stages of its production, preparation and consumption. If the tomato is shaped by "just-in-time" production practices, women workers make this supply-on-demand possible through their flexible labour.

The tracing of the tomato chain builds on the tradition of "commodity chain analysis,"[15] which examines three interlocking processes: 1) raw material production, 2) combined processing, packaging and exporting activities, and 3) marketing and consumptive activities.[16] The women workers who make the tomato chain come alive represent four different sectors of the food system — two in Mexico and two in Canada. In Mexico, they are the pickers and packers in Santa Anita Packers, a large export-oriented agribusiness, and the assembly line workers producing ketchup in Del Monte, a well-established multinational food processor. In Canada, the workers are cashiers in Loblaws supermarkets and service workers in McDonald's restaurants. How do these women workers (both as producers and consumers) reflect, respond to and resist the "flexible labour strategy" so central to corporate restructuring? There are, of course, obvious differences between the Mexican Indigenous workers moving from harvest to harvest to pick tomatoes and the Canadian women slicing these tomatoes and stacking them into a hamburger. Yet, since NAFTA, there are increasing similarities in the feminization and flexibilization of the labour force in all four sectors and in all three countries. One of the similarities is the increasing participation of young female workers, who, from the perspective of the companies, are seen as both cheaper and more productive than comparable male labour.[17] Gender ideologies, culturally entrenched and reinforced by managerial practices, strongly shape this socially constructed reality.

FLEXIBILIZATION: FROM ABOVE AND FROM BELOW

Key to global economic restructuring is the notion of flexibility. The term, however, changes meaning depending on whose perspective it represents. The perspective from above, from the vantage point of corporate managers, is different than the perspective from below, from the new global workforce. To some, flexibility implies "choice," but "*whose* choice" rules in a food system built on structural inequalities, which are based on differences of national identity, race, class, gender and age?

For large transnational corporations, flexibility has meant greater freedom (provided by NAFTA and increasing support from the Mexican government) to set up businesses in Mexico, where businesses are offered lower trade barriers, property laws that allow greater foreign investment, decreasing subsidies, decentralization of production through subcontracting and so forth. For large Mexican domestic producers such as Santa Anita Packers, trade liberalization has meant entering a globally competitive market with comparative advantages of land, climate and cheap labour. Once producing primarily for national consumption, Santa Anita has become ever more export-driven — it now produces 85 percent of crops for export and, in the case of greenhouse production, 100 percent for export. The fruit and vegetable sector is one of the few winners of NAFTA in Mexico.

The meaning of flexibility changes when set in the context of the new global marketplace, where borders and nation–states are less and less relevant, and where production is increasingly decentralized while decision-making is increasingly centralized. In this context, flexibility also refers to the shift from Fordist to post-Fordist production practices. Fordism was based on scientific management principles and organization of tasks in assembly lines for mass production, with the production of large volumes being the objective. Post-Fordist or "just-in-time" production responds to more diversified and specific demands in terms of quality and quantity.[18] It is ultimately very rationalized, of course, as demonstrated by the processes of workplace McDonaldization in which new technologies allow greater control of inventory and labour, while decentralization of production allows companies to shift many of the risks to subcontractors. In talking about the globalized corporate world, or "globalization from above,"[19] then, flexibility is ultimately about maximizing profits and minimizing obstacles (such as trade tariffs, government regulations, underused labour, trade union organization).

WOMEN WORKERS' EXPERIENCES OF FLEXIBILITY

What does flexibility mean, though, for the women moving the tomato through this continental food system, from Mexican field to Canadian table? If we first look at the consumption-end of the food chain, the fast-food and supermarket workers in Canada, and then move to the source, where women plant, pick, pack and process tomatoes in Mexico, we can learn how flexibilization has affected these women's daily lives.

McDONALD'S

"Flexible labour strategies" have been key to the model of production of McDonald's and its competitors. McJobs, whether filled by students, seniors or underemployed women, have always been primarily part-time (up to twenty-four hours a week). Part-time jobs do not require certain benefits and, because they are limited to short three- to four-hour shifts, do not require many breaks. Women student workers might be sent home after an hour or two if sales for the day are not reaching their predetermined quota. Karen, a university student, explains:

> They're supposed to make a certain amount of money an hour, say $1,300 between twelve noon and one p.m., and if they make less than that, for every $50 (under the quota), they cut half an hour of labour. Especially if you're newer, there's pressure to go home. It takes me an hour to get to work by bus, and I could be asked to go home after an hour of work.[20]

Flexibility of this temporary labour force is reinforced by the lack of trade union organization. Strong company-induced loyalty is fed by perks such as team outings, weekly treats and training that inculcate a family orientation. It is meant to dissuade employees from seeking unionization or from complaining about their hours. Nonetheless, there are increasing efforts to organize McDonald's workers and there have been recent union successes in BC and Quebec.

LOBLAWS

The experience of flexibility for women workers in the larger chains of the retail food sector, such as Loblaws in Canada, are just as precarious. Even though they are unionized, the working conditions of part-time workers have been eroded through recent labour negotiations. In the case of Loblaws, for example, the most recent contract negotiated by the United Food and Commercial Workers Union eliminated almost all of the full-time cashier positions. Part-time cashiers are dependent on seniority for being able to choose their working hours. This particularly affects new cashiers, such as Wanda: "When you are low on the seniority list, you are lucky to get any hours. They might call you in once every two weeks for a four-hour shift."[21] This restriction on available hours also affects the cashiers' earning power. A cashier must complete five hundred hours before being eligible for a raise. At this pace, she could work at the starting wage for over two years. From the company's perspective, this shift to primarily part-time flexible labour is a conscious strategy; it is part of "lean production."

DEL MONTE

What does flexibility look like in the Del Monte food processing plant in Irapuato, Mexico? The production of ketchup in Del Monte takes place during a four-month period, from February through May. In part, this coincides with the peak period for harvesting tomatoes; thus flexibility in the agromaquilas depends, in part, on the seasonal nature of agricultural production (becoming less pronounced with the increasing phenomenon of year-round greenhouse production).

Another reason that production is limited to one period is to maximize the use of the food processing machinery and the skilled labour force. Del Monte's ketchup production employs a combination of Fordist and post-Fordist processes: it is an assembly line production from the dumping and cooking of tomatoes in big vats to the bottling, capping and labelling on a mechanized line. Because other food processing (such as marmalade) uses the same machinery, the same full-time workers can easily shift from one product to another. Many are, in fact, multiskilled and are moved from one process to another, reflecting post-Fordist practices. Such multitasking is another form of flexibility in the experience of the new global workforce. Part-time women workers are brought on for the peak season only and for less skilled tasks. These women sometimes sit in the waiting room of the plant, hoping for a few hours of work, which are determined day by day. Flexibility reigns in a context where there is an oversupply of cheap labour, so companies can make such decisions on the spot, hiring and dismissing workers on a daily basis. This is another example of lean production, dependent on a disposable supply of female labour.

SANTA ANITA PACKERS

Finally we reach the source, Santa Anita Packers — the agribusiness that organizes production of tomatoes, from the importing of seeds to the exporting of waxed and packaged tomatoes in refrigerated trucks. Santa Anita, headquartered in Jalisco, in central Mexico, uses a mixture of production practices and diverse applications of the notion of flexibility. It is important to understand the historical development of the agro-export industry in Mexico[22] in the context of North–South political economic relations, which are based on ever-deepening inequalities, both between and within nations. Since the early part of the century, Mexican agriculture has been led by Northern demand for fresh fruit and vegetables, and by the use of cheap Mexican labour by US agribusinesses on both sides of the border. While the Depression in the 1930s led to American workers taking over farm labour jobs from Mexican workers in the US and also to a spurt of farm labour organizing, the availability of cheap Mexican Indigenous migrant labour fed the post-war development of large agribusinesses in both countries from the 1950s onward. This transnationalization of the economy was built upon institutionalized racism and sexism within Mexico and the US, employing Indigenous workers often as family units who were brought by the companies from the poorer states.

The sexual division of labour is seen most strongly in the packing plants, where a gendered ideology is used to justify the employment of women, as echoed by one of the company owners:

> Women "see" better than men, they can better distinguish the colours and they treat the product more gently. In selection, care and handling, women are more delicate. They can put up with more than men in all aspects: the routine, the monotony. Men are more restless, and won't put up with it.[23]

The feminization of the global labour force, and thus the feminization of global poverty, has been based on the marginal social role that women play and on a social consensus that their domestic duties are primary. As Lourdes Beneria argues, "the private sphere of the household is at the root of continuing asymmetries between men and women."[24]

In the case of Mexican agro-industry, women are among the most marginalized workers, along with children, students, the elderly and Indigenous peoples. Sara Lara notes that agribusinesses exploit their common situation of "mixedness," referring to the fact that these workers already play socially marginal roles based on their gender, race or age: "women as housewives, Indigenous peoples as 'poor peasants', children as sons and daughters, young people as students, all as the ad hoc subjects of flexible processes."[25] It is important to integrate national identity, gender, race, class, age and marital status[26] into any analysis of the new global labour force.

DEEPENING INEQUALITIES: FLEXIBILITY FOR WHOM?

In their restructuring, corporations have adopted a dual employment strategy that deepens the inequalities within the workforce and divides it into two groups: a "nucleus" of skilled workers who are trained in new technologies and post-Fordist production processes (quality circles, multiskilling and multitasking) and who have stable employment, and a "periphery" of unskilled workers whose jobs are very precarious. McDonald's and Loblaws both have a small full-time workforce, mainly male, while women make up the majority of the more predominant part-time workforce.[27] Tomato production in Mexico also mirrors this dualism. Small numbers of permanent workers prepare the seedlings and the land for production, and later pack and process the tomatoes; a large number of temporary part-time workers pick tomatoes during the harvest seasons. Santa Anita, for example, employs Mestizos from the local area for the jobs of cultivating the tomato plants, while hundreds of poor Indigenous workers, brought in by trucks and housed in conditions of squalor in makeshift camps, do much of the picking during the three-to-five month harvest season.[28] In this dual employment strategy, Indigenous workers are again required to be the most flexible, which is yet another form of discrimination and exploitation.

Such flexibility has been integral to labour-intensive and seasonal agricultural production for decades, though the composition of the migrant labour force has shifted over time. It is not uncommon for entire families to work together in the field, when the demand for labour is up. Children of local Mestizo peasant workers join their families on weekends during peak season, while children of Indigenous migrant workers, with neither school nor extended family to care for them, often work alongside their parents.[29] With increasing unemployment in Mexico, however, men are taking on agricultural jobs done previously by women, such as picking, and because the current economic crisis has increased the surplus of labour, companies choose the youngest and heartiest workers above the older ones (the ideal age seems to be fifteen to twenty-four, so workers in their thirties can already be considered less desirable). The flexible labour strategies of Mexican agribusinesses are predicated on race, gender and age. And once again, flexibility is determined by the companies and not the workers.

Technological changes within the production process are integral to the application of flexibilization. Differences among workers (of gender, race and skill) are accentuated with the increasingly sophisticated modes of greenhouse production and packing. Tomatoes in those plants, for example, are now weighed and sorted by colour in a computerized process, which at the same time records the inventory and monitors the productivity of the workers. Through these changes, foreign managers and technicians are reorganizing production relations and the workday in ways that are also shifting social relations, both in the workplace and at home.

In a Santa Anita greenhouse, unproductive workers are dismissed daily, as there is always a plentiful pool of surplus labour to choose from. There are echoes here of the McDonald's worker being sent home when quotas are down and the Loblaws cashier not being called for weeks when she's not needed, as well as Mexican women waiting for a few hours of work on Del Monte's ketchup production line. Flexibility serves the companies' need to maximize production and profits; it does not always serve the needs of Mexican or Canadian women in this food chain to survive, to complement their family income or to organize their lives and their double-day responsibilities. And as Sara Lara concludes, "Flexibility is not a choice for women," and "labour force management by companies is at the same time family management, that is, it reinforces particular family power relations."[30]

With NAFTA, the Mexican fruit and vegetable industry has been one of the only sectors to benefit from trade liberalization and has maintained an international competitiveness. Mexico has the advantage over its Northern partners in terms of land, climate and cheap labour. The expansion of the agro-export industry, however, reflects a basic North–South contradiction between a "negotiated flexibility" and a "primitive flexibility."[31] Large domestic companies in Mexico, such as Santa Anita, are becoming increasingly multinational, yet are still in the periphery of production decisions (controlled outside Mexico) and often lag behind in technological development. In the agro-export economy of Mexico, there is a growth of unstable and temporary employment in the still labour-intensive processes of production, sorting, packing and processing. In these jobs, women, children and Indigenous peoples (the most flexible workers in a rural labour market) are managed by "primitive flexibility." Transnational companies, however, are located primarily in the more industrialized North and control production through ownership, subcontracting and advanced technology (biogenetic engineering, sophisticated food processing, production of most of the inputs and machinery of production, and architects of the commercialization and distribution systems). These transnationals employ the "nucleus" of skilled workers, with relatively stable employment, and manage this workforce through "negotiated flexibility."

COMPARISONS ACROSS BORDERS: WOMEN WORKERS AS PRODUCERS AND CONSUMERS

Yet there are also increasing similarities between women workers in Mexican agribusinesses and food processing plants and women working as supermarket cashiers and fast-food service workers in Canada. They play key roles in the implementation of corporate flexible labour strategies. As a result, they experience similar contradictions in their efforts to fulfill their dual roles as salaried workers in the food system and as consumers or providers of food for their families. Wanda, a Canadian cashier, feels some common bonds with Tomasa, a Mexican tomato fieldworker:

> Tomasa used to make her own tortillas but now she has to go and work, so she buys ready-made tortillas. And she's feeling that pull

just like the North American women are: Should I stay at home with the kids? Should I go to work? She's feeling the economic thing, because everybody has to survive, everybody has to eat. She's taking care of the family, that's a priority in her life; I'd like to think that in my life that's a priority.[32]

Wanda has reached a point in her career, after twenty-three years as a part-time cashier, where she now has seniority and so may choose her hours. She "chooses" to work three eight-hour days instead of six four-hour shifts, for example, because she moved out of town a few years ago and must now commute one hour to work, adding two hours to her workday. That "choice" is framed by the fact that if she transferred to a Loblaws that was closer to her home, she would lose her seniority. She also "chooses" to work on weekends, because, as a single mother, it is the only time her former husband can take care of her children, saving her childcare expenses. Her "choice" of hours allows her to be at home during most weekdays:

> As a single parent, I'm taking my kids to school, doing the piano lessons, the Brownies, that kind of thing. So I know which days I don't want to come down to Toronto to work, because it's quite a ways for me. Or if they have a PD day [professional development day for teachers], I don't go into work that day.[33]

Here is where the flexibility of women's labour comes head to head with other social contradictions of an institutionalized sexist culture. Corporate managers, in fact, often point out that their flexible labour strategy suits women who "choose" to have more time with their families, and therefore don't want to work full-time. And there is certainly some truth to this. Even some feminists argue that flexibilization can be reappropriated by women and men, if it challenges the sexual division of labour in the home and promotes more shared responsibility, while also shortening the workweek. But it usually has little to do with "choice" and is often based on the assumption that women, not men or public childcare, will take care of children and feed their families.

In the Mexican context, there is even less of an illusion of "choice" for Indigenous women who are at the bottom of the hierarchy of workers, both locally and globally. While Santa Anita Packers brings Indigenous families to work during the harvest season, they provide neither adequate housing nor childcare, and it has been a struggle to get the children into the local school. It has been reported that company foremen became angry with Indigenous women workers who brought their children tied to their backs to the fields and who stopped work, periodically, to breastfeed them. Here, in the most basic sense, the primary role that women fulfill in feeding their children is regulated by the company's rules. And though they have little choice but to bring their children to the fields, they also take tremendous risks in doing so. When we visited their camp, one baby was reportedly dying because, as the Indigenous workers explained, pesticide residue on the mother's hand had entered the child's mouth during breastfeeding.

Since NAFTA, and with the deepening impoverishment of the rural population in Mexico, these Indigenous families are forced to migrate from one harvest to another for even longer periods of the year. Whereas previously they may have been able to remain home for a few months and raise some of their own food, they are now permanently moving, by necessity, ready to go to wherever there is work.

The Mestizo workers who live near the Santa Anita plant and only work seasonally experience the insecurity in another way. Due to erratic weather conditions, their work periods have been cut short, and the jobs available for them peter out. Describing the situation, Tomasa said:

> In the end, we were working one or two days a week, and then not at all. They don't even say thanks 'til the day that they return. Only when they begin to plant again in the next season, they come with their truck to take us back to the fields, no?[34]

This sense of never knowing when you are going to work, and often in the case of Indigenous migrant workers even where, is a permanent condition of agricultural fieldworkers. Canadian cashiers and fast-food workers may know a week or two in advance what their shifts are to be, but the constantly changing hours often affect family routines, interactions and, especially, eating practices. It is not uncommon for a family to have no time when they can all sit down to a meal together.

Whose interests are served by this flexible labour strategy? Flexibilization as it plays out in the continental food system, and particularly in the lives of women workers in this food chain from Mexico to Canada, must be seen as "an ideology propagated by firm owners as a desirable future end state, and supported by conservative pro-business forces and governments in order to assist the private sector in achieving this goal."[35] It is part and parcel of lean production, maximizing efficiency and profits and leaving the most vulnerable and marginalized workers bound to the shifting winds of just-in-time production. In the end, they become just-in-time workers with no time of their own.

And what are the real choices for women in this system? Wanda, the Loblaws cashier, has taken a keen interest in this study and has read the stories of the Mexican workers. She concludes:

> I feel an overwhelming sadness and connection to all the women in the "tomato food chain." We all play a seemingly small part, but the ramifications of our work are enormous ... We are all entrapped in the corporate workings of flexibilization. However, the dilemma still exists for all of us in the food chain: we're trying to survive.[36]

Deborah (centre) with Reyes Márquez (left) and Angeles Amezquita (right), members of the women's group in Valencianita, Mexico.

NOTES

I gratefully acknowledge the tremendous efforts of the graduate research assistants who worked from 1995 to 1999 on the Tomasita Project, helping to shape it and carrying out the interviews referred to in this chapter. Special thanks to Emily Levitt, Deborah Moffet, Lauren Baker (Mexican interviews), Ann Eyerman (McDonald's interviews), Stephanie Conway (Loblaws' interviews), Egla Martinez-Salazar (review of Mexican interviews), Karen Serwonka (McDonald's interviews), Anuja Mendiratta, and Melissa Tkachyk (glossary).

This chapter also refers to ideas more fully discussed elsewhere in this volume. See Kirsten Appendini, "From Where Have All the Flowers Come?"; Antonieta Barrón, "Mexican Women on the Move"; Ann Eyerman, "Serving Up Service"; Harriet Friedmann, "Remaking 'Traditions'"; Egla Martinez-Salazar, "The 'Poisoning' of Indigenous Migrant Women Workers and Children"; and Ester Reiter, "Serving the McCustomer."

1. Tania (pseudonym), interview with author, Toronto, Ontario, February 1998.

2. Tomasa (pseudonym), interview with author, Gomez Farias, Mexico, April 1997.

3. Sara (pseudonym), interview with author, San Isidro Mazatepec, Mexico, April 1997.

4. See George Ritzer, *The McDonaldization of Society* (Thousand Oaks, CA: Pine Forge Press, 1993). Ritzer notes that the new model of rationalization in our culture is no longer the bureaucracy, as Max Weber suggested, but the fast-food restaurant. He outlines the characteristics of this work organization based on 1) efficiency (from the factory-farm production of the ingredients to the computer scanners at the counter), 2) predictability (from the ambience and the personnel to the limited menu), 3) calculability or quantity, 4) substitution of non-human technology (the techniques, procedures, routines and machines make it almost impossible for workers to act autonomously), 5) control (the rationalization of food preparation and serving gives control over the employees), and 6) the irrationality of rationality (for example, we see McDonald's as rational despite the reality that the chemicals in the food are harmful and that we can gain weight from the high calories and cholesterol levels).

5. The four dimensions of maquilization, developed by J. Carillo as he observed restructuring in the auto industry, are elaborated by Kathryn Kopinak in *Desert Capitalism: What Are the Maquiladoras?* (Montreal: Black Rose Books, 1997), 13.

6. Gita Sen and Caren Grown, *Development, Crises, and Alternative Visions: Third World Women's Perspectives* (New York: Monthly Review Press, 1987), 25.

7. Kirsten Appendini, "Revisiting Women Wage-Workers in Mexico's Agro-Industry: Changes in Rural Labour Markets," Working Paper 95, no. 2, Centre for Development Research (Copenhagen, 1995), 11–12.

8. The categorizing of so-called "low-skilled" work needs to be problematized, particularly when describing the kinds of tasks allotted to women in food production.

Job tasks that correlate with women's domestic labour have almost universally been devalued and their counterparts in paid work have suffered a similar fate. While reigning gender ideologies purport that women are "naturally" more suited to certain tasks, Elson and Pearson argue that the famous nimble fingers are not "an inheritance from their mothers," but rather "the result of training they have received from their mothers and other female kin since early infancy in the tasks socially appropriate to woman's role." See Diane Elson and Ruth Roach Pearson, "The Subordination of Women and the Internationalization of Factory Production," in Nalini Visvanathan et al., eds., *The Women, Gender, and Development Reader* (Halifax: Fernwood Publishing, 1997), 191–203.

9. For a classic analysis of this development in the 1980s, see Swasti Mitter, *Common Fate, Common Bond: Women in the Global Economy* (London: Pluto Press, 1986).

10. For a further elaboration of this North–South contradiction, see Deborah Barndt, "Bio/cultural Diversity and Equity in Post-NAFTA Mexico (or: Tomasita Comes North While Big Mac Goes South)," in Jan Drydyk and Peter Penz, eds., *Global Justice, Global Democracy* (Halifax: Fernwood Publishing, 1997), 55–69.

11. While the presence of North American fast-food restaurants in Mexico is more visible, there has also been an incursion of the retail giants. Few are aware, for example, that the big Mexican supermarket chain, Aurera, is now owned by Wal-Mart, the Texas-based company that has become synonymous with corporate take-over, spelling death for smaller retail chains.

12. The "appropriation" of the "exotic other" is the subject of post-colonial theory and cultural studies examination of how difference is constructed within the politics of consumption to entice us into buying the mythical (and essentialist) look, the purity, the passion, the natural freshness of Southern peoples and lands. For an analysis of how Loblaws, and particularly President's Choice, has led the retail market in packaging difference, see C. Sachetti and T. Dufresne, "President's Choice Through the Looking Glass," *Fuse Magazine* (May-June 1994), 23.

13. Ecological economists contribute to unveiling the "hidden costs" in the production of the food we eat. William Rees, for example, advocates that we measure the "ecological footprint" of the goods we consume, and feminist ecological economist Ellie Perkins reminds us of the unpaid labour of women in managing the household. A more popular version of this analysis can be found in the cartoon story "Tomasita Tells All: True Confessions of Tomasita, the Abused Tomato," an ecofeminist tale told from the perspective of the tomato forced onto this continental conveyor belt. Parts of this story appear in *Tomasita's Trail: Women, Work, and the World in a Tomato* (forthcoming).

14. Ecofeminism offers an analysis that links the historical domination of women with the human domination of non-human nature. Although there are many different schools of ecofeminist thought, I support an analysis that proposes an integrative, historically and culturally contingent analysis of structural oppressions based on gender, race, class, as intertwined with the exploitation of nature as a "resource." I don't ascribe to the stream of ecofeminism that suggests women (as an essentialist category) are inherently (biologically) closer to nature. See Noel Sturgeon, *Ecofeminist*

Natures: Race, Gender, Feminist Theory and Political Action (New York: Routledge, 1997).

15. See Gary Gereffi and Miguel Korzeniewicz, eds., *Commodity Chains and Global Capitalism* (Westport, CT: Praeger Publishers, 1994).

16. See Laura Reynolds, "Institutionalizing Flexibility: A Comparative Analysis of Fordist and Post-Fordist Models of Third World Agro-Export Production," in Gereffi and Korzeniewicz, eds., *Commodity Chains and Global Capitalism*, 143–160.

17. Elson and Pearson, "The Subordination of Women and the Internationalization of Factory Production," 192.

18. For a useful discussion of Fordist and post-Fordist production practices, particularly in terms of the model of fast-food restaurants, see Ritzer, *The McDonaldization of Society*, 150–153.

19. Jeremy Brecher, John Childs, and J. Cutler, eds., *Global Visions: Beyond the New World Order* (Montreal: Black Rose Books, 1993).

20. Karen (pseudonym), interview with author, Toronto, Ontario, February 1998.

21. Wanda (pseudonym), interview with author, Toronto, Ontario, May 1997.

22. See Sara Lara, "La Flexibilidad del Mercado de Trabajo Rural," *Revista Mexicana de Sociología* 54, no.1 (January-February 1994), 29–48.

23. Conrado Lomeli, interview with author, Guadalajara, Mexico, December 1996.

24. Lourdes Beneria, "Capitalism and Socialism: Some Feminist Questions," in Visvanathan et al., eds., *The Women, Gender, and Development Reader*, 330.

25. Lara, "La Flexibilidad del Mercado de Trabajo Rural," 41. Translated from the Spanish by the author.

26. Single women are preferred as packers, for example, because they are moved from one production site to another and housed in company homes in women-centred families. In the case of Mexican farm labourers hired by the FARMS program in Ontario to pick and pack our vegetables during the Canadian growing season, however, widows are preferred, reflecting a machista attitude that they're safer than married or single women in a foreign job (Irena [pseudonym], interview with author, Miacatlán, Mexico, December 1998).

27. According to Statistics Canada, women are more likely to work part-time, by a ratio of 3 to 1, compared with men. *The Globe and Mail*, reporting on the study, states that "part-time employment was most prevalent among sales and service occupations, particularly in the food-service industry and among grocery clerks." The *Globe* quotes Gordon Betcherman of Canadian Policy Research Networks: "many employers want to hire staff to work less than 30 hours a week because they can be more flexible in scheduling around peak demand and because they have to provide fewer benefits" ("Part-time Work Stats Questioned," *The Globe and Mail*, 18 March 1998, 6). A related article notes that the most predominant female occupation is "retail sales clerk," with "waitress" as number seven on the list ("He's a Trucker, She Types," *The Globe and Mail*, 18 March 1998, 1).

28. The harvest season has varied tremendously lately, due to erratic weather conditions which are often blamed on El Niño. Unseasonal freezes have cut short the tomato season, causing companies financial losses and sending workers either on to other harvests or home to their villages where they seek casual labour to carry them through til the next harvest. In Gomez Farias, the workers lost three months of expected fieldwork and were eeking out a living making and selling straw mats (Tomasa, interview).

29. With the economic crisis in Mexico, and deepening gaps between the rich and the poor, agricultural workers are part of a "family wage economy," requiring all members to work for the survival of the family. In *Desert Capitalism: What Are the Maquiladoras?*, Kathryn Kopinak shows that while in 1981, 1.8 family members had to work to feed a family of 5, by 1996, the number was 5.4. Though Northern economies are described as "family consumer economies" rather than "family wage economies," it is increasingly the case that working-class families also depend on multiple salaries, which are often from combinations of part-time jobs.

30. Lara, "La Flexibilidad del Mercado de Trabajo Rural," 42. Translated from the Spanish by the author.

31. Ibid., 41.

32. Wanda (pseudonym), interview with author, Toronto, Ontario, October 1997.

33. Ibid.

34. Tomasa interview.

35. Kopinak, *Desert Capitalism*, 116.

36. Wanda (pseudonym), interview with author, Toronto, Ontario, August 1998.

Chapter Three

SERVING THE McCUSTOMER:

FAST FOOD IS NOT ABOUT FOOD

Protests in post-NAFTA Canada, such as the Days in Action in Toronto,
target the growing phenomenon of MᶜJobs.

SERVING THE MᶜCUSTOMER:

FAST FOOD IS NOT ABOUT FOOD

Ester Reiter

CITIZEN INTO CUSTOMER: CULTURAL AND IDEOLOGICAL IMPLICATIONS

PEOPLE ARE HUNGRY — for community, for nurturance. Young and old, we need and want to be cared for, cared about, loved. Our lives are difficult, and so we need some escape to a place where we will be valued, where our needs will matter, where we can play. For many families/households, gathering around a table to share a meal has been an occasion where emotional connections are affirmed. The soul as well as the belly needs feeding. It is no accident that the feast has often been at the centre of community events. However, in the past half century, the search to satisfy our needs has been fed increasingly by mass consumption of consumer goods. *We are on a treadmill and we know something is missing.* The more we need, the more we buy, but the more we buy the hungrier we are for something that will really satisfy, so the more we need. In this age of non-standardized work, where family members all have part-time jobs, one custom that has contributed to our well-being has become a special event rather than a regular occurrence — the family meal. We are now a society that grazes and snacks rather than a society that sits down with our families each evening. How and when did the commercialization of the family dinner occur?

During the Second World War, more people than ever frequented restaurants. Following the war, Canadian restaurant owners faced the end of their prosperous years, because eating at home was once again an option for families. Restaurateurs no longer had a ready clientele of people working odd hours and whose spouses were overseas. Some restaurant owners thought about how and where they could create a market for their food to keep themselves in business. Luring the average family into buying ready-made food held the promise of a new market that looked "like magic ... It's a magic that enables any restaurant to be as big as a city, to gather profits as big as the operator's imagination and to do these without major capital outlay." This, however, was no small challenge as it meant stiff competition with Mom. After all, "she puts love into her cooking."[1]

We can trace to the 1920s the attempt not just to sell what people want but to create a market by convincing people of what they need. As washing machines, dryers, televisions and dishwashers became available, the focus became selling one to each indivdual family. Individual women were encouraged to make themselves attractive through the consumption of cosmetics, the right shampoo, undergarments, seasonal fashion. These luxuries soon became essential. For example, the mass production of automobiles, the growth of suburbs and the lack of easily accessible public transportation made buying a car a necessity. During the Second World War women entered the paid workforce in greater numbers, but after the war, they were encouraged, even compelled, to leave their blue-collar jobs and return to their homes where they were encouraged to buy more consumer goods. However, the stay-at-home mom and the breadwinner dad became an economic impossibility for more and more families. From the 1960s to the present, women increasingly entered the labour force, and now, the income-earning wife and mother is more common than not.

These days, Mom is tired — she's working outside the home for pay and may have little or no time to cook. So she, like the rest of her family, needs a taste of the good life, the feeling of being taken care of. The call to "give yourself a treat today" is seductive and the affordability makes it possible. People flock to fast-food outlets — McDonald's, A&W, Burger King — for the golden fries boiled in oil, the brown bun (sweetened and nicely browned by the caramelized sugar it is dusted with), the hamburger. For many people, eating meat once constituted a rare treat. At one time only available to the wealthy on a regular basis, today meat is widely available as fast food, which itself has become comfort food — easy to eat, fun and, as the ads tell us, satisfying.

There's the rub. This bargain-basement instant solution that promises to fill our needs still leaves us hungry. So we buy more food, more things, hoping somehow to satisfy this need of ours. McDonald's, for example, promotes itself as a "fast, hassle free solution" to satisfying hunger, which simultaneously provides "value" that includes alignment with "community events, entertainment promotions and personalities that are important to our customers." Thus the purchased meal promises to provide something that "no one else can — the total McDonald's experience."[2]

McDonald's is one of the biggest success stories in recent history, having had its beginnings in the post–Second World War boom. In the 1960s, Ray Kroc took over the profitable hamburger stand in California and turned McDonald's into a global corporation. In 1997, it reported over US$33 billion dollars in sales in 111 countries around the world. McDonald's employees worldwide number more than one million, in 23,000 restaurants. The long-term prospects look brightest outside the US, where there are already 12,000 restaurants, with plans to add a few thousand more each year.[3] McDonald's is committed to expansion. In their words:

> McDonald's vision is to dominate the global foodservices industry. Global dominance means setting the performance standards for customer satisfaction while increasing market share and profitability through our Convenience, Value and Execution Strategies.
> — McDonald's Annual Report, 1995

As an example of this global expansion, McDonald's recently announced a one-billion-dollar investment in Latin America, where it plans to double the number of restaurants to two thousand by the end of the year 2000. Expansions into Bolivia, Lebanon and Sri Lanka are also heralded. According to McDonald's senior vice-president, Ed Sanchez, this is McDonald's contribution to economic development.[4]

Who benefits from this development? The World Bank defines the poverty line as the equivalent of US$370 a year. In the eight-year period from 1985 to 1993, while McDonald's became richer, the number of poor people in the world increased by 20 percent, to 1.2 billion. While poverty has increased, so has wealth. From 1960–1991, the share of the world's income for the richest fifth of the world *rose* from 70 percent to

85 percent, while the share of income for the poorest fifth *dropped* from 2.3 percent to 1.4 percent. These figures become even more dramatic when broken down by gender. The Human Development Report of the United Nations Development Program found that over 70 percent of the people now living in absolute poverty are women.[5]

As the consumer society has developed, freedom has come to mean the freedom to buy. We are led to believe that the more we consume, the freer we are. We are asked to see ourselves as private, individual and solitary, where there is no "we" only a "me." Our dreams, we are told by the banks, have no limits. Multinationals such as Nike tell us to "Just do it," as long as our imaginations stay within the confines of what can be bought. At work, we are downsized, re-engineered, organized into teams to enable even more intensification of work, and this is called "empowerment." We are freer then we have ever been, but within a range that empowers individuals in their decisions of which brand of running shoes to buy — as long as we don't ask the bigger questions, as long as we don't challenge the all-powerful primacy of the market and the corporations which run it. In the process of gaining all these new choices, collective action to defend public interests — such as environmental protection, social safety nets, health, education and the public sector — are becoming wildly unrealistic fantasies. And anyway, we are told they are infringements on our freedom, defined as an individual's right to choose. As privatization, deregulation and the rule of the "bottom line" deplete the resources available to the public sector in Canada, we see private fast-food companies moving in to fill the gap. At the same time, corporations promise to expand our freedom through offering us greater choice of different name brands. What gets lost in this brave new "McWorld" is the respect for what Ursula Franklin calls the "indivisible benefits" that form the basis of civil society.[6] Our sense of ourselves as citizens — with justice, fairness and equity as operating principles — is replaced by the "freedom" to become customers.

Fast-food companies present themselves as charitable, community-minded citizens (and perhaps sincerely believe it). They have tapped lucrative markets in schools, hospitals and other publicly funded resources such as zoos and sports arenas. For example, marketing gimmicks such as Pizza Hut's and McDonald's literacy programs reward first graders' achievements with fast-food certificates, promoting their product and their charitable image simultaneously. While the marketing image may be benign, the ideology is not. The fast-food industry does not much care about the health of either growing children or the environment. Nor does it concern itself with the poverty and hunger in the countries that provide the meat for the hamburgers North Americans consume. This benign and charitable image is a technique to reach the newest consumer — children.

Servicing customers under five years old is only profitable if they are targeted in selective ways. As John Hawkes, McDonald's chief marketing officer in the United Kingdom acknowledges, two-to-eight-year-olds are the age group to which hamburger ads are geared because it is among children as young as two that brand loyalty can be effectively created.[7] Promoting the well-being of this age group involves support for institutions such as affordable daycare and junior kindergarten. This kind of support, however, doesn't provide the same bottom-line advantage, so corporations such as McDonald's are not supportive of public funding that provides the resources children need.

Corporate sponsorship is spreading into other educational settings. In the US, Burger King has opened "Burger King Academies," fully accredited quasi-private high schools in fourteen cities. There are plans to do the same in London, England. In this new entrepreneurial model, with a voucher system where parents are given money and choices as to how to use it, schools don't teach so much as sell. They also shape a way of looking at the world, which engenders what education critic Jonathan Kozol calls "predictability instead of critical capacities."[8] Children are described as future "assets" or "productive units"; the child becomes "the product." This approach is also spreading into other sectors, such as healthcare. Can you distinguish which of the following quotes is about running a healthcare service and which is about hamburgers?

> As an *industry leader*, we provide *cost effective* services of *premier quality* in an environment which values our *people and partnerships* while focusing on our *customers* within a *profitable, innovative* organization positioned for the future.[9]

> ... we work together to take advantage of enhanced skills, attitudes, and behaviours of all our people and to share knowledge

across geographic and organizational borders ... As the industry leader, we're embracing change from a position of strength, challenging ourselves to reach even higher levels of excellence in understanding and meeting the needs and expectations of our customers.[10]

The first is MDS laboratory services, a for-profit healthcare company based in Ontario, which has healthcare investments in many previously publicly run facilities, such as hospital laboratory services. The second is from McDonald's 1994 Annual Report.

In the management literature, there is much talk of "serving the customer," obscuring the relationship between employer and employee and foregrounding the employee's responsibility to satisfy the consumer. The focus is not on equality and justice for the employee, but on satisfaction for the customer. This is touted as the road to good government.[11] It seems there is a new religion and it is called corporate self-interest, which benefits corporations with support from the state. In their very popular book *Reengineering the Corporation*, Michael Hammer and James Champy talk about the "shift of power from producers to consumers." According to them, it is the customer who now calls the shots and we are told individual customers — whether consumers or industrial firms — demand that they be treated individually.[12] Similarly, in *Reinventing Government: How the Entrepreneurial Spirit is Transforming the Public Sector*, David Osborne and Ted Gaebler praise competition that will give us "more bang for the buck." In the process, the citizen has become the customer and public interest is reduced to the needs of individual customers, and democracy is equated with cost efficiency.[13]

What does this discourse of democracy, of meeting people's needs through consumption, really mean? US critic Noam Chomsky describes democracy as really meaning "a system of governance in which elite elements based in the business community control the state by virtue of their dominance of the private society while the population observes quietly." In Chomsky's view, the key aim of democracy, US style, is not the freedom of speech and worship and the freedom from want and fear articulated by Franklin Delano Roosevelt, but the fifth unmentioned and well-documented "freedom to rob and to exploit."[14]

WORKING AT MCDONALD'S: EXPLOITED WORKER OR "THE PERFECT JOB"?[15]

McDonald's expects to expand its employees by the year 2000: the number of employees will increase 150 percent from one million at the end of 1997 to nearly two and one half million. The promotional pamphlet used by McDonald's Canada for hiring targets the young, who are out for a first job, and retirees. In the past, about 70 percent of the crew have consisted of young people. More than 50,000 employees have been through McDonald's international management training facility in Oak Brook, Illinois.[16]

Common to most fast-food training programs, managers drill their employees with "democratic" rhetoric: the employees are a team, the manager is the coach and their function is to work together to better serve the customer. "Counter hostesses" (cashiers) are to treat customers as guests and make them "happy." As one employee pamphlet says, "Your job is a sort of social occasion. You meet people — you want these people to like you."[17] These counter jobs are most often assigned to the female employees. The fast-food industry capitalizes on a gender ideology that takes the traditional division of labour in the home and locates it in a for-profit workplace. Thus women who are expected to care for others in the non-market sphere of the family are called upon to produce these feelings in their minimum-wage jobs. Such an approach works in a setting where the customer is always visible while the real boss is an abstract concept located in some head office far away. The omnipresent managers supervise the workers closely, ensuring that each micro step is performed according to the manual, but they have no real power over important issues such as wages or working conditions. The real decision-makers are nowhere in sight. Serving the "customer" is an effective management strategy, using the service aspect of a job to control labour and dependent on exploiting the good will of workers. It was pioneered in fast food but is now commonly found in many management manuals. It comes in some variant through other management strategies such as team concept, total quality management and continuous quality improvement. Meeting the "needs" of the customer are harnessed to the profit motives of management to make sure that surveillance of the worker is complete.

In what Arlie Hochshild calls the "managed heart," the fast-food companies attempt to harness human emotions for a dual purpose.[18] On the one hand, the "customer first" strategy is a good way to expand the market, and on the other hand, it is a very effective technique for monitoring workers' acquiescence to the very restrictive work practices imposed. Anyone who has worked in fast food or has been to a fast-food outlet has some idea of how the system operates. Virtually no cooking is done on the premises; rather each outlet is an assembly plant. Even the lettuce comes pre-shredded, and the eggs pre-scrambled in a carton. Each motion is timed to the second, and a labour schedule prepared in advance for each hour (half hour during the rushes), so that workers, rushing around at full speed, can serve the customer within the allotted time. Everything has been considered and preplanned — from the assembly of the food to getting it to the customer. All details are predetermined, such as the number of pickles (four, not three and two halves) on a burger, the amount and placement of the mustard, the number of fries that the scoop will hold (too much is cheating the store; too few, cheating the customer). The employees must follow the rules with not even the most minor of variations.

The "people skills" that managers must have make it their responsibility to ensure that morale remains high in an outlet. All kinds of social activities and the training system are designed to create the illusion that "McDonald's is a great place to work."[19] This special "experience" is meant to stimulate the notion of McDonald's as a family where one will be looked after. What remains unarticulated is that one may not unionize in one's family, although plenty of exploitation may exist. However, workers become aware that McDonald's is not their family, and that the working conditions leave something to be desired, the pay is low and the company does not really care about them. Thus, even though unionization in this industry is strongly resisted, organizing drives have occurred and continue to occur regularly. The goal is not so much monetary. Sarah Inglis, who led the almost-successful organizing drive of a McDonald's in Orangeville, Ontario, in 1994, explained that having a union can offer workers things such as dignity and self-respect, something she feels young workers are also entitled to.

In February 1998, over 82 percent of workers at the Mcdonald's outlet in St. Hubert, Quebec, decided that they needed a union to improve their deteriorating working conditions, so they signed up with the Brotherhood of Teamsters. In response, McDonald's Canada and the franchise owners suddenly decided that, after seventeen years in operation, the outlet was unprofitable and would have to be closed. The Quebec Federation of Labour (QFL) stepped in and offered to buy up this newly unprofitable franchise. Nothing doing. McDonald's refused to negotiate. The QFL and the Canadian Labour Congress considered a boycott of the chain and decided to engage in a major organizing drive in Quebec.[20]

In Montreal, the Brotherhood of Teamsters is applying for certification to represent workers at a McDonald's outlet. Montreal's labour commissioner has ruled in favour of the union by finding that the outlet had tried to tamper with its employee list by adding more anti-union workers to its crew to fend off certification. Accreditation hearings for this outlet and several other restaurants in the Montreal area continue. In Squamish, British Columbia, Jennifer Wiebe and Tessa Lowinger, Grade Twelve students, succeeded in organizing the only McDonald's outlet in the town with the Canadian Auto Workers (CAW). The union was certified by the British Columbia Labour Relations Board on August 19, 1998. These young women define their top bargaining priority to be a workplace with decent and safe working conditions, where employees will be treated with respect. (The CAW has organized eleven Starbucks and forty Kentucky Fried Chicken outlets in the province.)[21]

TAKING ON THE GIANT

Not only unionization but public outcry has presented serious challenges to McDonald's. Indeed, McDonald's guards its image as a company that gives to the community as basic to its functioning, and thus public criticisms are treated very seriously. In June 1997, the McLibel Trial concluded — this was the longest running trial in English history, representing a battle between the fast-food giant and Helen Steel and Dave Morris of North London. At issue was a pamphlet entitled "What's Wrong with McDonald's?" produced in 1986 by the London Greenpeace group. The pamphlet criticized McDonald's for promoting unhealthy food, exploiting workers, robbing the poor, damaging the environment, exploiting children through its advertising and murdering animals — not exactly previously unheard of charges. Eleven years after the pamphlet was first distributed, and two and one half years of trial testimony and many tens of millions of dollars in legal fees later, McDonald's made history. They had what one commentator called "the most expensive and disastrous public relations exercise ever mounted by a multinational company."[22]

The two defendants, who provided their own defence, faced the most high-powered lawyers money could buy. A technicality left the defendants having to prove not only that what their pamphlet claimed — that multinationals and the food industry do not promote health — but also that McDonald's itself directly caused conditions such as rainforest destruction and hunger in the Third World. The text in the pamphlet had to be treated as statements of fact to be proven with primary sources of evidence. The McLibel two did quite well despite this handicap. Although the high court judge, Mr. Justice Roger Bell, ordered the penniless defendants to pay £60,000 in damages, he found as a fact that McDonald's makes "considerable use of susceptible young children" in their advertising, is "culpably responsible" for cruelty to animals and pays low wages to its workers. The food was also found to have high salt and fat content and did not have the positive nutritional benefit claimed in advertisements and promotions.[23]

An Internet Website (www.mcspotlight.org) set up in the course of the trial was accessed over 24 million times in the first eighteen months of its existence by people from all over the world, and it continues posting news in cyberspace about anti-McDonald's struggles throughout the world. (This is an example of how the Internet can be an important tool for cross-border organizing. In this instance, it was very successful in mobilizing international solidarity.)

As well, Mr. Justice Bell pointed out, "McDonald's is strongly antithetic to the idea of unionisation of crews in their restaurants." UK McDonald's vice-president Sid Nicholson indicated that for an employee "to inform the union about conditions inside the stores" would be a breach of the employee's contract and considered "gross misconduct," and therefore a "summary sociable offence." According to Robert Beavers, the US senior vice-president of McDonald's, since the 1970s a "flying squad of experienced managers was dispatched to a store whenever word came of an attempt to organise it."[24]

Wal-Mart, with whom McDonald's has a retail partnership, is also working hard to oppose unionization. Wal-Mart offers McDonald's food "to go" in over eight hundred front check-out counters. The Ontario provincial labour board ruled that Wal-Mart had engaged in unfair labour practices in its Windsor store by threatening to shut down the store if employees voted for a union. As it was not legally possible to keep a union out, the conservative Harris government proceeded to change the labour law in Ontario by introducing a new labour bill called the "Wal-Mart bill," which made a certification vote mandatory. Judith McCormack, the former chair of the Ontario Labour Relations Board, called the bill an invitation to employers to engage in unfair labour practices by enhancing their ability to "jeopardize the credibility and authority of the law."[25]

The struggles to unionize McDonald's challenge us to look behind the scenes and to ask questions about the world of production, and they challenge the wisdom of accepting the marketplace as the determinant of how we should live. For unions, fast-food employees represent the new labour force — vulnerable workers, primarily women and young people in part-time jobs, working in small outlets for very large employers. Organizing in this sector requires some leadership. It is a time-consuming and expensive process. But we have enough examples of organizing attempts to know that it can be done. The majority of consumers eat fast food, and almost everyone has a relative or friend who has had firsthand experience with the labour process. There are growing alliances between all who have an interest in challenging fast food — workers, women's groups, environmental groups. Together we can redefine the nature of democracy to make it mean what we think it should. Why should corporations who make wealth immorally and unethically have the right to subordinate communities and their goals to individual private interests? Living in a civilized society means providing all members, waged and unwaged, with access to basic needs. Indeed it could be argued that one of the great achievements of this century is the creation of a public sector, flawed though it is, that will defend and protect our interests not only as separate individuals but as members of a community.

IS OUR FUTURE FRIED?

I think Marx described it best of all:

> The need for a constantly expanding market for its products chases the bourgeoisie over the whole surface of the globe. It must nestle everywhere, settle everywhere, establish connections everywhere ... In place of the old wants, satisfied by the production of the country, we find new wants, requiring for their satisfaction the products of distant lands and climes ...

> It compels all nations, on pain of extinction, to adopt the bourgeois mode of production; it compels them to introduce what it calls "civilization" into their midst, i.e. to become bourgeois themselves. In one word, it creates a world after its own image.

> All that is solid melts into air, all that is holy is profane, and man [sic] is at last compelled to face with sober senses his real conditions of life, and his relation with his kind.[26]

It should be clear that fast food is not about food. Rather, the idea behind fast-food corporations is to promote consumer consumption and allegiance to what, without the hype, could be seen as relatively dull, undifferentiated products. As blind tastings have proven, it is easier to tell a Whopper, a Big Mac or a Wendy's Single apart in television commercials than it is when you are eating them.[27]

The labour process in fast food, then, is not about the quality of the food produced, nor is it about how best to serve customers. It is about creating an illusion of participation in an authoritarian workplace. Carole Patemen refers to the difference between the psychological feel-good effects of what she calls "pseudo participation" and real involvement in one's workplace. Is a workplace where workers feel good an adequate substitution for one where workers have a say in how their jobs are organized? Democratization requires full participation at a higher level where important decisions are made. Rhetoric about empowerment, about workers and managers sharing a common goal in serving the customer, is not a replacement for the real thing. The real thing is an authority structure where the workers' role is not just to obey orders from on high, but one where workers will share in all the rewards of doing business well, including gain (profits), knowledge and power.[28]

Is fast-food corporatism our future? Perhaps it is. But we need to understand that there is nothing inevitable about a future based on the bottom line. And as a measure for future planning, for the survival of the planet and the peoples of the globe, this top-down approach to feeding the world has not worked very well. The proliferation of the golden arches has occurred in a world where over one billion people, 70 percent of whom are women, live in poverty; where neo-natal deaths due to maternal malnutrition number in the millions; where child labour proliferates; and where inequalities between the rich and the poor continue to increase. What is our responsibility? Perhaps we need to reconsider the efficacy of the consumer model used to sell hamburgers. How do we begin to build a more humane society in which we do not subordinate the goods of the community and the well-being of people to maximize gain for some individuals? How can we reclaim our place as active citizens rather than passive consumers?

Ester (second from left) joins Karen Serwonka
and Ann Eyerman at the May 1998 book retreat.

NOTES

This chapter also refers to ideas more fully discussed elsewhere in this volume. See Deborah Barndt, "Whose 'Choice'?" and Ann Eyerman, "Serving Up Service."

1. *Canadian Hotel and Restaurant*, 15 September 1955, 23.

2. McDonald's Corporation Annual Report, 1996, 9, 100.

3. McDonald's Corporation Annual Report, 1997. McDonald's posts financial results on a regular basis on its Website. These figures are constantly changing. See "Press Releases. Financial." *McDonald's*. <http://www.Mcdonalds.com>.

4. "Press Releases. Financial." *McDonald's*. <http://www.Mcdonalds.com>. April 1998.

5. United Nations Fourth World Conference on Women, *Platform for Action*, Beijing, 1995.

6. Ursula Franklin, *The Real World of Technology* (Toronto: CBC Enterprises, 1990; reprint, Concord, ON: House of Anansi Press, 1992).

7. John Vidal, *McLibel: Burger Culture on Trial* (New York: New Press, 1997), 141.

8. Jonathan Kozol, "The Sharks Move In," *New Internationalist* (October 1993), 8–10.

9. Emphasis in original. Vision '96. Press release from MDS announcing the "Clinical Laboratory Management Association (CLMA) 1995 Quality Management Award," 1995.

10. "Management Editorial," McDonald's Corporation Annual Report, 1994.

11. John Ralston Saul, *The Unconscious Civilization* (Concord, ON: House of Anansi Press, 1995), 96.

12. Michael Hammer and James Champy, *Reengineering the Corporation* (New York: HarperCollins, 1994), 18.

13. David Osborne and Ted Gaebler, *Reinventing Government* (New York: Plume Books, 1993), 80.

14. Noam Chomsky, *On Power and Ideology* (Montreal: Black Rose Books, 1987), 6–7.

15. "Come Join Our McDonald's Team," Pamphlet from McDonald's Canada.

16. "International McFacts," McDonald's Canada Promotional Package, 1998.

17. This was a handout given to employees at Burger King. Quoted in Ester Reiter, *Making Fast Food: From Frying Pan to Fryer* (Montreal: McGill Queen's, 1991), 86.

18. Arlie Hochshild, *The Commercialization of Human Feeling* (Berkeley: University of California Press, 1983).

19. Quoted from a McDonald's mini-application for employment.

20. Tu Chanh Ha, "McDonald's Closes, Workers' Union Bid Dies," *The Globe and Mail*, 13 February 1998, A3.

21. Dene Moore, "McChicken? Not These Two," *The Toronto Star*, 24 August 1998, A1.

22. Channel 4 News (UK), quoted in posting on the Website of the McLibel Support Campaign. "The McLibel Trial Story." *McSpotlight*. <http://www.mcspotlight.org>. September 1997. The Website provides a full history of the trial and updates on the 1999 McLibel Appeal.

23. Madelaine Droran, "Burger Chain Wins McLibel Suit," *The Globe and Mail*, 20 June 1997, A1.

24. Vidal, *McLibel*, 231.

25. Judith McCormack, "Bill Weakens Deterrent to Unfair Labour Practices," *The Toronto Star*, 23 June 1998, A19.

26. Karl Marx, *Communist Manifesto* (Toronto: Canadian Scholars' Press, 1987), 24.

27. *Nation's Restaurant News*, August 1984, 3.

28. Carole Patemen, *Participation and Democratic Theory* (New York: Cambridge, 1970), 77.

Part II

WOMEN WORKERS IN THE FOOD SYSTEM:

STORIES FROM

MEXICO TO

CANADA

Chapter Four

THE "POISONING" OF INDIGENOUS MIGRANT WOMEN WORKERS AND CHILDREN: FROM DEADLY COLONIALISM TO TOXIC GLOBALIZATION

An Indigenous boy joins his family in the tomato fields in Sayula, Mexico.

THE "POISONING" OF INDIGENOUS MIGRANT WOMEN WORKERS AND CHILDREN: FROM DEADLY COLONIALISM TO TOXIC GLOBALIZATION

Egla Martinez-Salazar

As a Mestiza[1] child member of a family forced by misery to migrate internally to overexploitative coffee and cotton plantations in Guatemala, I enter this analysis with a profound mark of the meaning of that experience. In fact, one of my sisters died because of exposure to pesticides and lack of proper food, medical care and adequate housing while working on the plantation. Her death was not even a statistic because migrant workers, one of the most unprotected and unorganized sectors of the working classes, are not represented in the mainstream media or in sophisticated analyses of labour issues. If these migrant workers are Indigenous peoples,[2] especially women, the silence around their lives is even more deadening.

In this chapter, I analyze how trade liberalization, with its vast flows of capital, has deepened the economic exploitation, political exclusion, racial and patriarchal discrimination of Indigenous women, their families and communities in Mexico, a discrimination that began five centuries ago with the Spanish conquest and colonization. An interlocking analysis based on race/ethnicity, class, gender and colonialist legacies is necessary for understanding the history and implications of the globalizing trend on Indigenous women's lives. An approach based on gender or class alone does not explain the complexities of their lives.

An analysis limited to gender supports the dominant Mexican nationalist ideology of *Mestizaje*, which sees European heritage as superior and which excludes Indigenous peoples, their ancestry and, therefore, their histories and rights. It also ignores the fact that racial, gender and class relations are mutually constituted and both shape and structure the subordination of differing groups of women,[3] and, I would add, Indigenous men, too. A class analysis alone, although very important and in recent years often forgotten, is also insufficient to understand how production, reproduction and relations of exploitation are mediated by race/ethnicity, culture, gender, sexuality and colonialism. As Chandra Mohanty pointedly argues, "class struggle, narrowly defined, can no longer be the only basis for solidarity among women workers. The fact of being women with particular racial, ethnic, cultural, sexual, and geographic histories has everything to do with our definitions and identities as workers."[4]

The lack of race/ethnicity analysis within gender or class theories has left Indigenous peoples, particularly women, invisible, forgotten or neglected. In classical class analyses, they appear as part of the rural proletariat, or semi-proletariat, or are not mentioned at all because their work in subsistence economies is not recognized as such, nor is their double duty as unpaid wives, mothers and caregivers.[5] In many gender analyses, Indigenous women are subsumed under the categories of rural workers, rural women or members of peasant societies.[6] The effects of blatant racial categorization that came with the Spanish conquest and subsequent colonization, as well as the imposition of policies of assimilation and integration, which deny Indigenous peoples' cultures and languages and homogenize them as "national citizens," are either minimized or ignored. In many anthropological studies, where ethnicity and culture are at the centre of analysis, the experiences and visions of Indigenous women are silenced. Privileged researchers tend to focus on Indigenous men's experiences, frequently portraying them, however, as the "exotic others," or naming their struggles for them.[7]

To understand how trade liberalization and the growing Mexican agromaquila industry[8] have affected the lives of workers, men and women, it is necessary to undertake an analysis based on interconnected systems of oppression (race/ethnicity, class, gender and colonialism).

Such an analysis helps us understand the particular struggles of Indigenous women and their families as migrant workers in the Mexican agromaquilas.

SPANISH COLONIZATION: THE HISTORICAL ROOTS OF INDIGENOUS PEOPLES' MIGRATION

Forced migration to Mestizo- and Creole-owned[9] plantations is not new for Indigenous peoples. After the brutal Spanish conquest in which millions of Indigenous peoples died from European diseases or were killed, the first massive forced migrations were organized by the colonizers. These took place in 1591, 1595 and 1601. Indigenous men constituted the majority of those who were brought to sugar plantations as slaves. Indigenous women sometimes accompanied their husbands to the plantations but very often they stayed back in their communities to cultivate their own crops and work in their homes, or to be exploited by the Spaniards as domestic workers or in the making of textiles.[10] In the 1700s, when the Indigenous workers began to die due to overexploitation and diseases, and the colonizers began to lose profits, they were replaced with African slaves, many of whom were eventually liberated during the nineteenth century.[11]

From the Mexican Revolution in 1910 to the present, the Mexican state, supported by the elites, has institutionalized assimilation as the policy through which Indigenous peoples' histories and cultures have been reduced to "The Indian Problem." The main premise of these assimilation policies was to get rid of Indianess and to bring European and North American "civilization" to the so-called "backward" Indigenous peoples. This ideology was based on the racist image created by the dominant culture — first the Spanish-Creole and later the Mestizo — that Indigenous peoples are inherently inferior and destined to be poor, so they do not deserve any better.

Indigenous communities have not benefited from industrialization or from the modernization of agriculture introduced in the 1940s. The communities have, in fact, been adversely affected by these changes and have coped with them by sending young men and women into forced migration to urban cities, within Mexico or to the United States, to find work. Mexican agribusinesses, modernization and the related Green Revolution (even though the Green Revolution brought some positive changes)[12] also made Mexico less self-sufficient in food production.[13] These trends and the more recent trade liberalization opened the way to export-oriented agribusiness, especially the growing and processing of fruit and vegetables in the northern Mexican states.

INDIGENOUS WOMEN AND THE NEW CONDITIONS OF FORCED MIGRATION

Particularly since NAFTA, Indigenous women, who have resisted the ongoing expropriation and erosion of their lands, increasingly migrate with their families from the poorer states to Jalisco, Sonora, Sinaloa and Baja California. Indigenous migrant workers in Sayula, in Jalisco state, for example, come precisely from the places where land reform, initiated by the Salinas government (in the late 1980s), "liberated" the *ejido* — in the states of Oaxaca, Chiapas Guerrero and Veracruz. The *ejido* was family-communal peasant land, which Indigenous peoples managed collectively. Before liberalization, this land could not be privatized, but under NAFTA, this land can now be bought by foreign interests. In Sayula, the Indigenous women pick the "beautiful and tasty tomatoes" that many of us purchase in Northern supermarkets.

The expropriation of this land is supported by racist ideologies that "naturalize" the poverty and marginalization of Indigenous peoples. The ideology is so entrenched in Mexican culture that many average Mexicans think that Indigenous peoples are marginalized because they do not work hard enough. It becomes easier for them to ignore Indigenous peoples' complaints and to forget their historical and contemporary rights for land, education, health, employment and adequate housing. Indigenous women, however, demonstrate what strong workers they are and how desperate their situation is when they travel with their families in crowded trucks to plantations in the central and northern Mexican states. Aware of the risks they are taking, these women go to the plantations anyway because they have to work, as they have always done, in order to feed their families.

The Indigenous migrant labour force in Mexico is family based.

Indigenous children accompany their mothers to the fields. On the Sayula plantation, Indigenous children officially start to work at the age of nine, although there are children who work at a much younger age. Because of their extreme poverty, Indigenous mothers cannot leave their children behind in their home villages and towns. Their relatives, equally poor or poorer, cannot afford to feed another mouth. Indigenous women, therefore, are obliged to bring their children, including their babies, with them to the fields where they are exposed to pesticides. A young Mestizo fieldworker revealed that male supervisors get mad at Indigenous women who bring their children on their backs and work with them all day long; yet they have no choice. Many children fieldworkers are paid less, even though they work all day.[14]

"Contractors" are hired by agribusinesses to, in turn, hire migrant labourers. These contractors very often promise Indigenous families good housing and wages. However, when they reach their destinations, they find very unhealthy living conditions waiting for them. The barracks on the Sayula plantation have been described by local journalists as "smelly ghettos that reproduce the misery of the places that Indigenous peoples come from. There, they live and die at the margins of a society that never understands them."[15]

Racist attitudes towards Indigenous women and their families help maintain these unhealthy standards of living. For example, Teresa Chavez, a Mestizo municipal employee, is very proud of the Lomeli, Valdes and Garcia Paniagua families who own the tomato agribusinesses in Sayula. She sees Sayula as a prosperous city, a city where "the best tomatoes are produced." Chavez defends the unhealthy conditions in which Indigenous women and their families live with the excuse that the climate is hot and "it is normal to have animals [insects] in the barracks." She also emphasizes that the agribusiness owners have done a lot to civilize "those people." The owners even built rustic toilets (latrines), but Indigenous workers defecate outside them. "Definitely," Chavez asserts, "these people do not want to become civilized."[16]

But Sayula health promoters and community activists see another reality. The few latrines that workers do have were only built after health promoters petitioned for more hygienic conditions. They also know that Indigenous women, men and children, already extremely poor, are brought to Sayula with the promise of decent houses. When they come, however, they either have to sleep in unhealthy barracks or they have to sleep outside in difficult weather conditions with no shelter at all, while they build cardboard houses or wait for huts to be built by agribusiness employees. Once built, cardboard houses are extremely dangerous because they are very flammable. Two serious fires recently destroyed whole rows of houses. In addition, the water that families must drink is not potable. All of these conditions breed cholera and other contagious illnesses.[17] For Chavez and for the company managers, however, these oppressive realities are reduced to a question of whether or not Indigenous people want to become "civilized," in western terms.

Mestizo women are hired in permanent positions as packers and moved by companies from one site to another. In most instances, they are better off than Indigenous women because they are protected from the sun inside the packing plants. They work longer hours, but their wage is three or four times that of Indigenous or Mestizo fieldworkers. Agromaquila managers (who are Mestizo) place the packers in better houses which are located in the town, while the camps for Indigenous workers are on the fringe of the fields or outside of town. Mestizo women have potable water, electricity and a little bit more space for cooking and laundry.[18] The agromaquila does not provide safety equipment (or even gloves, for example) to protect the workers against pesticide residue, but many Mestizo women are able to buy their own. Indigenous women cannot afford proper boots to work in the fields, as most Mestizo women can; therefore, they wear sandals or no shoes at all. It is not that Mestizo workers are responsible for their better housing and working conditions than Indigenous fieldworkers; it is that the structures in place racialize the labour force, which reinforces the stereotyping of Indigenous peoples and "normalizes'" their exclusion. And the agribusinesses justify this by saying "that's the way they [Indigenous peoples] live." In the United States and in Canada, the situation is similar. Agribusinesses do the same thing with undocumented Mexican migrants, poor Chicanos, people of colour and Aboriginal peoples.[19]

Because the majority of Indigenous women who are tomato pickers are monolingual (only some more privileged Indigenous men have been taught Spanish), they are neither informed of their rights nor given even minimum working instructions. A Mestizo woman field supervisor, one of the few females who holds this position in the agromaquila in Sayula, revealed that Mestizo clerical employees often deny Indigenous women health passes. They reason that Indigenous peoples do not need medical check-ups, because they cannot understand anything, as they do not speak Spanish. Only when this sympathetic field supervisor complained to company management were Indigenous women finally heard and sent to doctors. She felt it was very unjust that Indigenous women have to work under conditions that expose them and their children to cold weather and pesticides. Because the Mestizo supervisor was a single mother and was herself sick from the hazardous working conditions, she was more sensitive to the situation of Indigenous women. Male Mestizo supervisors, on the other hand, did not seem to care about the struggles of Mestizo women, much less Indigenous women.[20]

PESTICIDES: THE DEADLY POISONING

Marion Moses rightly says that work in agriculture poses many hazards, but one of the most insidious is pesticide exposure. Almost all commercial crops are heavily and repeatedly sprayed with dangerous pesticides, most of which are toxic chemicals that produce acute and chronic health problems among workers, especially women, the elderly and children.[21] The majority of Indigenous and Mestizo tomato pickers and packers are not given proper information about the toxicity of pesticides. In fact, such information is practically hidden. A study done in the Culiacan Valley of Sinaloa found that workers could not follow the instructions on the skull-and-crossbones labels. The instructions, which describe the chemicals as toxic and advise the use of special gloves and masks, are in English.[22] For many Indigenous women, even Spanish instructions would not help, because the majority have not had the right or opportunity to learn Spanish.

There is no data available in Sayula about pesticides poisoning. When I interviewed Mestiza workers, they did not feel safe talking openly about the effects of pesticides on their lives. Only two or three more outspoken workers acknowledged the health dangers they are exposed to, but conceded that they have no other choice but to accept them. Indigenous women seldom talked about their exposure to pesticides. In casual conversations, however, they acknowledged that very often they drink water from the containers used to mix pesticides. For Indigenous women who are pregnant, the risk to pesticides exposure is even greater. It has been documented that most of the pesticides pass through their skin very readily and can enter the placenta to affect the developing child.[23]

Generally, only acute symptoms of pesticide poisoning are recognized, such as the racing heartbeat, loss of consciousness, pounding headache, high temperature, nausea and burning skin. Less is known about the extent or magnitude of pesticide-related chronic health problems of agricultural workers — even among those who are protected — that result from low-level exposure over a period of months or years. Adequate longitudinal studies have not yet been done. One obstacle is that the time between exposure to pesticides and the development of a chronic problem ranges from ten to twenty years.[24] But pesticides also contain inactive ingredients which, unlike the active ones, are not required to be tested for their possible acute and chronic health effects and are not identified on the pesticide label. In the United States, their identity cannot be released to the public by state or federal regulatory agencies, even in cases of serious poisoning.[25] In Mexico, even where laws are in place, they are not enforced at all. If they are, agribusiness owners find ways to "influence" enforcers. Ultimately, it is the Mexican agromaquila owners who are responsible for this unhealthy situation as are their US counterparts, who supply capital to more than 40 percent of large-scale agribusiness in Mexico.[26]

PUTTING FOOD ON WHOSE TABLE?

Indigenous women working as migrant agricultural workers are the most forgotten and exploited actors in this global capitalist trend: a casualised almost clandestine economy, "where workers have little redress against either physical or economic exploitation."[27] My sister, a poor Mestizo girl who died after my family and I returned from a Guatemalan cotton plantation, represents only one more death in the long and endless list of poor children whose only crime was to be born the poorest of the poor. My parents as well as Indigenous women migrant workers, who were and are often condemned for bringing their children with them, are charged with being negligent parents. But what else can families do to survive, when historically they have been denied the right to exist?

To build solidarity with agromaquila workers, we have to understand that globalization is not a neutral process. It is a continuation of colonialism, a highly exploitative and unequal process in which relations based on race, class and gender shape the lives of the agromaquila workers and, among them, the most unprotected and marginalized labour force — Indigenous women and their families. Behind the perfect-looking tomato, there are thousands of hidden oppressive realities. There are also strong people who have resisted centuries of exclusion, people who want to work in respectful and dignified conditions, a right being eroded by trade liberalization and globalization.

It has been argued that agricultural workers are difficult to organize; they are seen as docile, domesticated and passive. But the referent of this traditional analysis is a gendered and racially privileged working-class worker, mystified as the (primarily male) breadwinner.[28] However, the reality of poor families and Indigenous families challenge this model because of the large proportion of unemployed or underemployed Indigenous male workers. Moreover, Indigenous families do not exhibit the classical split equating the private sphere with home life and the public with work. In order to survive, the whole family has to work; survival is also a form of resistance. For Indigenous peoples who have been repressed for centuries, survival has very often meant to resist in silence when the conditions are adverse. In some parts of Mexico, however, even at the risk of repression, Indigenous peoples are emerging as an important social movement. The January 1994 uprising of Indigenous communities in the southern Mexican state of Chiapas, led by the Zapatistas, coincided with the implementation of NAFTA and was a direct challenge to decades and centuries of such exploitative policies and practices.

Taking into account this context, it is problematic to say that agromaquila Indigenous and Mestizo workers are passive, docile and domesticated labour. Indigenous women, for example, are strong survivors, who are forced to work in subhuman conditions because of factors such as trade liberalization with all its structural adjustment policies and, in the case of Indigenous women, the persistence of colonial racism and patriarchy. Their priority is to put food on the table in a world where,

more and more, the distribution of wealth privileges the already privileged in the North, as well as the elites in the South. What, then, is our
responsibility in the North? How can we build solidarity? How can we
raise our consciousness so that we are aware of the food we are eating,
where it comes from and who, in fact, puts it on our tables?

*Egla (right) discusses her work with co-author Jan Kainer
while Antonieta Barrón rests at the May 1998 book retreat.*

NOTES

1. Mestiza/Mestizo. Conventionally in many anthropological and sociological studies as well as in everyday life, Mestiza/Mestizo is a person from mixed Spanish/ Indigenous background. However, due to the multiethnic and multiracial combinations in Latin America, a Mestizo person might not even have a European background at all. She/he can be a combination of different Afro and Indigenous *Mestizajes*.

2. Indigenous Peoples in Mexico are made up of fifty-six heterogeneous groups. Each group uses a different term to self-define themselves. For example, some use Pueblos Originarios (Original Peoples), ethnolinguistic groups and Native People. The majority, however, use their ethnolinguistic groups in naming themselves: Tzetzales, Tzotzhiles, Mayas, Tojolobales, Nahuatls, Chichimecas, Toltecas, Mixes, Yaquis, Huicholes, Lacandones and Tarahumaras.

3. Christina Gabriel and Laura MacDonald, "NAFTA and Economic Restructuring: Some Gender and Race Implications," in Isabel Bakker, ed., *Rethinking Restructuring: Gender and Change in Canada* (Toronto: University of Toronto Press, 1996),167.

4. Chandra Talpade Mohanty, "Women Workers and Capitalist Scripts: Ideologies of Domination, Common Interests, and the Politics of Solidarity," in Jacqui Alexander and Chandra Mohanty, eds., *Feminist Genealogies, Colonial Legacies, Democratic Futures* (New York: Routledge, 1997), 6.

5. See John Mason Hart, *Revolutionary Mexico: The Coming and Process of the Mexican Revolution* (Berkeley: University of California Press, 1989); and Tamar Wilson, "Theoretical Approaches to Mexican Wage Labor Migration," *Latin American Perspectives* 20, no. 3 (1993), 98–129.

6. See Lourdes Arizpe and Carlota Botey, "Mexican Agricultural Development Policy and Its Impact on Rural Women," in Carmen Diana Deere and Magdalena Leon, eds., *Rural Women and State Policy* (Boulder, CO: Westview Press, 1987), 67–83.

7. See Gary Gossen, "From Olmecas to Zapatistas: A Once and Future History of Souls," *American Anthropologist* 96, no. 3 (1994), 553, 570.

8. Agromaquila can be defined as massive intensive agricultural production oriented mainly to export but also covering national markets. In this kind of agricultural production, most of the labour force is temporal, seasonal, low waged with no benefits, racialized, feminized and exposed to pesticides. The term agromaquila derives from maquiladora, a Mexican term used originally to define the garment and electronic industry located in the northern border region of Mexico, and now applied to all free trade zones in Asia, Africa, Latin America and recently in North America. According to J. Carrillo, as elaborated in *Desert Capitalism*, maquilization refers to a process characterized by 1) the feminization of the labour force, 2) the high segmentation of skill categories, 3) the lowering of real wages and 4) the introduction of a non-union orientation. Kathryn Kopinak, *Desert Capitalism: What Are the Maquiladoras?* (Montreal: Black Rose Books, 1997), 13.

9. Creoles are Spaniards' descendents born in the Americas. They took control of the emergent nation-states in Latin America, after independence from Spain, in the nineteenth century.

10. Susan Deeds, "Double Jeopardy: Indian Women in Jesuit Missions of Nueva Vizcaya," in Susan Schroeder et al., eds., *Indian Women in Early Mexico* (Oklahoma: University of Oklahoma Press, 1997), 259.

11. El Colegio de Mexico, *Historia General de México*, Tomo I (México, DG: Harla, 1987), 397.

12. For more on the Green Revolution, see Harriet Friedmann, "Remaking 'Traditions,'" in this volume.

13. Arizpe and Botey, "Mexican Agricultural Development Policy," 74.

14. Anonymous, interview with author.

15. *Siglo Veintiuno*, 8 December 1996, 6.

16. Ibid, 7.

17. Petition signed by many Sayula citizens in January 1997.

18. Anonymous, interview with author.

19. Marion Moses, "Farmworkers and Pesticides," in Robert Bullard, ed., *Confronting Environmental Racism: Voices from the Grassroots* (Boston: South End Press, 1993), 141–160.

20. Anonymous, interview with author.

21. Moses, "Farmworkers and Pesticides," 162.

22. Esther Schrader, "A Giant Spraying Sound: Since NAFTA, Mexican Growers are Spraying Toxic Pesticides on Fruits, Vegetables and Workers," *Mother Jones* 20, no. 1 (1995), 34–36.

23. Moses, "Farmworkers and Pesticides," 166.

24. Ibid., 167.

25. Ibid.

26. Schrader, "A Giant Spraying Sound," 34–35.

27. Swasti Mitter, "On Organising Women in Casualised Work," in Sheila Rowbotham and Swasti Mitter, eds., *Dignity and Daily Bread: New Forms of Economic Organising Among Poor Women in the Third World and the First* (London: Routledge, 1994).

28. Patricia Hill Collins, *Black Feminist Thought: Knowledge, Consciousness, and the Politics of Empowerment* (New York: Routledge, 1990), 45.

Chapter Five

MEXICAN WOMEN ON THE MOVE:
MIGRANT WORKERS IN MEXICO AND CANADA

*Isabel Gomez comes to Ontario from Mexico every summer to pick
our locally produced tomatoes.*

MEXICAN WOMEN ON THE MOVE:
MIGRANT WORKERS IN MEXICO AND CANADA

Antonieta Barrón

The Political and Economic Context

In Mexico, structural adjustment has deeply affected the development of all sectors of economic activity. From the late 1980s and into the 1990s, agriculture has undergone profound transformations through structural adjustment measures that include a transfer by the state of its traditional role in directing the economy to private interests, the reduction of credit supports to small producers, the free reign of market mechanisms and an accelerated commercial opening to foreign interests. CONASUPO,[1] the national subsidy program for farmers, has reduced its role in grain storage, thus deregulating the prices of most agricultural products. These measures have had several results: the reduction of public financing and investment, the increase in costs of production and the creation of commercial policies that favour imports. Ultimately, there has been a drop in the agricultural GDP (Gross Domestic Product) and an increase of poverty in the countryside. As a consequence, peasant families have had to develop new survival strategies, including sending more family members out to seek employment as salaried workers in agribusinesses.

This chapter examines the fruit and vegetable labour market in two different regions in the NAFTA context: the San Quintin region of the Baja California state in northern Mexico, and the Niagara region in Ontario, Canada. I analyze the labour force from a feminist perspective, in terms of survival strategies, and from the employer's perspective, in terms of supply and demand. I hope to show how labour relations have been deregulated, and that this deregulation is not only limited to developing countries such as Mexico but is also occurring in more developed countries such as Canada.

Currently, women working in agricultural activities represent 32.2 percent of the rural female labour force. With 60 percent of the working population receiving the equivalent of two minimum wage salaries or less (minimum wage is 28 Mexican pesos or Can$9 per day), more members of Mexican peasant families have been forced into wage labour to compensate for such a low salary. Women are playing an increasingly important role in these strategies of survival. Rural women have two options: to work on the family farm (if they have one) while the husband and children migrate to work, or to migrate themselves — either alone or with their families.

Within the Mexican context, I argue that whether or not the agro-export market is more developed or less developed, the composition of the labour force by age and by gender is determined by the relation of *supply* of workers to *demand* for workers. When the employer has more choice of whom he hires, whether they are young or adult, men or women, working conditions and salary levels are restricted only by labour laws. The dynamic relationship between supply and demand determines the composition of the labour force as well as the work processes in Mexico. If demand is greater than supply, then all of the available labour force (men, women and children) works, especially during harvests. But if supply exceeds demand, then only adults (men and women) work,[2] depending on the activity. The work process is the first determinant of who is contracted. When physical strength is required, only men are contracted; when ability is required, either men or women can do it, and so the selection depends on supply and demand. In picking oranges, for example, where workers have to carry on their shoulders baskets that weigh as much as 100 kilos, women and children are not contracted; whereas for coffee picking, women and children are considered ideal.

In Mexico, there have recently been important changes in rural agro-export markets: a reduction in child labour, a shift from a daily wage to a piecework system and an increase in the participation of young women in picking, sorting and packing fruit and vegetables. The deterioration of living conditions for rural families and an increase of unemployment in both rural and urban areas have created an imbalance — *supply* now exceeds *demand* for labour. In other words, there is a surplus of labourers and not enough work for them. In the case of seasonal migrant labour to Canada, it is not supply and demand that determines who works in the labour force, but rather the ages of the workers. Employers can hire the workers they want with very few barriers in their way.

FEMALE AGRICULTURAL EMPLOYMENT IN MEXICO

Despite a recent trend towards a reduced workforce in the agricultural sector, the participation of salaried women workers is clearly increasing. For example, even though the number of men working in agriculture dropped between 1991 and 1996 from 7,185,900 to 6,732,200, women employed in agriculture increased from 1,003,800 to 1,189,500.[3] Even with NAFTA and the subsequent economic crisis, the percentage of women in the Economically Active Population (Población Economicamente Activa, or PEA) rose from 12.2 percent in 1991 to 15.2 percent in 1996.

If we analyze the working population by job position and gender,[4] we can find several possible explanations for this increase in female labour. It appears that women are replacing and not just complementing the male labour force; there is a kind of competition between men and women for jobs. Men are also leaving agriculture as production in certain traditional crops — such as corn, which once required male participation — has decreased, while production in crops that depend more on female labour — such as fruit and vegetables — has increased.[5] The number of self-employed women (women who have their own business in the informal sector), however, has dropped, while the number of those family members who help out without pay in the informal sector has increased disproportionately. (These are usually family members who work alongside other family members who are paid — daughters, for example, working alongside their mothers or fathers.) This shift can be explained by the increase of women in the salaried workforce in the formal sector. For many women, the economic reality often requires that they combine different kinds of work in both the informal and formal sectors. Many more women are developing small businesses in the informal sector as a survival strategy — for example, cooking and selling tamales on the street. As well, the migration of some members of peasant households has left the work of managing the family plot in the hands of the women. Not only do women compete with men in the national labour market, but the horizons are broadening as they become part of a highly regulated global labour market, participating not only in the agricultural sector but also in electronics and textiles, and even in the production of fruit and vegetables in Canada.

In general, more men than women work full-time in the agricultural workforce; still, 22 percent of the men work less than thirty-five hours a week. There has been an increase in the number of women who work thirty-five or more hours (as well as those working fifteen to twenty-four hours a week and less than fifteen hours), while the number of women working without pay has decreased. Women are thus moving more into salaried work, even though much of it remains part-time. In San Quintin, Baja California, almost half of women workers I interviewed gave "personal reasons" for working part-time, and 40 percent said it was because the job itself was designated as part-time.[6]

Agricultural workers' wages have traditionally been lower than those of industrial workers, who earn more than minimum wage. Of the large number of migrant workers who earn less than minimum wage, there are more underpaid women than men (approximately 60 percent women compared with 50 percent men in 1995).[7] In fact, the percentage of men receiving less than minimum wage decreased between 1993 and 1995, while the proportion of women increased. So it is clear that women's greater presence in the salaried labour force is also based on their being paid lower wages.

Deteriorating living conditions, due both to reduced working hours and low wages, have led rural families to seek new survival strategies, forcing more family members to enter the labour force. From 1989 to 1994, the national average of family members working increased from 1.63 to 2.67 per family; the average among migrant worker families was already 2.6 by 1991.

Mexican Case Study:
San Quintin, Baja California

The San Quintin region of the Baja California state in northern Mexico is a major producer of fruit and vegetables for the export market. The produce includes tomatoes, zucchini, peppers and cucumbers. Very little local labour is employed; 80 percent of the labour force is migrant labour. In contrast to what's happening at the national level, there are more men than women employed, approximately three men compared to every two women.

There is, however, a slight change in the composition of the female workforce. Between 1991 and 1995, the number of married women workers increased, while salaried employment for single women decreased.[8] It seems that as the traditional peasant housewife moves out into the salaried workforce and is no longer a traditional housewife, she becomes more a worker in her own right and less an assistant accompanying her husband in the fields.

Over 80 percent of the women I interviewed went to work with other family members. While the average salary fluctuated between 25 and 30 pesos a day (Can$5 to Can$6), more than half of the migrant workers made around 60 pesos. With a daily cost of living of about 20 pesos, and with housing provided, one would assume that they could accumulate some savings. If there are two members of a family working six days a week for six months, they should be able to save some money, but only by reducing what they spend to a bare minimum.

The increase of workers seeking migrant labour in the fruit and vegetable sector has also provoked changes in working and living conditions. In Baja California in August of 1996, the form of contracting migrant workers changed from a daily wage to a piecework system. As a result, most women reported working twelve-hour days, filling up to one hundred 20-litre containers at one peso per container; this shift is due to the increase in the *supply* over *demand* of the labour force.

According to standards set by the World Trade Organization, anyone who works at least one hour a week is considered part of the working population. Whether they work less than fifteen hours, or fifteen to thirty-four hours a week, or one to three days a week, they are considered part-time workers. Because of the working conditions in Mexico, migrant workers become so physically exhausted after three consecutive days of backbreaking work in the fields that they may decide not to go to work for the remainder of the week.

Whether they are migrant workers or from the region where they are working, once they finish their salaried workday, women must still cook meals, make tortillas, wash clothes, bathe their children and attend to various family needs. While some of the migrant labour camps in northern Mexico are more decent than others, with potable water and cooking fuel, the living conditions of most migrant workers in camps in other regions have deteriorated significantly. For example, in Baja California, three hundred migrant workers sleep on a patio without shelter, and families are separated only by sheets of plastic. The floor is earthen, and there is only one main water tap where the women go to wash their clothes and bathe their children. They cook on a makeshift burner made from a can. And this is what they face — after picking grapes from seven in the morning until five in the afternoon.

This story is repeated for thousands of women. When questioned about why he didn't provide better sleeping quarters, one producer replied: "Look, they're only here for a short time, and what's more, they're used to living like this. Who am I to change their customs?"[9] So for these migrant workers, there are neither laws nor rules, since it is believed that they don't live like human beings. They are merely the labour force that picks fruit. It is because of them that exports are increasing, yet this increase has not improved their living conditions; it has only increased the length of their productive and reproductive workdays.

CANADIAN CASE STUDY: MEXICAN WOMEN WORKERS IN ONTARIO

In comparing the per capita income (in US dollars) of the three NAFTA countries (according to 1995 data: $2,500 for Mexico, $26,000 for the US, and $20,000 for Canada), we must recognize that these figures reflect real structural differences in technology, productivity and institutional capacity. The social and economic conditions of the waged labour force have to do more with structural and political economic realities. For this reason, the differences in income between domestic and international migrant women have to be understood relative to the income levels of their respective countries.

The migration of Mexican workers to the Niagara region in Ontario is regulated by a 1984 agreement between the Governments of Mexico and Canada. Seasonal workers (from Barbados, Jamaica, Mexico, and Trinidad and Tobago) are contracted for the harvest and sometimes to cultivate and prune fruit, vegetables, tobacco and Christmas trees. This migrant labour force is separated by countries of origin, perhaps to avoid contact and cultural tensions: Mexicans work primarily in fruit and vegetables, bringing considerable experience and skill in agriculture to their jobs. The number of Mexican workers in Ontario rose from 3,825 in 1995 to 5,154 in 1997; only in recent years have women been included — 57 in 1997, and more than 150 in 1998. This is particularly interesting to study because of the feminization of the labour force in Mexico. Canadian producers also recognize that these women have skills in packing fruit and vegetables.

Of the women migrant workers we interviewed in our 1997 study,[10] the majority were single mothers (38.9 percent). They shared in common the fact that they had left small children or adolescents at home in Mexico (usually with grandparents), assuring the Canadian government that they would return to Mexico. The average age was thirty-eight; only 22 percent were older than forty, and they seemed to have gotten in because a specific farmer requested them, even though Canadian employers usually prefer younger workers.

Men and women make the same salary: between 1996 and 1998, this has been at the minimum wage of Can$6.90. Even though their workdays are regulated by labour laws (limiting the workday to eight hours), women workers are available for extra work if the farmer asks them to work overtime. Though the choice is theirs, all said they accepted overtime work, because, as one Mexican woman explained it, "That's why I came to Canada, to earn money, not to rest." The wage levels vary from Can$200 to Can$530 a week, depending on the hours they work; the cost of their airfare to and from Canada is deducted from their first paycheque.

The women hardly go out at all, except once a week when the boss takes them to buy food and supplies (only one of those interviewed had visited the well-known tourist attraction Niagara Falls, which is nearby). In contrast with Mexican women who migrate internally within Mexico, those who migrate to Canada often have worked previously in the service sector, in sewing or factory work, or as domestic workers, and don't have much experience as fieldworkers in Mexico (as the Canadian requirements suggest they should have). Nonetheless, they all soon become experts in fruit and vegetable work in the region. As one grape worker revealed: "You see, when I arrived, these grapevines were small and ugly, and after I worked with them, and encouraged them, look at them now, how beautiful they are!"

A normal workday is eight hours, yet the women often accept overtime up to twelve hours, and though they hope to be paid double for overtime, they are only paid the normal hourly wage, as in Mexico. The amount of money that the women are able to accumulate over their four-to-six-month stay in Canada gives them money to survive a few more months in Mexico. This has to be complemented with other earnings from low-wage jobs.

Perhaps because they make so much more in Canada, the women disregard some aspects of their working conditions. All the women interviewed, for example, talked about getting sick or having an accident and going to the doctor, but deciding not to take time out to recover for fear of losing work. As one woman told me, "I fell through a glass and had to have my leg stitched up, but when they told me I had to rest for two days, I went back to work so I wouldn't lose the money."[11] Lack of sick pay and time off also reflects the lack of unionization or workers' rights for migrant labour.[12] These women really have little choice but to accept the conditions of work — they have no one to advocate for them and speak little or no English. No matter how much they might complain among themselves about the treatment by the farmer who hires them, they seek to please him so that he will ask for them the following year.

It is difficult to compare the living conditions of migrant workers in Canada with the living conditions of migrant workers in Mexico. In Canada, they have a decent place to live, a bathroom, hot water, electricity for cooking, a refrigerator. And both men and women workers earn the same amount and work for the same amount of time.

MEXICAN MIGRANT WOMEN IN CANADA AND IN MEXICO: SIMILARITIES AND DIFFERENCES

The integration of women into the agricultural labour force is closely related to increasing poverty among rural families. Migrating to Canada is one way women can broaden their horizons and move beyond devastating economic conditions. Mexican migrant workers in Canadian fields are treated like second-class workers; their situation cannot be compared with Canadian workers doing the same kind of work. In Mexico, however, the material and physical conditions are much worse. While a workday in Canada may last for twelve hours, it isn't as exhausting as the same workday in Mexico, because in Canada workers are paid by the hour, while in Mexico, they're paid less and by the quantity picked, thus pressuring them into an accelerated pace of work. In other words, they must work much harder for much less pay.

Take, for example, a Mexican working in the Niagara region, picking peaches from seven in the morning until noon, when she stops for her lunch hour, and then continues working until seven in the evening. Her workday may be monotonous, but she doesn't have to fill a quota, is paid by the hour and may make around Can$82 a day. The same woman working in Mexico is paid one peso (in 1997, equivalent to Can$0.17) for each basket she fills (a container that holds 20 kilos of tomatoes). Working fast and hard for thirteen or fourteen hours, she fills one hundred baskets and thus makes 100 pesos, or Can$17.64, for an exhausting day's work.

Clearly, women working in the Mexican fields get the worse deal. They work under difficult conditions at piecework, earning just over Can$17 for a twelve-hour workday. As they migrate with their families, they have both long workdays as well as long hours of work in the home (fifteen to eighteen hours total). Both their working and their living conditions have deteriorated in recent years and they have little possibility of saving any earnings.

There are, however, some similarities in the experiences of women migrant labour, whether in Mexico or in Canada. Neither are paid overtime wages; they may receive medical attention, but any time taken out of the workday for medical visits or recuperation is not compensated.

And both groups work within the capitalist system, even though under different forms of contracting. One reflects a "crude capitalism" (which exploits workers without considering their physical capacity and limits), while the other is perhaps a less brutal capitalism, but one that nonetheless perpetuates inequalities. In both Mexico and Canada, and critical to the new geopolitical context of NAFTA, these "women on the move" reflect the deepening integration of the North American and Latin American economies. As free trade has expanded, it has forced them to follow the crops and the demand for their cheap labour, feeding not only Mexicans and Canadians but also the global food system itself.

Antonieta (left) discusses her work with co-author
Lauren Baker at the May 1998 retreat.

NOTES

This chapter was translated from the Spanish original by Deborah Barndt. This chapter also refers to ideas more fully discussed elsewhere in this volume. See Harriet Fried-mann, "Remaking 'Traditions'"; Egla Martinez-Salazar, "The 'Poisoning' of Migrant Women Workers and Children."

1. A government company, CONASUPO played an important regulatory role in the past, buying more than 12 percent of the national agricultural production and thus helping to regulate national price levels.

2. The US government recently passed legislation limiting the purchase of goods from countries who use child labour. This will surely affect rural migration in Mexico, since migrant workers often include their children in their fieldwork as families.

3. National Employment Survey by the National Institute of Geographical Statistics and Information, the Secretary of Work and Social Security, 1991, 1993, 1995, 1996.

4. Table 1: Working Population (in thousands) in the Agricultural Sector (1991–1996) by Job Position and Gender

	1991	1993	1995	1996	1991	1993	1995	1996
Position	Men				Women			
Employers	15.7	2.2	4.4	5.5	7.6	0.9	1.3	2.4
Self-Employed	36.3	49.8	42.2	39.3	13.2	8.1	13.2	13.1
Salaried	24.0	19.1	27.6	29.6	27.4	11.5	12.0	17.6
Unpaid	24.0	28.8	25.7	25.6	51.8	69.5	73.5	67.0
Total	100.0	200.0	100.0	100.0	100.0	100.0	100.0	100.0
Total	7185.9	7721.6	6922.1	6529.8	1003.9	1121.6	1182.5	1171.3

Source: Instituto Nacional Estadística Geográfica e Información (National Institute of Geographical Statistics and Information) — Secretária del Trabajo y Prevision Social (Secretary of Work and Social Security) — National Employment Surveys 1991, 1993, 1995, 1996.

5. With NAFTA, Mexico entered continental competition for grain production. As a result, the grain industry, which included corn, has suffered (to the point that, once self-sufficient, Mexico must now import most of its corn); the heavily subsi-dized US grain industry has continued to over-produce and increase its exports to Mexico. On the other hand, the fruit and vegetable market has thrived. It is in this sector that Mexico has the advantage of climate and cheaper labour.

6. In the fruit and vegetable business, workers may only have two to three days work when production is low. During peak harvest seasons, however, a "normal" work-day for women pickers and packers is twelve to fifteen hours. So part-time does

not mean only "part of a day" but can also refer to these fluctuations in working hours due to the dynamics of agricultural production (original research by author, San Quintin, Baja California, 1995).

7. Table 2: Working Population in the Agricultural Sector, By Gender, According to Wage Levels, 1991, 1993, 1995, 1996 (Percentages)

Income Level	Women				Men			
	1991	1993	1995	1996	1991	1993	1995	1996
Less than 1 minimum wage	44.4	53.2	59.9	25.9	43.7	48.0	44.2	16.4
1 to 2 minimum wages	40.2	31.3	22.1	29.3	39.7	36.3	27.8	32.6
More than 2 minimum wages	12.4	5.0	15.1	24.9	11.2	9.6	23.1	33.9
No Income	0.0	n.d.	29.2	17.3	n.d.	n.d.	21.5	13.3
Not Specified	3.1	10.4	2.9	2.7	5.3	6.0	4.9	3.9
Total	100.0	100.0	100.0	100.0	100.0	100.0	100.0	100.0

Source: Instituto Nacional Estadística Geográfica e Información (National Institute of Geographical Statistics and Information) — Secretária del Trabajo y Prevision Social (Secretary of Work and Social Security) — National Employment Surveys 1991, 1993, 1995, 1996.

8. Table 3: Civil Status of Salaried Women Workers

Civil Status	1991	1995
Single	43.9	39.6
Married	34.3	40.3
Common law	12.6	12.4
Single mother	6.1	4.7
Other	3.0	3.0
Total	100.0	100.0
Total numbers	(230)	(139)

Source: Compiled by author, based on original research in San Quintin, Baja California, 1991–1995.

9. Anonymous, interview with author, San Quintin, Baja California,1991.

10. The information in this next section is drawn from an initial survey and from interviews by the author with Mexican women migrant workers in Ontario in August 1997. Funding from the Canadian embassy in Mexico allowed an extension of this research during August 1998. Results of the most recent study are forthcoming.

11. Juana, interview with author, Niagara region of Ontario, August 1997.

12. Though there have been some attempts to organize the seasonal workers in Ontario, they have not been successful. It is very hard, in this case especially, because the workers are neither citizens nor landed immigrants, are only temporarily in Canada, and often don't speak English.

Chapter Six

"FROM WHERE HAVE ALL THE FLOWERS COME?"

WOMEN WORKERS IN MEXICO'S NON-TRADITIONAL MARKETS

The exotic flowers we've become accustomed to buying for our homes are probably grown and harvested by women in Mexico and other Southern countries.

"FROM WHERE HAVE ALL THE FLOWERS COME?"

WOMEN WORKERS IN MEXICO'S NON-TRADITIONAL MARKETS

Kirsten Appendini

BY THE END OF APRIL, flowers blossom from the balconies of Rome, combining the sweetness of spring air with the scent and colours of geraniums, petunias and pansies. My neighbours have been busy over the weekend, carrying home cardboard boxes filled with flowers to replant in their flower boxes. I have also been to the nursery several times and now have a lovely balcony garden to enjoy throughout the summer — with the proper care, of course. Every evening when I water my geraniums, I have to think of Ines, and all the other women, working with their heavy hoses, sprinkling the frail seedlings that are to be cut and sent off to Europe, Canada and the USA, in time to be planted and blooming in my Roman neighbourhood nursery by spring.

INES, FLOWER NURSERY WORKER

The little village in Morelos, Mexico, with sixty hectares of plastic-covered greenhouses, seems far away, but the thread of globalization links it to my balcony, to my joy of summer, to my delight of beautiful surroundings. Reversing the popular folk song of the 1960s, I stop to remember, "From where have all the flowers come?"[1]

When I first saw Ines at the geranium nursery in Morelos, she was "breezing" the small plants, carefully moving a heavy hose regularly back and forth during the eight-hour day in order not to drown the tiny plants that still had no roots. Ines explained the production process to me in great detail and with a genuine interest in the growth of the plants: "The female supervisor says the plants are like children and must be cared for in order to grow into beautiful plants."

Like the other two hundred and twenty women working in the nursery, Ines cares for the geranium seedlings from the beginning to the end, when the plants are sent off to the European partner that distributes them wholesale. Women are responsible for the entire production process, which is all manual work. The women's work is organized by groups, according to a post-Fordist model. Each group is responsible for an area within the nursery and follows the development of the plant — from preparing the beds for the seedlings to cutting the mature plants. Manual breezing comes at an early stage and has to be done very carefully so as not to damage the tiny seedlings; not until the roots are firm is the automatic sprinkling system turned on. Then, as the geranium plants grow strong and develop stalks, the cutting season begins.

Ines always looks forward to the cutting season, which starts in November. Cutting is done with a small sharp blade. The cuts are emptied into pails; six pails with one hundred and thirty cuts each is the hourly average. There are prizes for workers who cut the most. Ines hoped to gain more speed that year and win a prize.

After the cutting season, only a few women remain in the nursery. The beds are cleaned and new plastic bags are lined up. This is hard work: the small volcanic pebbles (*tezontle*) are thrown out, the bags are cleaned, disinfected and filled again. The bricks on which the pots stand must be lifted and cleaned. Ines said she was not sure if she would continue working then; the work at this stage is too hard and tiring, and pays only minimum wage. "It should be men's work, but it is women who do it," she complained.

Not that there aren't any men in the nursery. They are there, but they only help in the application of fertilizers and herbicides. They are also in charge of maintaining the equipment in the greenhouse — the irrigation equipment, electrical installation, ventilators — and undertaking any necessary construction and so forth. Since men are in charge of maintenance, they have permanent jobs, while women have "flexible" jobs, which start during the peak cutting season in November and end when the season finishes in March or April. The women said they were tired or bored, that they wanted "to stay at home for a while," help out[2] with household chores, or try some other job.

There is a gender division of labour in the nursery, a pattern found in other agro-industries and to a large extent confirmed by other studies.[3] This division of labour has been assumed by workers themselves and certainly by their employers. The gender discourse suggests that women have the attributes of caring, delicacy, speed, accuracy, and the skills for handling flowers and doing routine work. This means standing up in a damp environment, inhaling fertilizers and pesticides, pricking hands and fingers, and doing all of this during eight hours a day, six days a week, five to six months at a stretch for minimum wage (in 1993, equivalent to about US$4 a day).

Nonetheless, Ines plans to work here again next season. She even hopes to do so well that she might be selected as supervisor, the only promotion available for the women. In any case, she has already tried working as a factory worker in the industrial zone of nearby Cuernavaca. But though the wage is slightly higher, transport time and expenses eliminate the benefits. So she has decided to stay in the village, living near the greenhouse with her parents, brothers and sisters, helping out with housework, seeing her boyfriend, and giving some money, but not all of her salary, to her mother. She claims to "eat lots of vitamins and proper food, so as not to be affected by the fertilizer we work with."

This "gendered" portrait of a young working woman is repeated in the lives of thousands and millions of young women all over the world. Ines is as lovely as the blooming geraniums; were she a young Canadian worker she might work with proper equipment that would protect her from health hazards, work for one or two years in a nursery that grows the geranium seedlings for the market and save money to travel or to go back to school for further training. But most women in Mexico do not have such opportunities. They move along a horizontal dead-end labour market from domestic service to other low-wage service jobs, to factory work (if they live in an urban area) or to the agro-industry (in a rural area); it's the latter that offers the best daily rate.

Is the future really so bleak? That was not what I heard from the young women. They would joke about marrying, thinking that this was far off, not until their mid-twenties. By that time perhaps they will or will not want to work, but most agreed that their boyfriends would not approve of their working (even though some married women do work, breaking the custom that a married woman's place is at home). Female wage labour has been accepted for several decades, since the daughters of Mexican peasants became the nimble fingers of the strawberry industry in the states of Guanajuato and Michoacán. This was tolerated as long as women worked in gendered and controlled spaces in which employers assumed a gender ideology, reproducing the patterns of authority and subordination of a patriarchal society. Wage work both reinforced gender roles and altered women's bargaining position within the family, as girls gained degrees of freedom to dispose of their time and part of their income. Their income became an important source of cash for the rural family.[4] Certainly today nobody questions the presence of the single, young working woman, who represents 57 percent of the women workers in the agro-industries we visited.

The situation of married women was different, varying by age and region. In all, 20 percent of the women interviewed were married or in a stable relationship. In families just getting started, the women's income may also be important. This is especially the case when their husbands have no better employment than minimum-wage jobs, though men are likely to have more stable jobs or self-employment throughout the year.

ELSA, AVOCADO WORKER

Elsa, an avocado worker, lives in the outskirts of the city of Uruapán and works at an avocado packinghouse nearby. She is twenty-two and married. Elsa has attended high school. Her husband works at the plant and has work all year-round; formerly, he made wooden crates. They both live with their three-year-old daughter in a two-room house, on the urban plot where Elsa's father, a construction worker, has lived since her parents separated. A sister, who is a single mother, takes care of the father's household and of Elsa's daughter. Another sister works at the plant.

Elsa works a full day, plus overtime when she is needed. Often her work begins at eight in the morning and ends at ten in the evening, with a one-hour lunch break, during which time she goes home. Elsa began working at the packinghouse before her marriage and has worked there for several seasons. It is the only place where she has been employed. She did not work the year after her daughter was born, but then she returned to work again during peak seasons. However, she has now worked for a year and a half without interruption. When the export season is over, she will stay on and pack for the domestic market. Elsa hopes to keep her job, and her husband agrees to her working. They need both wages for household expenses and they want to save some money to finish building their house. Since they plan to have only one more child, Elsa does not consider her children to be obstacles to her having a job, especially with support from her extended family.

The working conditions in the avocado packinghouse where Elsa works comply with labour regulations. It is one of the larger and more established avocado packinghouses in the outskirts of Uruapán (on the slopes of the Michoacán highlands). This provincial city, with a lovely temperate climate, hosts one of the largest avocado producing regions in the world, with a thriving export business to Canada, Japan and Europe; Mexican avocados can be found in most supermarkets in these countries. The future challenge for avocado producers will be the competition with California avocado growers, a possibility since the ban on Mexican avocados has been lifted. (The ban was in effect following an act in 1914 that blocked avocados from entering the US due to sanitary conditions.) Or, perhaps, California growers will join Mexican growers in Uruapán and invest in the region's avocado production to take advantage of NAFTA. Some avocado entrepreneurs in Uruapán expect this will happen.

As an exporter, a company running a packinghouse must be registered and comply with government regulations on working conditions (health, safety standards and so on), on fiscal regulations and on labour regulations.[5] But companies do not always comply with all the regulations, particularly those regulations that concern working conditions and labour status. The degree to which packinghouses conform to or bypass regulations varies according to the crop, the size of the plant and the type of management. Non-enforcement of regulations is made easier by the seasonality of production — some packinghouses may be open only during the picking seasons, or have peak employment some months of the year. In the packinghouses I visited, minimum wages are enforced, and all employers and employees stated that they are enrolled in the social security schemes, though this is not clearly proven in some cases.[6] Payment for overtime can be less than the law requires as can payment for work on Sundays. Also, there is no indemnity for having worked over three months, as stated by Mexican labour regulations, nor are there written contracts for the workers. Women are dismissed by verbal notice from day to day when the peak season is over. The more fortunate in the flower and avocado plants might have a chance of staying on. This is what Ines hoped for and what Elsa accomplished.

Elsa is an experienced worker, a packer who has gained incredible speed at putting six to eight avocados into a cardboard box. Packing is one of the most desirable jobs, because it is paid by piecework, and a day's work can earn more than the standard daily minimum wage. It is also sought after, because skill in packing is especially valued for the delicate fruit for export. A good packer also has the best chances of continuing work when the export season is over. Avocados are grown all year in Uruapán, and after the export season, production is geared to the domestic market. Careful packing is not such an issue then, because the second-rate produce is kept and packed for national consumption. Even men (perceived to be less "careful") can be employed for this work. In fact, they are employed in one of the old packinghouses that is still under a union contract with one of those "bothersome" unions from the 1970s (which workers had organized before the era of "flexibility" and when men still dominated the labour market).

But there is little labour protection of full-time steady work nowadays. The classic working day of eight hours (six days a week at minimum wage) has given way to flexibility and has affected work in three areas. First, flexibility means the availability of work according to seasonal fluctuations and Northern consumer demands —geranium cutting peaks during the November months (to be sent off for spring), while roses peak in February (for St. Valentine's Day) and in May (for Mother's Day), and poinsettias in December (for Christmas). Mexican avocados alternate with Europe's Israeli imports, and, as we shall see, with mangos when the fruit is ripe for exports. Second, flexibility within each season means availability of work for long periods without days of rest. In the case of mango production, workers edure long hours and strenuous work under hazardous health conditions, as do workers in the nurseries. Finally, flexibility refers to the expectation that workers themselves can easily adjust their skills and adapt to changing production processes within the greenhouse or packinghouse.[7]

In the avocado packinghouse, as well as in the mango plants, the work process is organized along a conveyor belt, according to the Fordist model. This again translates into a rigid division of labour determined by sex. Men unload trucks, carry the fruit in boxes and load it on the conveyor belt. In the avocado plants, men also monitor the automatic rinsing and drying, while in the mango plants, women supervise the rinsing and drying of the fruit and are also in charge of scalding the fruit in boiling tubs, a requirement of the US Food and Drug Administration to kill any possible larvae. Women stand in fixed positions as the fruit rolls by on the conveyor belt; they select the mangos and pack them into boxes. Sometimes they may change to putting together the cardboard packing boxes. This is usually a beginner's job or done to fill in dead time, and men may participate. Otherwise, men move around, stacking the boxes of fruit onto the trucks that are to carry the merchandise to the border towns of Matamoros or Laredo, where the boxed fruit is handed over to US brokers.

Perhaps Elsa will remain in the avocado packing plant. As an experienced packer, she could even be employed at the small food processing unit, which operates in a few plants, processing avocado for "guacamole," a mashed and flavoured avocado dip used in the local fast-food industry and also exported. Perhaps Elsa and her husband will build a small house. Elsa is part of the working class in urban provincial Mexico. How is she any different from peasant women — daughters, widows or abandoned women? They still feel the burden of a gender ideology in which women's work is "subordinate" to their role as daughters, as mothers and as household managers, and so their jobs are seen as temporary and their income complementary. Are they working only because they are very poor?

PETRA, MANGO WORKER

From Uruapán down towards the Pacific Coast, we come to the low-lands of Michoacán, the fertile and irrigated valley of Apatzingán, known as the Tierra Caliente, for the intense heat in the region. An exporting region since the beginning of the century, especially during the era of the haciendas (a broad term referring to both small and large agricultural plantations), it was here that land reform was radicalized when the then president Lázaro Cárdenas divided these prosperous haciendas into worker co-operatives in 1936.[8] A cotton boom, followed by growth in melon exports, brought cash to the region from the 1950s to the late 1970s. Land tenure patterns often changed in a non-legal market of leasing and outside investment, while migration to the North became established as it became increasingly difficult for renter *ejidatarios* to survive only from their small plots of land.[9] Their sons sought new ways of earning an income. Today, trucks, boots, cowboy leather jackets and Mexican rock predominate the scene on a Saturday night at the *zocalo* (main plaza), "machismo" vibrates in the air, stories of flashy money mingle with drug trafficking. It can be a "dangerous place," people liked to tell us.

The plump yellow-red mango has become familiar in Northern supermarkets and grocery stores, like the one I visited on Bloor Street near Spadina in Toronto! Mangos became a new export crop for Mexico in the 1980s and now predominate the valley agriculture along with lemons, which are destined for the domestic market. We interviewed women in seven packinghouses in this region. Some are large plants with over one hundred workers, modern management and working under contract with transnational corporations. Others are smaller plants, run by an *ejido* co-operative or as a family business. I met Petra in one of the small plants.

Petra lives in the village of El Ejido. She is responsible for the support of five (out of twelve) children and two grandchildren. Petra lives in utter poverty and her wage barely stretches to feed her family. She keeps some chickens and a son looks after a few goats, but on the day of the interview she had no money to buy *maize* (corn) to feed the chickens. Petra deplores being a widow and is one of several we interviewed whose husbands were killed in brawls. When her husband was alive, she would help weed the small plot of land he cultivated, but did not work outside the household. "With a husband, you do not have to work. When there is no one to support you, you have to work, otherwise there is no food," she lamented, referring of course to salaried "work" and the never-ending domestic work that is also her fate. Petra feels the weight of being a woman on her own and of dealing with the difficult situations of her children (one daughter has been imprisoned on charges of drug trafficking, another was abandoned by her husband). She considers herself lucky to have gotten a job. She talked to *la administradora* (the manager) of the mango agro-industry, whom she knows well from the village, and got a job right away.

At the packing plant, Petra stands at the beginning of the conveyor belt, pushing the mangos as they come rolling in, and she sorts them manually. Sometimes, she puts together cardboard boxes. During the mango season, which lasts from four to five months, Petra works at the packing plant. It is a seven-days-a-week job and she often works late at night, because the mangos that come cannot remain unpacked, they cannot continue hanging on the trees either, just because it is Sunday. The mango is a delicate tropical fruit and has to be shipped off right away. After the summer, when the plant closes, Petra takes a job as a domestic servant in a private house in the nearby town of Nueva Lombardia. Though the work is lighter, the pay is less, and she prefers the plant.

Most of the workers, female and male, come from the village. There is no special contract, people know when the season opens and ask for work. "They are like a family" is an expression frequently used by the employers. Petra also feels that she can rely on the employers in the case of personal need, which is important to her because she is on her own. The fact that the plant manager is a woman makes it easier to talk about her personal problems, Petra said.

The female manager, Sylvia, is an example that the division of labour is not only gender biased but also cuts across class. Sylvia is the younger sister of the *ejido* bosses who run the packing plant and she is known, among the mango growers, to be a tough buyer to deal with and a competent manager, though she is always surrounded by her brothers.

The gender ideology in Tierra Caliente — with the intertwining of working women who want to be independent, the discourse of virility and the violence of machismo — presents a complex reality. Women work to "help their families," and young girls perceive marriage as far off in the future, when they're in their mid-twenties. Only the thoughtless ones elope with their boyfriends. And who would want to work after marrying? "It is the man's obligation to take care of his family. If I work, he will become lazy, or not bring home the money and start seeing other women," was a common refrain. "Marry?" queried Sylvia. "How can I find a man here in Tierra Caliente? I am a free woman with a good job. Here all the men are 'macho'; they won't accept my independence."

Uncertain Futures

Women workers are aware of the gender bias, both at work and at home, and although they appear to accept the discourse, they are also contesting it. But it is totally reinforced by the employers: within the nursery and the packinghouses, jobs are sex-typed and demand for workers favours women for a process that relies on unskilled, routine and basic labour. Within the agro-industry, women have access to a larger number of jobs than men, but men occupy the more stable and better paid ones. However, in the present situation of an economic crisis, loss of formal jobs in industry and the disruption of small-scale agriculture, the working conditions of men are also changing. They are moving into more informal work, increasing migration and even into illegal activities. Certainly, the dynamics of these processes will lead to changes that affect the lives of both women and men.

Daily survival is hard in a world where the luxury of buying tropical food and flowers in the North is based on cheap labour of women in the South and made available by a labour market that leaves many unemployed. This is reinforced by the gender ideology of employers and by deeply entrenched social norms. Change may not be a linear trend towards better conditions, but rather a twisted and complex movement, as women cope with new and difficult situations, yet at the same time opening new spaces for themselves within their working environment and their homes.

Kirsten visits Niagara Falls following a collaborative research meeting in October 1996.

NOTES

This chapter is based on "Revisiting Women Wage Workers in Mexico's Agro-Industry: Changes in Rural Labour Markets," Working Paper 95, no. 2, Centre for Development Research (Copenhagen, 1995), and was written while I was a guest researcher at the Centre. The research on women workers was carried out at El Colegio de México and sponsored by the Ford Foundation. I am indebted to the three institutions and to Deborah Barndt, who made valuable suggestions for this version.

1. "Where Have All the Flowers Gone?" was a folk song popularized in the United States by folk singer Pete Seeger and by the folk group Peter, Paul and Mary in the 1960s.
2. Older daughters often "help out" with household and childrearing chores. This reflects the large extended family and the family wage system in Mexico. It also refers to working alongside another member of the family at work. The family member who "helps out" isn't paid for their work, while the member they are helping out is paid.

3. See Lourdes Arizpe and Josefina Aranda, *Las Mujeres en el Campo* (Oaxaca, México: Universidad Autonoma Benito Juárez, 1988); Jane L. Collins, "Gender and Cheap Labor in Agriculture," in P. McMichael, ed., *Food and Agrarian Orders in the World Economy* (Westport, CT: Greenwood Press, 1995); Sara Lara, "La Flexibilidad del Mercado de Trabajo Rural," *Revista Mexicana de Sociología* 54, no. 1 (January–February 1994; M. de la Luz Macías, "Demanda de Fuerza de Trabajo Feminina en Cultivos de Exportación Seleccionados," in K. Appendini, B. Suarez, and M. de la Luz Macías, eds., *Responsables o Gobernables? Las Trabajadoras en la Agroindustria de Exportación* (México: El Colegio de México, 1997).

4. Arizpe and Aranda, *Las Mujeres en el Campo*.

5. Manual Castells and Alejandro Portes, "World Underneath: The Origins, Dynamics, and Effects of the Informal Economy," in A. Portes, M. Castells, and L. Benton, eds., *The Informal Economy: Studies in Advanced and Less Developed Countries* (Baltimore: The John Hopkins University Press, 1989).

6. This was in evidence, for example, when the answer was that workers would not go to the public clinic but rather "see a private doctor," because they didn't trust the social security service.

7. For an elaboration on flexibility in post-Fordist production models, such as those applied in flower production, see Sara Lara, *Nuevas Experiencias Productivas y Nuevas Formas de Organización Flexible de Trabajo en La Agricultura Mexicana, Procuraduría Agraria* (México: Juan Pablo Editores, 1998).

8. Lázaro Cárdenas was the Mexican president who carried out a radical and extensive land reform from 1936 to 1938; half of all the agricultural land was expropriated and handed over to peasants throughout the country. In Tierra Caliente, the most technologically advanced haciendas in Mexico were expropriated, destroying a vast agricultural empire that raised cattle and produced lemons and other crops.

9. *Ejiditarios* refer to those who were "renters" on collectively owned property. For more information, see Harriet Friedmann, "Remaking 'Traditions,'" in this volume.

Chapter Seven

PUTTING THE PIECES TOGETHER:

TENNESSEE WOMEN FIND THE GLOBAL

ECONOMY IN THEIR OWN BACKYARDS

Amanda Hope joins a protest against sweatshop-made garments bought and sold by Sears, organized by TIRN and UNITE, October 1991, Knoxville, Tennessee.

PUTTING THE PIECES TOGETHER:

TENNESSEE WOMEN FIND THE GLOBAL

ECONOMY IN THEIR OWN BACKYARDS

Fran Ansley

From the Belly of the Beast

In the United States, as in Canada and Mexico, the effects of globalization on women, their families and their communities are both profound and uneven. This "US chapter"¹ offers a window on to some of these dynamics as they are playing out in one community in the United States. The view from the window will, of course, be affected by its frame, so I should begin by sharing a bit about my own peculiar vantage point. I am a university-based legal scholar involved in a long-term research and education project with Tennessee factory workers who want to better understand and more effectively respond to "the global economy." For the past eight years, I have worked with an organizational partner, the Tennessee Industrial Renewal Network, to organize and document a series of worker-to-worker exchanges between factory workers here and in the export-processing zones of northern Mexico.

The project has brought me and my blue-collar collaborators into international networks where we can trade stories and compare notes with other labour unionists, academics and community activists in the NAFTA countries and beyond. Although these experiences have brought home to us the significant gaps and differences between workers in the world's North and South, they have also impressed us with the strong parallels and intersections between what is happening to local workers and local communities in very different places around the world.

We have become convinced that the process of trading stories across NAFTA borders can help people on both sides to develop and communicate a deeper and more practical analysis of globalization and its effects. This chapter is conceived in the spirit of such exchange. Not a systematic survey, rather it offers a set of interrelated but often disparate events and developments that my collaborators and I have discovered in the course of exploring the impacts of globalization in our own backyards. While the US government and US-based multinationals wield tremendous influence as players on the world stage, we see daily the impact of these corporate strategies on the poorer communities living within this powerful country, the "South within the North." They speak from within the belly of the beast.

SHIFTING FOOD AND WORK PATTERNS IN AN APPALACHIAN COMMUNITY

The community these stories come from is in the foothills of southern Appalachia. It is in an area of green rolling countryside, with a range of small towns strung along highways, neither blessed nor cursed with the coal that has left its mark so strongly in some other parts of this region. Some of these towns are large enough for a weekly paper; one town I can think of is busy enough to boast a movie theatre. Most of the people who live in this eastern, more mountainous end of Tennessee are white, though some are African-Americans. Some households here are doing well. More are getting by, but uncomfortably close to the margin. Other households — tucked away up valleys and down creeks, or in a rundown neighbourhood back behind the cemetery, or living in cheaply built public housing already going to seed — are poor. These households in poverty are not small in number, though if one were looking for them in the aggregated economic statistics for the county or state or region as a whole, their existence and condition would often be elided and obscured.

Independent family farms are increasingly rare here. Still, many people continue to make some portion of their living from the land, both by raising a part of the food they eat (though that part is generally shrinking as the women in the families find themselves with less time for the slow, hard work of preserving garden produce), and by raising a crop or two for cash, most often cattle or tobacco.[2]

On the consumption-end of the food chain, fast-food restaurants are now a common feature of the landscape in our area and are, of course, a key employer of women here, as elsewhere. Yearly, the franchises seem to extend their reach further from the region's cities and deeper into the countryside, and they are now a common sight even in relatively depressed communities. From town to town they sprout and proliferate, in all their tediously varied monotony, showing up as part of the strip development along highways in smaller and smaller population centres throughout the area.

In the larger and more prosperous towns in this mix, some of the fancier grocery stores have begun to spruce up their offerings. Cut flowers and snow peas, mangos and Bibb lettuce are now available to discriminating shoppers, enabling even those out here in the boondocks, where there is still a discernable surviving regional cuisine, to try the latest recipe they saw last week on cable or satellite TV, despite its intimidating list of exotic ingredients. In one town, the newest development is a grocery store located inside a Wal-Mart. Within a large, well-lit structure which also houses its own miniature McDonald's restaurant, the housewares and automotive supplies blend seamlessly into the food sections, and consumers can purchase their pop-tarts and pillowcases, frozen French fries and fishing tackle, tomatoes and Malaysian-sewn T-shirts, all at the same commodious conveyor-fed check-out scanner, conveniently open twenty-four hours a day.

Nowadays, a mother shopping at this particular Tennessee Wal-Mart can also buy *chipotle* and *masa harina*. The recent increase in Latina and Latino immigration is something very new for most communities in our area. Most towns have never had a Spanish-speaking teacher, police officer, judge, emergency room doctor or driver's licence examiner. Up until recently, even to hear a foreign language spoken on the street or in a public place was a considerable novelty. But over the past five to ten years, something new is happening in many small towns and rural areas of Tennessee. New groups of Mexican and Central American workers are arriving here, just as they are in similar areas of the Southeast and Midwest. Some come as seasonal agricultural workers (in our area they are now important contributors to both the tomato and the tobacco harvests). But others come to stay year-round, often in jobs like chicken processing, in the hardest, dirtiest and lowest-paid reaches of the local economy. And although grocery stores, Western Union and shady "legal advisors" have begun to figure out ways of serving and profiting from this new low-end market, most public and private community institutions have been slow to follow with support of or outreach to the new Spanish-speaking residents.

Many people here work in factories, even though manufacturing as a percentage of total employment has long been declining in relation to services, and even though many factories have partially or totally shut down in recent years.[3] There is a dwindling array of sewing factories, long a backbone of employment opportunity for women without much formal education in our region. Those sewing factories that do remain are shrinking in size and degree of capitalization. There are furniture plants, auto-parts facilities and factories that make household electric products, all of which have steadily employed women, albeit they have been concentrated in the lower-job categories.

Most of these firms arrived in the 1950s, '60s or '70s from "up North," when manufacturers found it profitable to leave behind the higher wages, stronger unions, steeper taxes and less business-friendly regulatory climate of the industrialized Northeastern and Midwestern parts of the country. In that era, communities like the ones I am describing became favourite destinations for runaway shops. In those days, many of the communities chosen — as well as big chunks of the workforce — were new to manufacturing and (from the employers' point of view) relatively unsullied by prior contact. Further, small town and rural county governments often tended to be more grateful for and compliant towards investment than were large urban centres.

In any event, people who lived in the area were glad to see industrial jobs arriving. Many were aware that the factories came from more unionized and higher-paid locations in the North. Many had heard that Northern workers were unhappy with the fact that a bunch of hillbillies were "stealing" their jobs. But Southerners took pride in the strong mountain work ethic that local economic developers so often praised them for. In some plants workers succeeded in organizing unions, in some they did not. In either event, a regional wage differential remained. And before long, people say, the plants came to seem a natural part of the landscape. It seemed that they had always been here, and always would be. As things turned out, people were wrong on both counts.

THE NEW WORLD ECONOMY
AT WORK IN TENNESSEE

In 1989, in response to a wave of factory shutdowns that was then hitting our state and region, the Tennessee Industrial Renewal Network (TIRN) was born.[4] It represented a joint effort by the Amalgamated Clothing and Textile Workers Union, the Commission on Religion in Appalachia, the Highlander Research and Education Center, and other organizations. Organizers encouraged individuals, unions and communities to contact TIRN if they were hit by a total or partial industrial closing, or if they had reason to believe they were vulnerable to one in the near future.

Sure enough, the calls began coming. One was from a group of women and men who worked at a large foreign-owned multinational electronics plant in the area. (For purposes of this chapter, I refer to the firm as "Electroworld.") Hourly employees at the plant told TIRN they were apprehensive about their future. They explained that trouble had been brewing for several years: the firm had begun moving parts of what used to be Tennessee production to low-wage locations in developing countries. At first, one small production line was taken off to the Mexican border, to a town they had never heard of and whose name they found difficult to pronounce. But within a few years, it was clear that things would not stop there.

In grievance meetings or during informal conversations on the shop floor, if union members showed reluctance about management proposals, company representatives began to drop remarks. "You're going to drive us to Mexico," they'd say, or "This is the kind of thing that will force us to move to Mexico." This refrain eventually made itself felt in contract negotiations as well, and local union leaders decided to call the company's bluff. They announced that they wanted to see Electroworld's Mexican facilities for themselves. An opportunity was arranged, the union bought airplane tickets for the negotiating committee, and from the workers' point of view, the trip turned out to be a decided success. The facilities they toured in Mexico were clearly second-rate. Engineering problems appeared to be substantial, and issues around quality were much in evidence to the educated eyes of the union visitors. That year the committee returned to the US, held fast in negotiations and obtained a contract they were proud of.

However, during the next round of contract negotiations three years later, the outcome was quite different. After making another union-paid trip to Mexico to have a second look, the workers found themselves staring open-mouthed at a vastly upgraded operation. The facility was large, efficient and running smoothly, with a quality finished product pouring steadily off a high-tech line. The union officers found themselves remembering all too keenly some of the engineering changes they had been watching in the plant back home, changes that made production lines more segmented, flexible and easy to dismantle, perfect for loading onto tractor-trailers at a moment's notice.[5]

At the conclusion of this tour, the leadership of the local returned home to negotiations deeply frightened about their ability to preserve jobs for their members. They ended up agreeing to a "two-tier" contract that did little more than narrowly preserve previously existing benefits for current workers. New hires would come in at substantially lower pay and benefits. Even worse, all those on layoff status at the time the contract was negotiated — a significant number of workers towards the bottom of the seniority rolls, due to slack production at the time of negotiations — were assigned to the lower tier. These people were also declared ineligible to vote in the contract ratification process. One such woman ("Judy," I'll call her), had over twenty years seniority with Electroworld at the time of these events. However, she was on layoff because she had been bounced from one Electroworld plant to another as the company closed nearby facilities, and with each bounce, she had lost her accumulated plant seniority. She was so angry when she heard the terms of the contract, that she took layoff status rather than stand next to someone on the line making twice her wage for the identical work. She called her adult kids and told them she would start babysitting their children so they could go to work.

After that, Judy and her good friend ("Carol," I'll call her) got into arguments over the union. Carol told Judy it wasn't the local president's fault that workers were put into a two-tier system, that he had tried to do what he could. But Judy felt like punching him in the nose. The women didn't let the argument get in the way of their friendship, but it wasn't an easy time. Judy was about as mad as she could ever remember being. "I was shafted. That's it, plain and simple. Just *shafted*. It's not fair."

Judy was not the only one. Many workers on both tiers were furious at this turn of events, and blamed the bad contract on the union's leaders. Membership in the union dropped from over 60 percent to less than 40 percent. The union local tried to fight its way back to health, but it had a difficult time recovering from the wounds of that concessionary contract. "Sharon" and "Linda," two energetic and feisty members of the union, both with past experience as shop stewards, took on the job of editing the union local's newsletter. They hoped to use it to educate and mobilize the membership. But it was an uphill battle. Members knew only too well that Electroworld now had multiple subsidiary plants in Mexico, and others in Asia and Eastern Europe.

Workers say that being on the receiving end of all this restructuring often felt like riding a roller coaster: one month the company would complain that it was losing money and that workers must redouble their efforts to increase productivity. The next month, stories in the business section of the local paper would report record profits for Electroworld and would regale readers with tales of the profit-generating "scorched earth" tactics of its latest CEO. And meanwhile, management was reorganizing Electroworld into a "new paradigm," team-centred workplace. (Sharon and Linda said the talk about "teams" and participation was mostly a sham. Job ladders had disappeared, and it was hard to see how that was good for team members.)

Eventually workers at this plant found themselves caught up in another dynamic characteristic of today's economy. The parent company divested itself of the Tennessee factory, not moving these last production lines overseas, but simply shedding its US production functions altogether. Except for a few remnants, the Tennessee enterprise was sold to a mix of smaller buyers. The resulting entities would continue to produce the same products and, at least initially, would still sell them to the same company, but no longer from "inside" the parent company's corporate structure. From that time on, the parent would simply contract (or not) for production, thus shifting the risks to the smaller producers.

In this way, permanent employment in one multifunction company was "contracted out." The former employees of the multinational were offered jobs at the new companies, but their benefits were slashed. Workers at the plant were not to be in a formal employment relationship with any branch of Electroworld and were to have none of the legal protections or entitlements that had come to accompany that status under the existing American system of labour and employment law. "Welcome to life in the virtual corporation," one sympathizer remarked.

And she was right to see this as a pattern. The move to hollow out parent corporations, to create a lean and "agile" centre while relegating more and more workers to a newly evolving periphery, is another hallmark of today's restructured economy. Women, often perceived as less attached and more marginal to the enterprise than men, are particularly vulnerable when contracting out begins.

Not all restructuring is a direct result of "globalization," and not all displaced workers have lost their jobs as a result of capital flight: many workers are laid off, demoted or marginalized as a result of organizational restructuring and technological innovation as well. But increasingly TIRN members have come to view these changes as related to one another, as part of a series of worldwide developments in the ways that corporations and financial institutions are mobilizing their economic and political resources both at home and abroad to capture profits and reduce costs, and also in the ways that national governments relate to that mobilization. Although these developments are very large and are often played out on a world stage, TIRN has become increasingly conscious that their mark is evident in the smallest and closest details of what happens at home.

NEW FAMILY SURVIVAL STRATEGIES IN THE GLOBAL NORTH

Unlike most urban factory workers, some people in the communities I am describing here are rural property owners. If they lose their foothold in industrial production, such people may be able to turn to their relatively small landholdings as a possible foundation for survival. Old-style subsistence farming is not a viable alternative. It was long ago marginalized and then virtually eliminated, when railroads and highways linked the area with the rest of the industrializing economy, first penetrating and then destroying most local markets in their path. Nor are many local landowners familiar with newer-style alternative agricultural options. (Some sincere and creative efforts at community-supported agriculture and environmentally conscious land stewardship do exist in this area today, and these efforts undoubtedly point towards important futures. But thus far they have had limited success in attracting traditional small farmers, blue-collar or low-income people into their networks.)[6]

However, other less benign strategies for gaining income from land are available. Another way for small rural landowners to produce an income-stream from their acreage has recently surfaced, accompanied by aggressive marketing from agribusiness. Company representatives and agricultural extension agents have fanned out in target areas to promote "contract poultry growing." Their goal is to recruit a battery of small landowners into the business of growing chickens for the burgeoning poultry industry.

The new recruits enter a system which has been steadily pressing towards vertical integration since the close of the Second World War, while control of the industry has become concentrated in fewer and fewer corporate hands. Large companies known as "integrators" organize and assemble the various inputs and components of poultry production. Their growing concentration and vertical integration shifts entrepreneurial risk away from the core enterprise, resting it instead on the shoulders of those towards the bottom of the web of relationships that make up the whole.[7] When all is said and done, those who take the most risk are the small landowners who supply the land and labour to grow the birds, and the line workers employed in the plants where the birds are killed and processed. Also adversely affected are the human and ecological communities (including, of course, the birds themselves) that are forced to absorb many of the severe environmental and other insults associated with mass poultry production.

TIRN first learned about this new development in the area almost by accident. Carol, Judy's friend from Electroworld, started talking in TIRN meetings about what was going on with her at home, and TIRN staff became interested. Carol had worked for Electroworld during its corporate roller-coaster ride. In fact, she had been so concerned about whether her job would be moved to the maquiladoras, she had paid her own way to go on a TIRN-sponsored trip to Mexico. Carol's brother ("Isom," I'll call him), had over twenty years' seniority at another industrial plant in the area, but when management introduced new technology there, he was told he could either accept layoff or start sweeping the factory floor for $6 per hour. Under those conditions, Isom — already over fifty and suffering from emphysema — decided, with encouragement from Carol and other members of the extended family, that contract poultry growing looked like a better alternative. This use of the family land also appealed to Carol as a way to achieve some independence from Electroworld and the uncertainties of her post-Electroworld employer, and she agreed to join Isom as a partner in the business.

Brother and sister soon realized that they would have to mortgage the family land in order to finance the expensive, highly automated, single-purpose buildings that house chickens in this system, buildings that had to be constructed to the precise specifications required by the integrator, each costing $40,000. (These days one building houses 20,000 birds, and landowners are encouraged to put up four buildings on the theory that one person can handle routine chores for that number.) They learned that they would have to depend on the integrator for pick-up and delivery of the highly bred, fast-growing chicks suited for this type of production, and also for the regular and timely delivery of the required feed via tractor-trailer, as well as for medications and growth-enhancing feed additives, for general know-how and trouble-shooting, and ultimately for a series of contracts that would be renewed (or not) largely at the discretion of the integrator. They were warned that disposal of the large amounts of manure, dead chicken carcasses and other waste generated would be their responsibility. The company predicted, however, that, for a limited period, their neighbours would likely constitute a ready market for the chicken waste. They were assured that after that market was exhausted, there were technical solutions to the problem, which they could learn about later. The couple attended company-organized training sessions to learn how the integrator would calculate their earnings after each crop of chicks had completed their "grow out" and had been picked up, weighed and taken to the processing plant. Apparently all would hinge on a number, Carol and Isom's "conversion factor," for that particular crop of birds. The number would take into account both the total amount of food the birds had consumed and the total weight they had achieved by the end of the grow-out period. As Carol joked, "If only you could get them to grow without food, you could really do pretty good."[8]

The integrator in the poultry business has control over a bristling array of variables in its relationships with growers, and this control raises a very real potential for both favouritism and abuse. Grower advocates charge that instances of ruinous retaliation against "troublemakers" have indeed occurred,[9] and switching to a different integrator is often not an option for growers, due to the high level of concentration in the industry.[10]

Despite their economic vulnerability, some contract poultry growers have begun to organize in the Southeast, and elsewhere.[11] The industry is new to this part of the state, however, and many growers here are still just learning the ropes, still hoping that they will be one of the longed-for achievers, still hoping that things will work out as well as their "liaison man" with the company assures them it may. Certainly some contract poultry growers do manage to come out ahead, so the dream of individual success is not entirely hallucinatory.[12] Having recently embarked on this post-NAFTA, post-downsizing strategy, Carol and Isom are determined to look on the bright side as to its future. But whatever the outcome in their individual case, problems with this industry are substantial, and the problems are not restricted to the chicken-growing phase of the process.[13] They occur further down the line as well.

FAMILY SURVIVAL STRATEGIES
IN THE GLOBAL SOUTH

Further down the production chain are factory hands who work in the plants where the chickens, once grown, are killed and processed. Conditions for line workers in these plants, as in meat processing in general, are notoriously brutal. Pay is low, the pace of work is relentless, health conditions are poor and injury rates are high.[14] Reported conditions include stressful line speeds, repetitive motion problems, cold temperatures, degrading and abusive supervisory practices and denial of reasonable bathroom breaks. Moreover, there are few unions to challenge these conditions.

Jobs like these are typically held by the least privileged segments of the workforce. In Appalachia they have traditionally been reserved for poor whites. In parts of the Southeast with a larger Black population, they have often been filled almost exclusively by African-Americans. In either case, women are usually strongly represented. In recent years, men and women immigrant labourers — mostly from Mexico and Central America — have become the employees of choice in meat and poultry plants in the Southeast. Poultry processing has been one of the occupational gateways through which a new and largely unanticipated wave of Latina and Latino immigrants has escaped the seasonal migrant stream and settled into year-round employment in rural communities in the region.

Immigrants come to Tennessee from Mexico and Central America for different reasons. In some instances they are escaping economic crisis, war or political repression. Sometimes they are believers in the American dream. Not a few have a taste for adventure. Some Tennesseeans have been learning from their new Mexican and Central American neighbours about the ways that extended families south of the border often use migration to the US as part of a larger survival strategy. We see the lines at the post office on Friday afternoons, and are realizing that seasonal and permanent workers are often sending substantial remittances home. Such income from the States may enable a Mexican family to buy construction materials for a house in an economy back home where access to credit for residential housing is non-existent for the non-affluent. It may enable younger siblings to finish high school or college. It may help a single mother purchase a long-needed wheelchair for her adolescent child. It may support sick or disabled parents. It may enhance a family's political prestige in their home community.

As such varied needs, dreams and ambitions have propelled immigrants onto the road North, these travellers have encountered occupational niches ready to take advantage of both their intense motivation and their social isolation in their new-found homes. The arrival of this new Latina and Latino workforce has been accompanied by downward pressure on wages, resistance to unionization and continued deterioration of working conditions.[15] Once again, companies are profiting.

Latina and Latino immigrants have developed a reputation for enduring hard work for long hours while maintaining high rates of productivity. Further, their often precarious legal status in the US makes it extremely risky for them to speak out or defend themselves even in those instances when they are aware of their putative rights under labour, employment or civil rights laws.[16] All of these features make the new Latin American workforce attractive to employers bent on lowering the costs of production and can trigger real fears and even racist reaction among native-born workers faced with new and formidable competition.

ORGANIZATIONAL RESISTANCE: WORKER-TO-WORKER EXCHANGES

In response to these complex dynamics and their impact on blue-collar workers, both immigrant and native-born, the Tennessee Industrial Renewal Network and other economic justice groups in the United States have sought to develop strategies of collective resistance to some of the worst dynamics of the new world economy. One of TIRN's most direct responses to global change has been the sponsoring of a series of two-way, cross-border exchange trips between Tennessee and Mexican factory workers.

Since 1991 the organization has sponsored visits by Mexican workers and labour activists to Tennessee, and has arranged trips to the Mexican border for Tennesseeans who have lost their jobs or who, like Carol when she first went on such an exchange, are still working, but in industries threatened by capital flight to the maquiladoras. These trips have provided amazing learning experiences for the individuals who participated and for the organization as a whole.[17] Carol, for one, says she will never be the same. When times get rough for her up here, she thinks about Mexican women she met and how they had to keep moving on, working and living in much more precarious conditions.

Individuals who participated in the TIRN trips have spoken to their union locals and church congregations around the state of Tennessee.

They have written letters to their editors and testified before the Office of the US Trade Representatives. They have lobbied their members of Congress and argued with their teenage sons about "those Mexicans." Some of them have also reported looking with new eyes on the Spanish-speaking people they find standing with them in the shopping line at Wal-Mart.

The trips also introduced TIRN members to a wider world of allies and teachers. After TIRN's first exchange trip (to Matamoros, Mexico, in 1991), the organization found itself naturally drawn into the fight to block passage of NAFTA in the US Congress. In fact, in a town near Carol's, a whole delegation of Electroworld workers joined with other industrial workers in a motorcade against NAFTA. It was the largest demonstration of its kind ever held in that business-dominated community. A member of Carol's local union described a trip to Juarez, Mexico, and how capital flight was harming Tennessee workers. An African-American woman who had been on a trip to Matamoros, Mexico, told about the terrible wages and working conditions of Mexican workers and about the serious environmental problems at the border. She questioned the claim that NAFTA would be good for Mexico, saying that NAFTA would make all of Mexico into one big maquiladoras zone, exploiting cheap labour while benefiting multinationals.

Although the campaign was unsuccessful in blocking the deal, it put TIRN in touch with the diverse internationalist groupings that have emerged in opposition to the agreement in the US, Canada and Mexico. These trinational networks have continued to collaborate in the building of an expanded campaign against a "Free Trade Area of the Americas," a proposed extension of the neoliberal NAFTA regime to the whole of the hemisphere,[18] and TIRN members have continued to be active on these issues.

TIRN hardly claims to have a handle on how to achieve international solidarity among workers in a globalizing economy. The organization is painfully aware of the modesty of its efforts compared to the enormity of the problems facing those who want a more democratic, egalitarian and sustainable world. Many TIRN members also recognize that the disproportionate wealth and power held by the US government and by US-based multinational corporations has often made it hard for people born and raised in this country to even understand how the world looks to other people, much less to work with them to develop just and effective alliances across international and racial boundaries. Nevertheless, more and more of us involved in this work are convinced that the prospects for a healthy environment and a just economy depend exactly on this dream. We believe that the positive side of NAFTA is the opportunity it has opened for popular movements to start learning and acting in more internationalist ways — sometimes perhaps, even in the writing of internationalist books like this one.

Fran engaged in conversation during our May 1998 book retreat.

NOTES

This chapter also refers to ideas more fully discussed elsewhere in this volume. See Kirsten Appendini, "From Where Have All the Flowers Come?"; Deborah Barndt, "Whose 'Choice'?"; Antonieta Barrón, "Mexican Women on the Move"; Harriet Friedmann, "Remaking 'Traditions'"; and Egla Martinez-Salazar, "The Poisoning of Indigenous Migrant Women Workers and Children."

1. Editor's note: This essay by Fran Ansley is the only contribution from a feminist academic/activist working in the United States (though the "Canadian" contributors include three US-born writers), because the Tomasita Project, which gave birth to this volume, focused primarily on food production in Mexico and food consumption in Canada as two ends of the NAFTA food chain. Ansley was, nonetheless, one of the original four research collaborators and has helped continually to reveal links, not only between workers in the three countries but also within the processes that depend upon and exploit the cheap labour of the poorer populations of all three. And her work has reinforced for us the importance of including US collaborators, who truly are speaking from within the "belly of the beast."

2. These days tobacco is looking less and less dependable, especially given the fact that the genius of tobacco from the small farmer's point of view was the regulatory system that protected farmers from price fluctuations, a system that is inconsistent with today's "free market" policies in agriculture.

3. For some early classic sources on deindustrialization generally, see Harrison Bennett and Barry Bluestone, *The Great U-Turn: Corporate Restructuring and the Polarizing of America* (New York: Basic Books, 1988), and Barry Bluestone, *The Deindustrialization of America: Plant Closings, Community Abandonment, and the Dismantling of Basic Industry* (New York: Basic Books, 1982). Subsequent observation suggests that "*re*industrialization" is probably a more accurate term. Significant manufacturing remains in the US (albeit on seriously altered terms), even as labour-intensive manufacturing in selected Third-World, low-wage havens has surged.

4. For the Canadian reader of this volume, it is important to recognize a similar phenomenon in the North and the links between the dynamic deindustrialization/reindustrialization of Canada and the US. With the first Free Trade Agreement between the US and Canada in the late 1980s, many Canadian garment factories fled South, first to Appalachia and the deep South, and then — if not directly, often eventually — to Mexico and Central America.

5. Secretariat of the Commission for Labor Cooperation, *Plant Closings and Labor Rights: The Effects of Sudden Plant Closings on Freedom of Association and the Right to Organize in Canada, Mexico and the United States* (Dallas, TX: Secretariat of the Commission for Labor Cooperation, 1997).

6. Two organizations working on these issues in our area are the Narrow Ridge Earth Literacy Center in Grainger County, Tennessee, and Rural Resources in Greeneville,

Tennessee. For an overview of US groups working on alternative policy and local practice, see Elizabeth Henderson, "Rebuilding Local Food Systems from the Grassroots Up," *Monthly Review* 50, no. 3 (July-August 1998), 112–124.

7. Large-scale hog farming brings similar problems. See "Carolinas Tackle Pollution Problems of Hog Industry," *Southern Communities* (July-August 1996), 8, and John Lang, "U.S. Staggers Under Weight of Farm Animal Waste Problem," *Knoxville News-Sentinel*, 23 April 1998, A11. The risk-shifting arrangements in this type of agribusiness are also reminiscent of agro-export regimes now being developed in Mexico and Central America. For an analysis of the analogously integrated "new herbs" industry in Guatemala (featuring North-bound non-traditional agro-exports like snow peas and cauliflower), see *Growing Dilemmas: Guatemala, the Environment, and the Global Economy* (1992), a publication jointly produced by AVANCSO (Asociación para el Avance de las Ciencias Sociales en Guatemala) and PACCA (Policy Alternatives for the Caribbean and Central America), available in English from Documentation Exchange, Austin, Texas.

8. In a conversation with a contract poultry grower in another state, I learned that at least one of the big chicken enterprises has an even more elegantly designed system for determining the contract grower's return. Under this system, each time a grower receives a new batch of chicks, he or she is placed in a "class" with all other growers who received chicks at the same time. At the end of the grow-out cycle, an average conversion factor is calculated for that particular class. Those who achieve the average are paid the standard rate. Any grower who achieves better than average is paid a bonus. The bonus is financed by docking the pay of all growers in the class who achieved less than average. In this way, growers are put on continuing competitive rounds to increase production, reiteratively pitted against a fluctuating group of their peers. The person I spoke with was particularly troubled by the size of the difference in pay levels under this scheme, a difference which he felt was unjustified by any difference in the effort expended or skill applied by the growers.

9. One author mentions the following variables controlled by the integrator in a typical poultry contract: the number of flocks delivered to a grower during the year; the requirement that a particular grower install expensive new equipment; the timing of feed deliveries; the diagnosis of illness in chickens; the type of medication provided in case of illness; the declared weight of the feed delivered and the chickens picked up; the quality of chicks and feed delivered; cancellation of a contract or refusal to renew a contract. Since poultry growers are viewed as "independent contractors" rather than employees, they are not protected by labour and employment laws. Federal laws governing agriculture, including statutes pertaining to meat production and processing, have done little thus far to protect contract poultry growers from abuse. See, for example, Clay Fulcher, "Vertical Integration in the Poultry Industry: The Contractual Relationship," *Agricultural Law Update* (January 1992), 4; and Randi Ilyse Roth, "Contract Farming Breeds Big Problems for Growers," *Farmers Legal Action Report, Minnesota Family Farm Law Update* 7, no. 1 (Winter 1992), 1.

10. In 1985, for instance, the ten largest poultry processing firms controlled almost

three-fourths of all broiler production, and the three largest controlled 40 percent (Fulcher, "Vertical Integration in the Poultry Industry," 5).

11. An important though struggling group that advocates for growers is the National Contract Poultry Growers Association. See "Mississippi Farmers Score Partial Victory in 'Chicken War,'" *Southern Communities* (July-August 1996), 8, and Steve Bjerklie, "Dark Passage: Is Contract Poultry Growing a Return to Servitude?," *Meat and Poultry* (August 1994), 24. The group can be contacted at National Contract Poultry Growers Association, P.O. Box 824, Ruston, Louisiana 21273, USA, (800) 259-8100. Additional information is also available from the Rural Advancement Foundation International (RAFI), P.O. Box 640, Pittsboro, NC 27312, USA, (919) 542-1396.

12. See, for example, the cover story for *Progress Report: The Tuskegee University Small Farmer Outreach Training and Technical Assistance Project* (October 1997), 2.

13. See also R.C. Lewontin, "The Maturing of Capitalist Agriculture: Farmer as Proletarian," *Monthly Review* 50, no. 3 (July-August 1998), 72–84.

14. See Marc Linder, "I Gave My Employer a Chicken That Had No Bone: Joint Firm-State Responsibility for Line-Speed-Related Occupational Injuries," *Case Western Reserve Law Review* 46, no. 1 (Fall 1995), 33–143.

15. See, for example, Alexander Rhoads, "Shattered Promises: Immigrants and Refugees in the Meatpacking Industry," *Poverty and Race* 1, no. 5 (November 1992), 5 (newsletter of the Poverty and Race Research Action Council, Washington, DC), describing recruitment of immigrant workers and African-American workers from the Southeastern US for jobs in Midwestern meatpacking; Barry Yeoman, "Spiritual Union: A Case Study," *The Nation*, 1 December 1997, 15, describing the amazing union organizing efforts of Guatemalan immigrants at a chicken processing plant in North Carolina. For a more general look at conditions and wages in the industry, see David Griffith, *Jones's Minimal: Low-Wage Labor in the United States* (Albany, NY: State University of New York Press, 1993). For an introduction to the "growing numbers and widespread settlement [of Latinos] throughout rural America," see Refugio Rochin and Emily Marroquin, *Rural Latino Resources: A National Guide* (East Lansing, MI: Julian Samora Institute, 1997).

16. Many but not all unskilled Latina and Latino immigrants working in the US economy are undocumented. Lawyers in my part of the country know little about immigration-related laws. Further, they are often ignorant of how those may or may not intersect other laws more familiar to them. Given that few immigrant workers have access to helpful information about their rights, that most are too poor to pay for legal assistance, that federally funded poverty lawyers in the US are prohibited from representing undocumented workers, and that few of the slender protections that do exist for immigrant workers carry provision for statutory attorney fees, legal rights traditionally conceived are scandalously ineffective for assuring the well-being of this population. More promising at present are efforts that treat legal rights as a site for education and self-directed action rather than as a place of refuge. See Jennifer Gordon, "We Make the Road by Walking: Immigrant Workers,

the Workplace Project, and the Struggle for Social Change," *Harvard Civil-Rights Civil-Liberties Law Review* 30, no. 2 (1995), 408–450.

17. I have written about these trips elsewhere, and find it hard to overstate how helpful and challenging they have proven for me in my own efforts to make sense of globalization and its (il)logic. See, for example, Fran Ansley, "Southern Women and Southern Borders on the Move: Tennessee Workers Explore the New International Division of Labor," in Barbara Ellen Smith, ed., with Susan J. Williams, *Chains of Iron, Chains of Gold: Women, Race and Class in the U.S. South* (Philadelphia: Temple University Press, 1998); "What's Globalization Got to Do with It?," in Joel Handler and Lucie White, eds., *Hard Labor: Women and Work in the Post-Welfare Era* (Armonk, NY: M.E. Sharpe, 1998); "The Gulf of Mexico, the Academy, and Me," *Soundings* 78, no.2 (1995), 68–104; "North American Free Trade Agreement: The Public Debate," *Georgia Journal of International and Comparative Law* 22, no. 2 (1992), 329–468; "U.S.-Mexico Free Trade from the Bottom: A Postcard from the Border," *Texas Journal of Women and the Law* 1, no. 1 (1992), 193–248.

Other stories and educational materials on TIRN's exchanges have appeared as well. See, for example, Luvernel Clark, "We Need to Get Together More," *Labor Research Review* 11, no. 1 (Fall 1992), 91–93 (a now-discontinued publication of the Midwest Center for Labor Research in Chicago) and "From the Mountains to the Maquiladoras," a 20-minute videotape available from the Tennessee Industrial Renewal Network, 1515 East Magnolia, Suite #403, Knoxville, Tennessee 37917, USA, (423) 637-1576, and from the Highlander Research and Education Center, 1959 Highlander Way, New Market, Tennessee, 37820, USA, (423) 933-3443.

18. Some recent descriptions of oppositionist activity related to the Free Trade Area of the Americas include Alejandro Bendana, "The Santiago People's Summit," *The Progressive Response* 2, no. 16 (16 May 1998) (a joint publication of the Interhemispheric Resource Center in Albuquerque, NM, and the Institute for Policy Studies in Washington, DC); Victor Menotti, "Santiago's Other Summit," *San Francisco Bay Guardian* 29 (April 1998); and "MAI for the Americas?," *The Morning NAFTA: Labour's Voice on Economic Integration* (11 March 1998), 1 (a publication of the Canadian Labour Congress, Ottawa).

Chapter Eight

SERVING UP SERVICE:

FAST-FOOD AND OFFICE WOMEN WORKERS

DOING IT WITH A SMILE

Women working in offices and in fast-food restaurants have been similarly affected by new technologies.

SERVING UP SERVICE:

FAST-FOOD AND OFFICE WOMEN WORKERS

DOING IT WITH A SMILE

Ann Eyerman

[Work] is about daily meaning as well as daily bread.
For recognition as well as cash;
for astonishment rather than torpor;
in short, for a sort of life rather than a
Monday through Friday sort of dying.

— Studs Terkel, *Working*

WE ARE INDEED IN THE MIDST of a revolution in work, a revolution that has significantly changed the workplace in a relatively short period of time. New organizational processes combined with new technology are creating employment settings that barely resemble the norm of less than a generation ago. The restructuring and downsizing of the labour force demand leaner and meaner employees who can (and will of necessity) produce the same amount of profit for a lower outlay (that is, lower personnel costs). This chapter explores how two groups of women — office and fast-food workers — are being influenced by these changes and how they are responding to them.[1] These women's stories reveal how the organizational processes and structures that first affected fast-food workers are now permeating the lives of office workers and how the vision pioneered by McDonald's is becoming the norm for the office (and indeed, for many other kinds of workplaces).

In his autobiography, Ray Kroc, the founder of the McDonald's fast-food empire, tells a story of the two McDonald brothers. Kroc tells this story with a humorous admiration for his company's namesakes. As the two California brothers were making plans to turn their hamburger stand into a "fast-food" joint, they spent a Sunday drawing out the model for their store in chalk on their tennis court and walking through the process, erasing and making changes when there were too many steps between hamburgers, French fries and milkshakes. When Ray Kroc bought the McDonald brothers' operation in the early 1950s, these original tennis court drawings were adjusted and adapted and became the model for Kroc's McDonald's and almost every other fast-food restaurant we have today.[2] Except for one obvious difference: the McDonald brothers believed that to guarantee the efficiency and cleanliness of the operation, only young men, dressed in white, should be hired. Young girls, they thought, would attract the wrong kind of crowd — rowdy boys who would distract them from their jobs and thus cut into the profits of the restaurant.[3]

From this tennis-court model, Ray Kroc developed a system that has become far more than an efficient and profitable way to make hamburgers. The golden arches have become one of the most recognized symbols in the world, surpassing even the symbol of the Christian cross, and the words Big Mac need no translation anywhere.[4] But for workers, and especially women workers, what is more important is the mindset of the McDonald's philosophy and its procedures and organizational structure that ensure not only a profitable hamburger business but a continuation of a certain corporate mentality. The success of the system depends upon a workforce that can be quickly trained not only in hamburger-making but in the proper McDonald's attitude. As Lucy, a McDonald's worker, explains:

> Everything is McDonald's. The way McDonald's does it is the way you have to do it. It's got to be done the same way, they got to taste exactly the same. That's why we do it that way ... I think it's a good place to work ... it's so great, you make so many friends and everyone's so happy and cheery, so you have to be [too]. It's like a happy environment. You got to have a good attitude or you can't work there. You'd be miserable, like there's a lot of people who are unhappy and they don't like the job because you have to

be happy, right? It's part of customer satisfaction. Everywhere you go people look at your attitude.[5]

This system requires workers who are flexible enough to fit their personal schedules into McDonald's and who are "trainable." Trainability extends beyond the basic steps for putting together a Big Mac. This is how Sarah describes it:

> You have your Mac sauce, you have your onions, your lettuce, a slice of cheese, two pickles and your meat. It gets to be automatic ... it's like you're a machine. You know everything has a specific place within the dressing table, a specific order, so you don't make mistakes, you go from that order.[6]

But more important, the McDonald's worker has to become a person who is dependable and eager to serve customers with a smile, even while being paid a very low wage. This combination of mechanized training and service with a smile has made Kroc's formula a very successful model. Enough so that these same "rules" are now being adopted in workplaces beyond the food industry.

The McDonald's model is considered feasible and attractive by both public and private workplaces that are forced into downsizing in order to compete in the new global market or forced to trim bureaucracies to reflect the new global corporate ideology — an ideology driven by market competitiveness and flexibility. Labour forces have little choice but to restructure along with the marketplace, as political policies reinforce what appears to be an uncontrollable yet simple economic fact of life — what is good for big business is good for society. This agenda requires just about every institution and its workers to either restructure or find themselves on the wayside, victims of their own inability to change.

The introduction of microchip technology, labelled the "Great Enabler" by Michael Hammer and James Champy, gurus in the religion of downsizing,[7] has allowed business to restructure workplaces and downsize employees. As Ursula Franklin explains so elegantly in *The Real World of Technology*, the tools, not the people who use them, have come to define work and workplaces.[8] This new world of work, as dictated by the demands of a global marketplace being driven by a corporate agenda, requires workers to readjust their working (and home) lives to stay competitive and employed. The McDonald's model has set the standard for other organizations, especially offices, where technology combined with reorganizational schemes have precipitated a revolution in the work process.

Perhaps the most obvious and significant parallel that can be drawn between office and fast-food workers today is the demand for flexibility, not only in when they work but also in the skills that they bring to their workplace. In January 1996, *Business Week* predicted that within a very short period of time, a large proportion of the labour force would consist of contingent, part-time, contract or temporary workers.[9] Workers will become part of the "just-in-time" reserve army ready to move into jobs when they are needed and out again when they are not. Workers' control over their hours and such things as overtime are no longer considered "choices" to be made by the workers but "requirements" imposed by the employer. In the shift work of McDonald's employees, it is a very familiar world. Sarah, a swing manager, explains:

> Part-time really depends on what your availability is and what hours you'd like to work, but it also depends on the sales, right? If sales are low then you may not get as many hours as you wish to get, and if sales are high and McDonald's needs you, then you get tons of shifts.[10]

But this demand is more difficult to accept for workers who are accustomed to greater control over their hours — this is especially true for older office workers caught in the transition. Meg, a temporary legal secretary, expresses her loss of control:

> They'll pay you [overtime], and it's supposed to be voluntary. But boy, oh boy, do they really hate it when you don't agree to stay. I got a job assessment just before I quit the last job. I was told that I was the best secretary this person had ever had, but he couldn't put up with my not being willing to work late. And when [they] say late, [they] don't want you to pick up and leave at seven o'-clock, [they] need you to work until midnight. And it was like [they're] doing you a favour, [they're] giving you a job! That's another thing that I found about [them]: "Honey, you don't like it,

bye, there's the door. We got ten people waiting in line for your job!"[11]

Meg now recognizes that she is no longer in control of her time at work, and that if she says no to overtime, she could well be out the door. Flexible hours, then, represent a mixed blessing for women workers. They offer the tempting opportunity to fit work schedules into life schedules; however, that usually means no control and low wages. So, in general, flexible hours reinforce gender-stereotyped roles at work and at home and often mean the end of permanent employment for most women. Norma, a long-time temporary secretary, explains:

> I'm flexible by choice but also by necessity. I would love to get into a job and be there for five years, but it's not available. Whether it's the way that I see the world or the way the world is right now, permanent work means a year at a stretch. I like the flexibility, I hate the downside of it. Because if you're too flexible, it means you're not working all the time and it's hard to stay ahead. [Now I work] short-term, mid-term contracts.[12]

Joan, who has worked as a legal secretary for many years, expresses a kind of resignation to this new kind of employment, and a sense of powerlessness:

> We can't look at our positions as being long term or stable any longer, that's just not a given. It isn't you who necessarily decides when your job ends, where you'll work. Your employer decides that.[13]

While these three office workers may not be having their shifts changed every two weeks, they are experiencing the same "uncertainties" and pressures demanded by the marketplace and their employers today. What McDonald's managers and employees have always known, that there are more teenagers out there to replace the ones who leave, has become part of the office workplace. As Joan explains, "There's also a great deal more competition, and the kids that are coming out of school now, they'll work for less. They have more skills than some of the older workers, like computer skills."

Thus, workers must not only be flexible in when they work but also in what skills they bring to a workplace. Jobs may now involve multitasks, many of which had not been combined before. Some jobs bear little resemblance to what they were just a short time ago. For example, office receptionists are now often required to know accounting software or desktop publishing in addition to having a pleasant phone voice. And bank tellers, as Loretta explains, are much more than money processors:

> When I started with the bank, you were there to serve your customers. I'm not a sales person and [now] that's basically what they want all staff members in the branch to be — tellers, everybody. You have contact with the customer, then that's your time to make a sale. Sell, sell, sell! Every time there's a campaign, you're expected to try to sell to each customer at your wicket. And you have monthly quotas, sales targets, and if you don't meet them, they're not very happy. I never considered myself a sales person. I can't hype-up things that I don't believe in myself.[14]

This multiskilling of employees allows the employer to move workers around to respond to just-in-time demands and to operate at maximum efficiency. But it also creates an opportunity to use (or misuse) an employee at various jobs. As Sarah explains:

> I'm sure a store manager would prefer to have crew trainers that know all stations, therefore they're more flexible and can work all stations even when they're not training. You can use that person if you're maybe minus a person on window or minus a person in back. You can use that person in a place to help out.[15]

This is not much different than what some workers in law firms, like Joan, are experiencing:

> I'm a floater. I'm assigned to whoever needs me, so if someone wants me to cover their phones but there's not a particularly huge amount of typing, I'm also assigned to cover other people's overload. Most people work in dedicated positions, but if their lawyer is out, they are automatically assigned somewhere else.[16]

Whether working part-time or full-time jobs, this multitasking and multiskilling create a greater intensification of the work process. The belief in the efficiency of technology (not to mention the financial investment made by a company) is so prevalent that it demands an equal expectation of efficiency in workers. Workers are expected to be able to perform tasks that in a previous era might have been done by several employees. This logic that technology allows for a downsizing of the workforce does not address the question of what happens to those who are left when they are faced with an overload of work. Loretta discusses her current work in insurance:

> It's a two-person job, it really is, and there's only me doing it. It was a person who came in part-time who did it before me, but she didn't do all the work that I do. I guess they figure now they have somebody full-time. I get bombarded with everything, and on top of that, I think the claims have doubled or tripled. If you could see my desk you'd die, because it's just stacks and stacks, and on top of that there are time frames involved. So as I get closer to the deadline my blood pressure gets higher and my nerves get shot, and it's not worth it. It's just their unrealistic expectations, and it's throughout the whole office. Everybody you talk to there just feels terribly overwhelmed most of the time, because there's too much work and too few people.[17]

This intensification of the work process does not allow the space or time to develop or use the creative and personal knowledge that a person carries with her into a workplace to get the job done. As work is intensified and workers are required to do more, plugging themselves into a variety of jobs and work situations, this tacit knowledge is devalued. But what is lost by its omission is an office culture based on the passing of knowledge and information among workers through informal conversation with one another.[18] In today's restructured workplace, as in the fast-food establishment, that culture is being replaced by one that fits within a perceived model of mechanical efficiency. There is no downtime to develop anything different. If there's a quiet period, the "Clean, don't lean!" motto applies whether tables, files or a co-worker's overload are involved.

This motto was poignantly described by Maria about working at McDonald's: "You always got to be moving. [No] standing around, you got to clean. Move, move, move. Stock salt and pepper or fill in the milk shakes." Lucy synthesizes it this way: "If it's dead, you have to clean."[19] And the motto is echoed by office workers such as Joan:

> You are not allowed downtime. That is the big change, and I sometimes resent that, because occasionally when you've been working really hard you need some time to take a breath and do your filing. But to be obliged to respond immediately to shifting demands ("OK, your lawyer is away, you're going to be assigned to work for so and so") makes it very tough. So it means you have to keep up all the time. Everything has to stay up to date all the time, and you're doing that catch up work on overtime.[20]

The McDonald's model of a just-in-time workforce that can be sent home when customers are scarce and called in when the need arrives has spread to other workplaces. Take, for example, the experience of an accountant who was called in for a temporary position (for which she had to be interviewed) that was to last for four months. Her own efficiency shortened the just-in-time need for her services, so she was laid off after two weeks.[21] And in the case of Loretta, her employer did not see that she needed assistance to do her two-person job. The company had just installed a new computer system and decided her problem would disappear after she received more training (on her own time and paid for from her own pocket). Persuasive arguments are often made that the latest technology is the only and best way to deal with the current work situation, especially if there has been an enormous outlay of funds to purchase it. To repeat what Ursula Franklin said in 1990, the tools, not the people who use them, too often define the work problem in a culture that is fascinated with technological fixes.[22]

There may be another connection between McDonald's and women office workers. Pat Bird and Alice de Wolff, in their recent study on clerical work in Metro Toronto, noted the shocking fact that 92,600 clerical jobs were lost between 1989 and 1997, approximately 10,000 of those since 1994.[23] These jobs are not just temporarily unfilled, they no longer exist. It is logical to expect that as service jobs, and especially those in fast food, increase, at the same time that clerical work decreases, there will be a downward mobility of these discarded office workers into lower-wage service jobs. Part of McDonald's success has been to hire marginalized people (for example, teenagers, retirees, minorities, untrained women) and make them into "happy" employees who will not complain about low wages and unpredictable hours. As more workers, especially women clerical workers, become marginalized, the golden arches may look more appealing as a workplace, especially if there is little else in the job market. Already the demand for fast-food jobs has increased, as have the requirements for such jobs. Sarah comments:

> The application forms have changed, too. You know, before they used to be a small little application form with your name, your number, where you live and that's basically it. You'd get a phone call and you'd come in for an interview and if they liked what they saw at the first interview, then you went through a second interview process. Now you have on the application forms "availability." You can put in what hours you are available to work. Now the manager can see if the person is very flexible or not flexible. A lot of people now are even sending in their résumés. Before it used to be just a plain application, now with every single person you get that résumé coming in. They're desperate for work, that's right.[24]

The question remains, however, whether the downwardly mobile clerical workers can find happiness in McJobs. Those who matured within the norms of the past may always feel the degradation of the new workplace, whether in the restructured office or in the fast-food outlet. But as a younger generation replaces this group, the McJob becomes the norm. Their job expectations were not formed at a time when there was long-term job security and benefits. Unlike older workers who are ready to slow down, they are more equipped physically to respond to the demands of the workplace.

Just as the Luddites[25] revolted, not against new technology per se, but against the degradation of their work culture, so women workers are resisting in ways that stop short of threatening their job security. Joan, as many other women in the workforce today, took what she considers a legitimate route of resistance. When I met her, she was taking time off her job on a stress week and had gone to her doctor for an extension of another week. She told me that it gave her a "breather place" to make a decision about the next step to take. While this form of resistance may not dramatically change the work structure, it does allow one person some control within her own work world.

Other McDonald's workers have tried to resist by organizing unions in their stores, only one successfully in North America.[26] There are also the small daily acts of resistance taken by individual workers. Sarah told the story of giving a free cup of coffee to a homeless man who carried an old McDonald's cup with his belongings. He would come in for a free refill, and when she was on duty as swing manager, she always filled his cup for free:

> You still have your own way of thinking, your own personality, they don't change you. They don't change you, but they like their ways, you know. They like their ways and you have to obviously oblige some of their ways, because you work for that company. But if there are certain things that you can do within your power, you can do it. No one is ever going to come down to me and say you shouldn't have given that guy a coffee. They may say this, but they're not going to come and document me and my file. They may just make me aware of the situation.[27]

Where will the future avenues of resistance emerge from, and how successful will they be in helping women office and fast-food workers maintain a level of control over their work? It is a perplexing issue and one to be considered by labour organizations and social justice groups, especially now as McJobs become the norm and not the exception in workplaces (including unionized ones). Unions will have to find new strategies if they hope to organize such women workers, workers they have basically ignored in the past. Perhaps organizers need to listen to the voices of private sector office workers and fast-food workers in order to understand what that strategy should be.

These are also important issues for feminists to take up. The needs of these women workers must be addressed not only from the perspective of such basic issues as equal pay and working conditions but also in terms of how this upheaval is affecting their fundamental sense of self in the workplace, home and community. The voices of the women who have spoken in these pages are demanding more humane work and workplaces, where human dignity is valued as much as the bottom line.

Ann interviews a fast-food worker in Toronto, 1997.

NOTES

This chapter also refers to ideas more fully discussed elsewhere in this volume. See Deborah Barndt, "Whose 'Choice'?"; Ester Reiter, "Serving the McCustomer."

1. The McDonald's workers' quotes used in this chapter came from interviews I conducted as part of the Tomasita Project. The office workers' quotes are from interviews I conducted during research towards my master's degree in Environmental Studies, York University, 1998. Both groups of women preferred to remain anonymous; thus only pseudonyms are used throughout the chapter.

2. Ray Kroc, *Grinding It Out: The Making of McDonald's* (New York: Berkley Books, 1977), 89–90.

3. Max Boas and Steve Chain, *Big Mac: The Unauthorized Story of McDonald's* (New York: New American Library, 1977), 19.

4. "Golden Arches Better Known Than Cross," *Anglican Journal* 121, no. 8 (October 1995), 5.

5. Lucy, interview with author, Toronto, Ontario, September 24, 1996.

6. Sarah, interview with author and Deborah Barndt, Toronto, Ontario, February 7, 1997.

7. Michael Hammer and James Champy, *Reengineering the Corporation: A Manifesto for Business Revolution* (New York: Harper, 1993), 83.

8. Ursula Franklin, *The Real World of Technology* (Toronto: CBC Enterprises, 1990; reprint, Concord, ON: Anansi, 1992), 56.

9. G. Koretz, "U.S. Labor Gets Flexible," *Business Week*, 15 January 1996, 22.

10. Sarah, interview.

11. Meg, interview with author, Toronto, Ontario, March 20, 1997.

12. Norma, interview with author, Toronto, Ontario, March 7, 1997.

13. Joan, interview with author, Toronto, Ontario, March 15, 1997.

14. Loretta, interview with author, Toronto, Ontario, March 20, 1997.

15. Sarah, interview.

16. Joan, interview.

17. Loretta, interview.

18. Heather Menzies, *Whose Brave New World? The Information Highway and the New Economy* (Toronto: Between the Lines, 1996), 105.

19. Maria, interview with author, Toronto, Ontario, September 14, 1996; Lucy, interview.

20. Joan, interview.

21. Anonymous, informal discussion with author, Toronto, Ontario, July 31, 1996.

22. Franklin, *Real World of Technology*, 56.

23. Pat Bird and Alice de Wolff, *Occupational Analysis: Clerical Occupations in Metropolitan Toronto* (Toronto: The Clerical Workers' Centre, 1997), i.

24. Sarah, interview.

25. The Luddites, followers of the mythical Ned Ludd, were a group of labourers who rioted in the industrial areas of England in the early 1800s. They destroyed textile machines to which they attributed high unemployment and low wages. In *Progress Without People: New Technology, Unemployment and the Message of Resistance* (Toronto: Between the Lines, 1995), David Noble emphasizes that the Luddites were not against the technology per se. What they were protesting was the dominance of the "economy" over society and those who controlled it. Society was nothing more than a reservoir of supplies for production. People, along with the land and trees, were treated as commodities to be used and disposed of as economic expediency required. The machines that the Luddites destroyed were the visible and tangible manifestation of this social upheaval.

26. "B.C. McDonald's First to Unionize," *Canadian News Facts* 32, no. 15 (August 1–August 31, 1998), 5733.
27. Sarah, interview.

Chapter Nine

NOT QUITE WHAT THEY BARGAINED FOR:

FEMALE LABOUR IN CANADIAN

SUPERMARKETS

Wendy Rogers (right) promotes Loblaws' magazine to Karen Serwonka, research assistant.

NOT QUITE WHAT THEY BARGAINED FOR:

FEMALE LABOUR IN CANADIAN

SUPERMARKETS

Jan Kainer

THE RETAIL FOOD SECTOR[1] in Canada is a large employer. More people are employed in this sector than in auto manufacturing.[2] The size of the retail food sector is important not only because it reflects the growing significance of the service economy but also because it is a major employer of women.[3] Like many private service industries, it is dominated by part-time women workers. The gendered structure of the retail food workforce is critical to understanding what is occurring in the sector today. Jobs are undergoing significant restructuring — full-time jobs are disappearing or being converted to part-time, and lower-wage tiers are being applied to part-time workers.

This chapter examines the gendered consequences of restructuring in the retail food sector. It explains how in one crucial component of the food retail system, the supermarket, management has reduced labour costs through a highly structured gender division of labour. Post-Fordist managerial practices, especially in the 1990s, have intensified gender inequality in the sector as supermarket management increasingly turns to labour flexibility strategies, such as the use of part-time work, to lower the cost of wages. Many of the workplace changes that are detrimental to women have emerged in recent rounds of collective bargaining between labour and management at supermarket chains. Concession bargaining has occurred in almost every province in Canada and has seriously eroded wage rates and job security of supermarket workers, especially those employed part-time.

In the current period of restructuring, managerial reliance on women

as low-wage and part-time workers is deepening systemic gender inequities in the sector. As feminist analyses of restructuring indicate,
there is an intensification of non-standard employment for women in a
range of occupations and industries.[4] Employers recruit women as part-
time and temporary workers not only because they are cheap to hire
but also because of historical patterns of gender organization that assign
women to gendered work and social roles. As Jane Jenson points out,
"[a]n employer's decision to create part-time jobs is a choice that expresses an existing set of culturally shared assumptions about gender relations, about women's social roles, about men's social roles, and about
the relationship between work and family."[5] The case of supermarkets is
illustrative of gender patterning in work relations in which women have
traditionally been assigned part-time work — work that is socially constructed as feminine and consequently devalued.

As explained in the next section, the gender composition of the supermarket workforce has always been divided between men performing
higher-paid occupations designated as "skilled" and women performing
lower-paid occupations designated as "unskilled." In the present context, this historic gender division of labour provides the basis for management to extend the use of cheap, flexible female labour. Gendered
skill definitions that were introduced in the early twentieth century
continue to permeate the organization of the supermarket workforce
and are used, consciously or unconsciously, by employers to subordinate women in the supermarket industry. In the restructuring process
this gender-based ideology is evident in various labour flexibility
strategies implemented by management. A brief overview of the history
of the retail food sector reveals how the gender division of labour was
created, and especially how gender-typing has shaped jobs in the
industry.

Historic Gender Inequities in
The Retail Food Sector

From its very beginnings, the workforce of the retail food sector has
been rigidly divided by gender. Nona Glazer's historical analysis details
how, in the early twentieth century, women were inserted into the retail

sector as low-wage, deskilled and part-time workers.[6] In the shift from full-service to self-service retailing that occurred prior to the Second World War, women replaced men first as store clerks and then later as cashiers. Self-service retailing entailed transferring work performed by the store clerk to the customer. In the early years, the store clerk was responsible for customer service including "salesmanship" and locating and packaging merchandise for the customer. The shift to self-service meant the customer was expected to fetch the merchandise and take it to the cashier, which was facilitated by the growth of product standardization (prepackaging) and product recognition brought about by national advertising. But the greatest impetus for self-service retailing was its effect on lowering the cost of wages. Retailers quickly learned that the advantage of self-service was a reduction of their workforce requirements. The need for full-time workers, especially, was decreased by hiring part-time store clerks and cashiers, many of whom were (white) women who could be paid less than men (because they were not unionized), and who were perceived by management to be better suited to perform customer-service roles. Thus the evolution of the gender composition in the retail food sector, as in other types of retailing, resulted in women dominating the lower-paid service jobs.

Men, on the other hand, had historically performed craft-based occupations, such as butchering, that were controlled by an apprentice system and by craft unions. Male workers in the growing retail food sector were assigned "masculine" roles such as managing the store and stock and produce jobs, which required a great amount of physical labour. These predominantly male positions were typically full-time. Male workers were better remunerated because their work was perceived to require more skill or physical strength, and they were more likely to be unionized.[7]

Because men were the first to be organized in the retail food sector, they were able to protect their privileged positions within the store, reinforcing a sexism that existed at home as well as at work. When women began to fill positions during the transition to self-service, the male-dominated unions did not advance a bargaining strategy to improve working conditions or to win equal wages for women.[8] Moreover, when food stores moved to complete self-service in the post-war era (becoming the supermarkets we know today) and began to expand the use of part-time labour, the unions did not oppose the loss of full-time employment.[9] And since part-time workers were largely women,[10] they became overrepresented in part-time jobs from that point forward.

During the 1970s, supermarkets diversified to include deli, bakery and floral departments. These service departments were added to broaden customer service, and, because they could garner higher profits than general grocery merchandise, they also enhanced store profitability. Service departments required more workers than did other areas of the store, "both for in-store production and for direct customer service."[11] Women were recruited to these service departments because management could pay them less than men, and because the ideological assumption was that women, not men, could better perform the domestic and human relations work the jobs required. For instance, duties performed in the deli and bakery departments required food preparation, cleaning and personal interaction skills. It was assumed that women learned how to do this work in the home and that on the job it required very little ability and know-how. As a consequence, these jobs were undervalued by the primarily male management.[12]

The gendered workforce has remained firmly intact to the present day. In today's supermarkets, women are predominant in the service jobs of cashier, meat wrapper and deli attendant. These female-type jobs are lower-paid and are concentrated in the part-time category. Men continue to be employed in production jobs — defined as jobs that generate profit-creation in the store and that include meat cutter, stock/produce clerk and department manager. Historically, production jobs have been viewed as profit-creating because they are an integral part of the process by which merchandise is physically prepared and placed on the shelf, whereas service jobs are far removed from the "preparation" of merchandise and cater to customer needs. (The exception here are the mostly female meat wrappers whose job is to "prepare" the meat by wrapping it for the customer.) This gender-based distinction between production and service jobs, as discussed in the next section, is highly questionable. Nevertheless, based on this rationale, jobs held by men are higher paid and are more likely to be full-time. However, it must be stressed that the vast majority of supermarket workers today, both male and female, are employed part-time. Retail unions[13] estimate that approximately 75 to 85 percent of their membership in supermarkets are now in the part-time category. Significantly, too, the majority of the part-time workforce is female.[14]

The Gender Implications of Supermarket Restructuring

The following section describes changes in workplace reorganization that directly or indirectly affect women in the supermarket workforce. The significance of the gender division of labour in this sector is evident in the case examples of work reorganization discussed here. The examples also demonstrate that part-time and service work categories are particularly sensitive to reduced hours, wage reductions and job displacement. In every instance, supermarket management strives to retain the boundaries of the gender divided workforce in order to maximize profit. Upon close examination of the new managerial practices and recent collective bargaining outcomes, it is evident how the process of restructuring has gender-specific implications.

Reduced Hours: Working Lean

A key feature of supermarket management is control over the workers' assigned hours.[15] Labour flexibility is achieved by manipulating the distribution of hours among different departments and by dividing hours between full-time and part-time employees. The distribution of hours is highly gendered because store managers typically assign production departments more hours than service departments. The work performed in production departments (meat, grocery, produce) is seen as essential to a supermarket's operation, and a core number of hours is assigned for production work. Service departments (deli, bakery, meat wrapping, cashier) are viewed as less important for generating profit and are the first to experience reduced hours during slow business periods. However, the assumption that production is more important for profitability is not entirely accurate since the service departments have higher profit margins than those in production.[16]

In spite of the fact that some service departments earn higher profit margins, the women workers in these areas are more likely than men to experience reductions in their hours of work. Meat wrappers, the majority of whom are part-time female workers, are especially vulnerable. For example, I interviewed a woman with six years seniority in the meat department (working part-time) who was receiving no scheduled hours at the time of our meeting. Her part-time male co-worker with less seniority was given hours because, as she explained, "part-time males do heavier work; they clean the machines, the grinder, the chopper and the meat cooler."[17] The gender division of labour was working against this female meat clerk; men, who are allowed to perform a broader range of tasks, from weighing, wrapping and selling meat to more physically demanding work, are given priority. Managers thus prefer to schedule part-time male workers because they are able to perform a wider variety of tasks.

Cashiers are also losing hours because they perform work that retail management determines is not profit-creating; management therefore minimizes staff in this service department. A typical response about loss of work hours is expressed by a cashier employed at a supermarket chain: "Over the past six months I've only received sixteen hours of work. I'm not entitled to benefits. I'll never get a [wage] increase."[18] In her workplace, part-time employees have to have worked a total of four hundred hours and have one year of service before they can receive benefits under the collective agreement. The reductions in hours in the cashier department is limiting work opportunities for cashiers with fewer years of service, while at the same time intensifying the work of high seniority cashiers who are assigned hours. Female-dominated service departments are typically allocated fewer hours overall relative to the male-dominated production departments. As a result, part-time cashiers, meat wrappers, bakery and deli clerks are losing out to their male co-workers.

While part-timers are in competition with one another for hours, it is usually the "core workforce" that absorbs some of the hours of part-time or peripheral workers. For instance, management is now requiring full-time workers to engage in multitasking whereby they are asked to perform tasks normally done by part-timers (or by full-time employees in other departments). A stock clerk may work at the cash register during busy periods of the shopping day; not only does this intensify the work of the full-timer, but it reduces the number of hours available for part-time workers in the store. There is a specific gender dimension to this arrangement — management uses male stock clerks to replace women cashiers.[19]

Increasingly it is becoming difficult, if not impossible, for part-time workers to move to full-time work. Companies are not replacing full-time employees who quit, retire or are on disability pension with full-time positions, because they are higher paid and receive substantial benefits. Through this process of attrition, more and more work is being assigned to part-time workers. Women are especially disadvantaged by this policy because almost all of the full-time jobs available today are departmental managerial positions, and the majority of these are occupied by men.

REDUCED WAGE RATES: THE EMERGENCE OF WAGE TIERS

In the 1990s, competitive pressures have increased in the retail food sector. Poor sales growth, deflationary pricing and increased competition from alternative store formats (for example, warehouse clubs) have affected profitability. In response, supermarket chains have focused on reducing labour costs through wage concessions at the bargaining table. Recent contract negotiations in Canada reveal that significant wage decreases have been implemented through two-tiered and multitiered wage structures and lower-rate contracts, in which workers are paid wage rates below industry standards.[20] These newly negotiated wage tiers particularly affect women. Because women are disproportionately represented in the part-time workforce, combined with the fact that hours are being reduced in the service departments where the vast majority of women work, they are losing out compared with male workers in the supermarkets.

For example, Loblaws, a major supermarket chain based in Ontario, established a new part-time wage tier in 1990 that significantly prolongs intervals between pay raises — raises are given according to total hours worked annually, rather than through an automatic wage increase based on months or years of service. Under the previous system, an employee *automatically* moved up the wage tier every six months, irrespective of the number of hours worked. Now, when the hours of part-time employees are reduced, it can take years before they receive an hourly wage increase. For instance, in the 1996 round of negotiations between

Loblaws management and a large local of the United Food and Commercial Workers Union, a four-year collective agreement created a new part-time wage tier for new hires (that is, those workers hired after the date of ratification of the contract). This wage tier requires a new part-time worker to register 8,751 hours to reach the new top wage rate of $12.50 per hour. However, other part-time workers who were on the job before the contract must accumulate a total of 7,001 hours to reach the top rate of $15 per hour, operating on a different tier. Not only does this create a systemic inequity between "new" and "old" hires but it also constitutes a gendered inequity, given that women experience decreased hours of work in the service departments and therefore progress through the tier at a slower pace. As a consequence, women are unequally affected by this type of part-time two-tiered wage structure. In the same agreement, Loblaws also offered a buyout program to full-time workers who could opt to convert permanently to part-time status and return to work earning a wage rate of $8 per hour; this effectively lowered their wages and moved them into a less stable employment category.

At other major supermarket chains in Ontario, such wage concessions have become the norm since the mid-1990s. Negotiations at Miracle Food Mart resulted in across-the-board wage reductions of $1.75 per hour for both full-time and part-time workers, as well as for workers on lower-paid wage tiers in the part-time category. These wage reductions were part of a buyout program at the chain.[21] A&P[22] also negotiated wage reductions for workers accepting buyouts, and $4-per-hour wage reductions were applied to employees at their smaller stores.[23] Finally, at all of the major supermarket chains, double-time pay for Sunday work was eliminated and replaced with a lower rate of premium pay. It is important to note that Sunday work creates specific problems for women workers who must juggle childcare and other family responsibilities with their paid employment.[24]

In order to decrease their labour costs, employers have pressed for lower wage tiers in the part-time category. Retail unions, which have a history of protecting the male-dominated full-time workforce, have resisted implementation of wage tiers for full-time workers.[25] As a result, wage tiers have not appeared in the full-time category, but they have proliferated in the part-time category. Since women are concentrated in part-time jobs, they have absorbed many of the losses associated with wage concessions.

JOB DISPLACEMENT: EMPLOYEE BUYOUTS

As mentioned, bargaining concessions have included employee buyouts. Retail food corporations have offered both full-time and part-time workers layoff buyout packages. Most of these offers allow an employee to accept a one-time payout based on years of service; in exchange, the employee either gives up seniority (accumulated years of service) or the right to full-time employment. The corporate objective of employee buyouts, of course, is to eliminate higher-waged workers. Both full-time and high seniority part-time workers have been targeted by supermarket management, but the thrust of these programs has been to eliminate full-time jobs, which receive higher rates of pay and superior benefits than do the part-time jobs. Buyout programs, like wage concessions, have been offered by most major supermarket chains in Canada, including Safeway, A&P, Miracle Food Mart and Loblaws. Clearly, management wants to extend hours in stores to part-time workers, while cutting back on full-time staff.

This strategy was particularly evident in negotiations with the Miracle Food Mart chain in Ontario that culminated in a three-month province-wide strike.[26] At the end of the three-month strike, the parties negotiated a buyout program that was intended to eliminate seven hundred full-time jobs from the Miracle Food Mart chain. However, following the strike, only five hundred full-time employees had opted to take the buyout package. In an effort to downsize full-time jobs, the company unilaterally eliminated full-time female-dominated positions in service departments in every store across the province! Specifically, the company terminated full-time cashiers, meat wrappers and deli attendants. It is very likely that these traditional female service jobs were singled out for elimination because they had received province-wide pay equity adjustments in 1990 and were thus more costly to the chain.[27] The expansion of part-time employment was another important consequence of the Miracle Food Mart strike. It was agreed in negotiations that 60 percent of the hours freed up from the elimination of full-time positions was to be allocated to new part-time hires.[28] These new part-time hires were paid under a lower-wage tier and restricted to working a maximum of sixteen hours per week.

The Miracle Food Mart strike is a remarkable demonstration of how the food retail industry relies on the gender division of labour to restructure and reorganize the workplace to reduce labour costs. To gain greater labour flexibility in the 1990s, management continues to rely primarily on women workers, who comprise the majority of the part-time workforce and who dominate in lower-paid service occupations. Supermarkets are pursuing a distinctly gendered low-wage strategy — female-type jobs are the first to experience reduced wages and reduced hours, or face elimination altogether.

THE CHALLENGE AHEAD

Changing economic and labour conditions have strong implications for women employees. It is clear that the gender division of labour in supermarkets, which historically has segregated women in lower-paying service and part-time jobs, continues to be used by management to promote flexible specialization — a managerial strategy to reduce the cost and amount of labour.[29] The fact that women mainly occupy positions in the service departments especially disadvantages women because these jobs have been labelled unskilled and are undervalued by supermarket management.

Women, as the majority of part-time workers, are increasingly marginalized as flexible workers. Because part-time workers provide managers with optimal flexibility in assigning hours and because part-time workers are less costly to employ, management continues to rely heavily on this contingent workforce to keep labour costs down. While part-time work is proliferating, women's full-time positions are also disappearing, as demonstrated in the case of Miracle Food Mart. Full-time female-type jobs that have traditionally been devalued, such as the service work performed by deli workers and cashiers, as compared with jobs performed by men, are identified by supermarket management as too costly and are stamped for elimination, only to be replaced by part-time positions. Men are still more likely than women to be employed full-time (even though full-time jobs overall are shrinking) and to receive higher wages than women. The process of work reorganization has reinforced structures of gender inequality in an industry that has traditionally been characterized by systemic gender inequities. Women in gender-typed service jobs have borne the brunt of recent work reorganization. Even through labour negotiation processes, the results have been "not quite what they bargained for."

Historically, these jobs have been marginalized and devalued because of prevailing gender ideologies about skills and women's role within the family. The definition of skills needs to be challenged. The struggle to remove gender inequalities will require ongoing and concerted efforts in this highly feminized sector. It will require a continued challenge to the male-dominated unions to ensure that they take into account the tremendous impact that wage concessions have on female workers and that they address gender inequities within the workforce as well as gender discrimination within unions themselves. To date, the union leadership in the retail food sector has inadequately protected its female membership, through collective bargaining, from the consequences of restructuring.[30] Unlike other unions, such as the Canadian Union of Postal Workers, which opposed a two-tiered wage structure and negotiated pro-rated benefits for part-time workers, the retail food unions have accepted wage differentials for part-time workers.[31] As Jane Jenson comments, the proliferation of part-time employment "sets limits on the political space for women to achieve economic equality."[32] The case of workplace restructuring in supermarkets clearly illustrates the constraints in which women are operating, and represents the enormous challenges ahead that are needed in order to counter its forces.

Jan (left) and co-author Ann Eyerman in conversation at the May 1998 book retreat.

NOTES

This chapter also refers to ideas more fully discussed elsewhere in this volume. See Fran Ansley, "Putting the Pieces Together"; Deborah Barndt, "Whose 'Choice'?"; and Harriet Friedmann, "Remaking 'Traditions.'"

1. In this chapter, I use the term retail food sector, which includes supermarkets and other small retail food stores. The majority of retail food stores are small owner-managed businesses. For example, of a total of 29,987 grocery stores in Canada, only 1,641, or about 5 percent, are supermarkets. Supermarkets, however, dominate in dollar sales.

2. In 1991, 402,080 people had jobs in food stores, while only 152,850 were employed in the auto sector. 1991 Census of Canada: Industry and Class of Work. Cat. No. 93–152, 93–326. Cited in Judy Fudge, unpublished manuscript, 1995, 29.

3. The 1996 Canadian census reports that retail work is the most common occupation for women. A total of 339,025 women were employed in retail sales while cashiers, who ranked third as the most common job, numbered 235,585 (*The Toronto Star*, 18 March 1998, A1, A9).

4. See Marjorie Cohen, "The Implications of Economic Restructuring for Women: The Canadian Situation," in Isabella Bakker, ed., *The Strategic Silence* (London: Zed Books, 1994); Ann Duffy and Norene Pupo, *Part-Time Paradox: Connecting Gender, Work and Family* (Toronto: McClelland and Stewart, 1992); and Jane Jenson, "Part-Time Employment and Women: A Range of Strategies," in Isabella Bakker, ed., *Rethinking Restructuring: Gender and Change in Canada* (Toronto: University of Toronto Press, 1996), 92–108.

5. Jenson, "Part-Time Employment and Women," 94.

6. Nona Glazer, *Women's Paid and Unpaid Labor: The Work Transfer in Health Care and Retailing* (Philadelphia: Temple University Press, 1993), 68–86.

7. In the US, the Amalgamated Meat Cutters, representing butchers and meat cutters, was chartered in 1897, the Retail Clerks International Association was founded in 1898. See John Walsh, *Supermarkets Transformed: Understanding Innovations* (New Brunswick, NJ: Rutgers University Press, 1993), 31, and James Mayo, *The American Grocery Store* (Westport, CT: Greenwood Press, 1993), 184.

8. See Glazer, *Women's Paid and Unpaid Labor*, 82.

9. See Mayo, *The American Grocery Store*, 185.

10. On the issue of women part-time workers in the retail food sector, see Glazer, *Women's Paid and Unpaid Labor*, 84–85.

11. Walsh, *Supermarkets Transformed*, 53.

12. According to John Walsh, women in service departments of supermarkets earn over $2 less per hour than men working in supermarkets (Walsh, *Supermarkets Transformed*, 141–144).

13. The two unions in Canada representing the vast majority of workers in the super-

market sector are the United Food and Commercial Workers (UFCW) and the Retail Wholesale Canadian Service Sector Division of the United Steelworkers of America. Both of these unions are American internationals with their head offices located in the US.

14. For a detailed discussion of the gender division of labour in supermarkets, see Jan Kainer, "Flexibility and Low Pay: Restructuring in Ontario's Food Retail Sector," Working Paper Series, no. 14, Centre for Research on Work and Society (York University, Toronto, Ontario, June 1997). An analysis of the grocery industry workforce can also be found in *Human Resource Study of the Grocery Distribution Industry — Phase I* (Ottawa: Canadian Labour Market and Productivity Centre, February 24, 1995). The CLMP reports that in 1995, 60 percent of all retail food employees work part-time, but the data is not broken down by gender.

15. The profit-hour ratio allocates a precise number of labour hours in a week as per dollar of sales and is dependent upon sales volume, specifically sales per worker hour.

16. Deli departments with hot-case sales can earn particularly high margins of between 60 to 100 percent. See Louise Leger, "Deli Demand," *Grocer Today* 10, no. 7 (September 1996), 59, 61. See also Walsh, *Supermarkets Transformed*, 118.

17. Anonymous (part-time meat clerk), interview with author, Toronto, Ontario, September 17, 1992.

18. Notes from meeting, UFCW Local 1000A, Toronto, Ontario, May 24, 1992.

19. See Kainer, "Flexibility and Low Pay," 12.

20. For a discussion of the competitive pressures within the supermarket industry as they relate to labour costs, see Janet Collins, "The Changing Face of Labour," *Grocer Today* 10, no.7 (September 1996), 13–14, 17, 62.

21. These wage reductions were reached as part of the outcome of a bitter three-month-long province-wide strike at the chain in 1994. Workers were represented by the United Food and Commercial Workers, Locals 175/633.

22. The Great Atlantic and Pacific Company of Canada Limited, known as A&P, is a foreign-owned company operating a large chain of corporate supermarkets in Canada. The corporation owns A&P stores; it acquired Dominion stores in 1985, and purchased Miracle Food Mart from Steinbergs in 1990. A&P, Dominion and Miracle Food Mart are banner store names.

23. A&P converted the "B" stores (or smaller stores) to a discount format, which is similar to a franchise, but is not a franchise. In this conversion process, new management hired both full- and part-time workers, who are paid a lower wage rate than workers employed at the larger "A" stores.

24. Sunday shopping legislation permitting retail stores to open was passed in 1992 in Ontario. The provincial Select Committee on Retail Store Hours concluded from their hearings that Sunday shopping put "a strain on the family structure," especially for families of retail employees, "many of whom are women, who might be required to work on Sunday" (*Second Report* [Toronto, 1987], 6).

25. On this issue, see Jan Kainer, "Gender, Corporate Restructuring and Concession Bargaining in Ontario's Food Retail Sector," *Industrial Relations/Relations Indus-*

trielles 53, no. 1 (1998), 183–206.

26. The union was United Food and Commercial Workers, Locals 175/633, representing Miracle Food Mart stores. The strike took place during the winter months of 1993–94 and occurred at sixty-three Miracle Food Mart stores in Ontario, representing 6,500 workers — 1,700 full-time and 4,800 part-time.

27. Pay equity negotiations were conducted with United Food and Commercial Workers and A&P in 1989–90 to comply with Ontario's *Pay Equity Act*, which required unionized firms with more than five hundred employees to negotiate pay equity plans by January 1, 1990. At the Miracle Food Mart chain, full-time cashiers, meat wrappers and deli attendant positions were compared with production (that is, stock) clerks and received about a $60/week wage adjustment. Albeit, only 621 full-time workers out of a total 2,065 received a pay equity adjustment in 1990. See J. Kainer, "Cashing in on Pay Equity? Negotiating Equal Pay in Ontario's Food Retail Sector" (Ph.D. diss., York University, 1996), 293.

28. The total number of hours represented by 700 jobs is equal to 25,900 hours; 60 percent of this number is 15,540 hours or 971 part-time positions, assuming sixteen scheduled hours per week.

29. A flexible firm operates with a segmented workforce, which is divided between core and peripheral workers. Typically, the core workers are highly skilled or multi-skilled, or both, and are higher paid. Peripheral or flexible workers, encompassing workers who are employed part-time or on short-term and temporary contracts, are lower paid and are more disposable. In the supermarket, the full-time workers constitute the "core" and the part-time workers the "peripheral."

30. For a detailed discussion of the weak role of the retail food unions in protecting its female membership, see Kainer, "Gender, Corporate Restructuring and Concession Bargaining in Ontario's Food Retail Sector," 183–206.

31. See Julie White, *Mail and Female: Women in the Canadian Union of Postal Workers* (Toronto: Thompson Educational Publishing, 1990).

32. Jenson, "Part-Time Employment and Women," 96.

Part III

SIGNS OF HOPE:

WOMEN CREATING
FOOD ALTERNATIVES

Chapter Ten

PUTTING FOOD FIRST:

WOMEN'S ROLE IN CREATING A GRASSROOTS

FOOD SYSTEM OUTSIDE THE MARKETPLACE

Native women and children join an anti-poverty march in Toronto in the late 1980s.

PUTTING FOOD FIRST:

WOMEN'S ROLE IN CREATING A GRASSROOTS

FOOD SYSTEM OUTSIDE THE MARKETPLACE

Debbie Field

IN THE MIDST of global restructuring, the virtue of the marketplace, with its mysterious capacity to express human need on the one hand and organize economic production to satisfy it on the other, seems to have become the guiding principle for all aspects of life. Environmental and economic regulation, state spending and the inefficiencies of public services are all seen as barriers obstructing the otherwise efficient performance of the market. How has this trend affected food access? Hunger continues to be a global problem. In the so-called developing world, half a century of promised economic growth has not reversed chronic food insecurity. Successive "Green Revolutions" have failed to increase food access. If we place the food system in the wider historical context, the logic of the marketplace begins to look not just inadequate, but destructive to the basic elements of food security.[1]

Herman Daly and John Cobb[2] describe environmental "externalities" — the consumption of resources and the damage to the natural world — as costs that never appear in the accountant's ledger. The cleanup of the Exxon Valdez oil spill registers as an increase in the Gross National Product (GNP); jobs are created and money is spent. The opposite occurs when we tread lightly on the earth. In food production there are also human externalities associated with the development of global agribusiness. For example, millions of people are displaced from traditional fishing and agriculture in much of the developing world.

This registers as a net gain even though subsistence peasant farmers once fed themselves and their families outside the cash economy. GNP rises when agricultural workers, in the current Mexican example, find themselves working all day on a tomato farm, earning too little to buy food now only available in the marketplace. Vandana Shiva describes how this situation has affected women in many countries of the South:

> The privatization of land for revenue generation displaced women more critically, eroding their traditional land use rights. The expansion of cash crops undermined food production, and women were often left with meager resources to feed and care for children, the aged and the infirm, when men migrated or were conscripted into forced labour.[3]

FOOD INSECURITY IN THE 1990S

Displacements from the land, food insecurity and periodic mass starvation are all part of the narrative of the twentieth century. As delegates to the 1996 World Food Summit declared:

> More than 800 million people in the developing countries are chronically undernourished. Millions more suffer debilitating diseases related to micronutrient deficiencies and to contaminated food and water. Every day one out of five people in the developing world cannot get enough food to meet their daily needs.[4]

Even in the West, the last two decades have been marked by an accelerated slide into food insecurity. The now seemingly permanent feature of urban hunger can be traced directly to the powerful and successful campaign to reassert the logic of the capitalist marketplace in every sector of society. Following the Second World War, Europe and North America developed a social contract committed to a comprehensive social "safety net." With variations between countries, the safety net included public healthcare and education, full employment at high wages, universal social assistance and old age pensions. Although the new social services system never successfully delivered on its promise, the elimination of poverty was initially one of the explicit goals of postwar social policy.

In the early 1980s, a dramatic reversal took place as western governments began to slash spending on a range of social programs. The results in Canada have been a permanent unemployment rate of 10 percent, wage stagnation, a widening gap between low- and high-paid workers, a steep descent into poverty for millions who relied on income supports and the expulsion of hundreds of thousands from the formal economy and permanent housing who have taken up residence on society's fringes. Against this backdrop, poverty levels have actually increased. By 1996, those without adequate income to buy the basics increased in Canada from 14.2 percent to 17.9 percent. Despite strong recoveries from recession in the early 1980s, and again a decade later, the tendency for poverty to decline as a function of economic growth was actually reversed.[5] When food exists primarily within the marketplace, food insecurity is directly related to lack of income. In an urbanized environment in which people do not garden or farm, food access is maintained by cash purchases at retail outlets. No money, no food. This simple truth becomes more widespread as high rents absorb close to all available income.

One of the signs of increased hunger is the birth of food banks in the early 1980s, and the growth in their use ever since. In 1989, 1.4 million Canadians were using food banks; by 1997, close to 3 million, or 2.24 percent of Canadians were visiting food banks.[6] But hunger is even more widespread than food bank use. Only 15 to 25 percent of those who are food insecure use food banks, with the remainder going without even finding a food bank or other charitable support.[7] This means that close to 10 percent of Canadians are not able to adequately feed themselves and go hungry at some point every month.[8]

It is nothing short of astounding that in just twenty years a massive food crisis has taken shape in North America. Images of starving children from around the world are now broadcast into homes where men, women and children themselves go to sleep hungry. And what do world leaders say about this irrational problem of continued food insecurity in such a wealthy world, a problem which really seems to make no sense? While paying lip service to fighting hunger, the documents resulting from the 1996 UN World Food Summit in Rome proposed few solutions. The South was warned against state intervention in food production or distribution and advised to follow the lead of industrialization. The problem in the North was minimized:

> Recognizing that even though food-insecure people do exist in North America, for the majority of the population, domestic food security has been achieved in the United States and Canada. This reflects the success of both nations' agricultural and fisheries production processing and distribution sectors that have provided abundant supplies of food in a variety of forms during all the seasons of the year at increasingly affordable prices. [9]

Cold comfort for the hungry: the food is there, but it is not available to many who need it.

THE FOOD SYSTEM DOESN'T WORK TO MAKE US HEALTHY, EITHER

The current food system does not ensure universal food access, nor does it make nutrition a priority. The highest level of profit is made on the most processed, usually the least nutritious, food. The food industry is under pressure to specialize in value-added foods, rather than in unprocessed healthier foods, such as fruits, vegetables, grains and beans. In the agricultural sector, the logic of the marketplace encourages farmers to increase their pesticide use, to experiment with genetically altered seeds and to focus on export options rather than growing for local markets. Using Daly and Cobb's analysis, there is more economic activity when a farmer purchases expensive herbicides, fertilizers and pesticides. Likewise the GNP increases when we buy imported potato chips (containing the fake fat "olestra") and pop, while it decreases when we consume a bowl of locally grown organic cherries. Yet which is healthier? Which is tastier?

The marketplace is also destroying generations of food behaviour. Where individual cultures and regions historically used food to define themselves, there is now strong global pressure to replace local food rituals with homogenized fast and prepared food culture, exemplified in the global growth of McDonald's. On a personal level, we connect human freedom with having enough money to buy the food of our

choice in the marketplace. And in an interesting twist, human liberation, particularly that of women, has been identified with being released from generations of food drudgery in the kitchen. Our mothers
and grandmothers spent their lives preoccupied with food and cooking;
why would modern women follow suit?

Has this rejection of home cooking enhanced the quality of life for
the majority of people? Yes and no. Certainly for those of us who can
afford it, it's wonderful to have the option to buy some prepared foods
and not to have to reproduce all our food with our own hands each
day. Yet at the same time, we have lost important values in this commodification process. Alarming numbers of North Americans rarely experience commensality, the anthropological description of the human
habit of sitting down to eat as a group. Deskilling in food growing and
preparation is evident as each successive generation is more alienated
from farming and cooking talents formerly taken for granted, and as
take out and prepared food become more popular. Who benefits from
these trends? Certainly not low-income people, caught in a constant
struggle to find enough money to play the marketplace food game. And
not the majority of women. Most women are poor, and all over the
world, poor women struggle on a daily basis to find the food they and
their families need to survive.

DEVELOPING PUBLIC POLICY FOR
EQUITABLE FOOD ACCESS

Founded in 1985, FoodShare Toronto is a community based, non-
profit organization with the mission of working with low-income communities to improve access to affordable and nutritious food. Our goal
is to develop social policy and community projects that will alleviate
the growing problem of urban hunger. From our point of view, the current global food system isn't working very well to eliminate hunger or
to promote optimum health. Drawing on the work of Brewster Kneen,
of British Columbia's The Ram's Horn, and Rod MacRae, of Toronto's
Food Policy Council, we wonder if solutions to chronic and continued
food insecurity could come from allowing basic healthy foods to exist
outside fluctuating market relations. This could occur through marketing boards, which set stable prices for farmers on the one hand and

consumers on the other, or from convincing society and governments that it is time to invest in subsidizing basic food so that, for the first time in human history, we can eliminate hunger.

Kneen[10] originally proposed that healthy foods be made available through the Canadian social healthcare system. Each provincial health card could provide individuals with credits that could be used to obtain foods, depending on the number of family members and whether there are any special needs, such as pregnancy, or medical conditions that necessitate increased healthy food. At the grocery check-out, the allocated amount of healthy food would be free, and the individual would pay full prices for processed foods or food that went beyond each individual's allowable health-card limit. Pointing to growing international evidence, MacRae suggests that diet is a significant risk factor in close to 60 percent of diseases, ranging from hypertension to stress, cancer and diabetes:

> All of these chronic diseases are related to nutrition. They affect the food-rich (those with sufficient income to acquire whatever foods they desire) and the food-poor (or those experiencing food insecurity). Very significant percentages of the Ontario population are at risk of these diseases because they do not eat in a manner optimal for health. We all pay, through publicly funded health insurance, for the costs of individuals' poor food choices and for hunger. The food system, through which most people acquire food, carries no responsibility for the consequences of consumption of these products. Yet estimates of avoidable mortalities and costs associated with poor nutrition show that millions of dollars can potentially be saved annually.[11]

One possible model, then, is the healthcare model. We at FoodShare propose that to end hunger and promote health, basic foods should become available through government supported mechanisms. Prepared or fast foods would continue to be the main focus of the marketplace food system, but basic food, fresh fruit, vegetables, grains and beans, would be available outside the marketplace. The Canadian healthcare example provides some hope and direction. Healthcare becomes a right when everyone has access to health coverage free of charge through government mechanisms, rather than buying medical services of their choice through the market system. A quick look south of the border reveals that a fully privatized market-based system of healthcare is incapable of delivering universal healthcare to all citizens. Isn't this also the case for food?

Perhaps a public policy strategy could be built around assuming wholesale healthy food for all of society, not just the poor. What would happen if a fraction of the funds now spent in the medical system were invested in ensuring that healthy food is available free or wholesale to the entire population? Or if agricultural policy were driven by a desire to reduce local hunger, increase healthy food production, stabilize the income of farmers and reduce environmental damage? Public access to good food is indeed a contradiction to the marketplace approach to food distribution. Whether in the South or in the North, agricultural policy is driven by trade concerns rather than local food access priorities. Farmers end up growing crops for export, depleting the soil and using expensive fertilizers and pesticides.

Yet several countries have experimented with various government interventions connected to a strategy proposed in 1995 by Agriculture Canada:

> Food should be produced as close as possible to where it will be consumed ... Producing the principal subsistence foods locally not only reduces household food costs but also supports local food traditions, and preserves indigenous seed varieties and sustainable food production methods.[12]

For example, the municipal government in Izmir, Turkey, operates staple stores;[13] India's Kerala State subsidizes grain for the entire population;[14] New Zealand, along with many countries in the South, provides subsidies of local staples; marketing boards in Canada and the industrialized world regulate supply; the Department of Supplies in Belo Horizonte, Brazil, operates open-air markets selling fruit, vegetables, grains and beans at wholesale prices to a third of that city's population;[15] and Toronto's Good Food Box program[16] sells produce at cost through a community-based co-op, which is subsidized by government and the voluntary sector. All of these efforts promote urban and rural linkages, generate demand for local agriculture and work to decrease urban hunger. In Toronto we describe this approach as "Field to Table," the Brazilians call it "Direct from the Producers."

FoodShare is analyzing these and other examples of government commitments to putting food first, either through social planning or fiscal initiatives. Our efforts (which are funded by the Atkinson Charitable Foundation) are directed by this question: What will it take for everyone in Ontario to have adequate access to affordable, nutritious food by the year 2002?[17] Because of the potential benefits of using some market and cash means to help people express both personal choice and responsibility, we are particularly intrigued by models in which foods are available at wholesale prices, rather than free, to the entire population through government-subsidized community-based mechanisms.

From our reading of the international experiments, it seems that those programs that are open to the entire population, rather than just to those who lack food security, are the most successful. The net benefits of everyone having the incentive to purchase healthy foods at wholesale prices seems to far outweigh the cost of subsidizing food for the entire population. As well, successful Canadian initiatives, such as the baby bonus and the social healthcare system, demonstrate that programs only survive when they are universal. Finally, a multisectoral alliance based on self-interest is central to achieving a more equitable food system that exists independently of the marketplace. Only a broad-based coalition of interests — people of all classes concerned about their health, low-income people concerned about their basic needs, farmers and supporters concerned about a local food system — can move social policy in such a direction.

WOMEN'S ROLE IN CREATING
A NEW FOOD SYSTEM

Any massive effort to make major food policy changes will surely be important to women, and will involve them as key players, for several reasons. First, women are more vulnerable to food insecurity because they are more likely to be poor:

Families led by women are more likely to be poor than those headed by men ... Even with recent improvements, women still earn only 64% of men's average wages. In addition to gender, marital status is a key factor. Single-parent families — most of which are led by women — face a higher risk of poverty. In 1996, 60.8% of families headed by single-parent women were poor compared with 11.8% of two-parent families.[18]

Second, women often make feeding their children a priority, putting themselves at even higher risk of hunger. When there is too little food, women will often deprive themselves of food so as to ensure that their children do not go hungry. A University of Toronto study discovered that women using food banks experience a variety of nutrient inadequacies, ranging from iron to minerals to protein. The study provides further evidence that women and children are going hungry, and that current solutions, including food banks, are not working:[19]

> ... the results of this study raise serious questions about the health and well-being of families using food banks in Canada. The inability of most households in this study to meet their food needs despite obtaining charitable food assistance attests to the inability of an ad hoc, community-based system of charitable food assistance, to compensate for the large and growing holes in our social safety net. Adequate income support programs are urgently needed to ensure the most basic of health needs are met for those Canadians unable to participate in the employment market or unable to garner sufficient income through their participation.[20]

Third, on the family and personal level, women all over the world still shoulder the major responsibility for meal preparation, even in households where men and women both work outside the home:

> Women are the key players in food utilization, making up most of the care-taking labor required for maintaining the health of household members, especially children and the elderly.[21]

There is a vigorous debate about how to view women's involvement in cooking. On the one hand, many see women's continued overrepresentation in the kitchens of the world as a clear indication of the distance that still needs to be travelled to achieve women's equality. The double day of work, in which many women work many hours after they come home from their paid job outside the home, remains a constant threat not only to women's equality but also to their health and well-being. At the same time, some feminists are working to develop a culture which sees women reclaiming their attachment to cooking as a gratifying experience, in which women's past relationship to cooking and food is celebrated in the same way that many women celebrate childrearing.[22] And it must be acknowledged that many women have never had much choice leaving the kitchen; for them the challenge is not to reclaim but to embrace these daily tasks with support and dignity. Regardless of which side of this debate is chosen, any social policy that puts food first should have a positive effect on the lives of women, since most women are either poor and food insecure or food stressed by their responsibility for food.

Women have traditionally offered leadership to alternatives that have promoted the socialization of food needs. On the political level, women have been at the forefront of struggles to demand that governments ensure adequate food access, sometimes leading demonstrations for subsidized staple products. They have also been at the centre of movements to organize prenatal, infant, school and child-feeding programs. At the community level, the majority of participants in grassroots food projects such as community kitchens, community gardens and bulk-buying clubs are women.[23]

Since most low-income and working-class women spend their lives trying to figure out where they will find the money for the next meal, making basic food available to everyone wholesale, would certainly reduce pressure on women. As well, women continue to take major responsibility for food preparation. Socializing some aspects of food — for example, establishing collective or community kitchens — would help to take pressure off women and spread the responsibility around. The availability at workplaces and schools of low-priced, high-quality home-cooked meals that provide healthy alternatives would certainly take the pressure off women's double day. Employers have come to recognize the importance of providing quality subsidized childcare, and some are adding staff lunchrooms and cafeterias. Turn-of-the-century American feminists dreamed of redesigning homes so that women could share kitchens and laundry rooms, and generations of socialist-feminists have seen communal food as a part of a future utopia.

MOVING AHEAD — FOCUSED ON FOOD SECURITY

The struggle to reduce hunger in Canada, and internationally, is at an impasse. The anti-hunger movement strategy that demands an increase in income for the most vulnerable in society, though valid and to be supported, does not currently enjoy mass approval. All over the world, food is still not a right, and hunger is on the rise in most countries. The United Nations calls for food to be a right. But what does this mean as distinct from income or housing being a right? As we build new coalitions to change public opinion and government policy so that more resources flow to the poorest, we may do better if we can separate food security from the complex struggle for income security.

On one level, everything is connected: hunger, poverty, homelessness are clearly interdependent. Social justice victories occur when progressive changes are ready to happen at the broadest political level. At the same time, victories are often won when movements isolate their specific problem from the struggle for income redistribution. Proponents of both universal childcare and socialized medical care were successful because they did not connect their issue to the more difficult goal of income redistribution, but in fact mobilized around a single issue, without denying this long-term goal. Childcare and healthcare activists were able to organize the needs of low-, middle- and upper-income communities, which for different reasons were all interested in quality childcare, or in the second example, a quality healthcare system.

If the movement for food security could convince society that it's time to put resources into socializing basic food, we will have made an important gain for social justice and equity. This will not eliminate the need to fight against the problems caused by continued income disparity and poverty. But in the meantime, social measures that give priority to the importance of food will improve the lives of millions. We cannot know what this will actually look like until we have undertaken much more analysis and research. It may in fact be that food sold at wholesale prices is the most effective and efficient model. Or it may be that farmers and producers reject the wholesale food option as involving too much government intervention.

Whatever option is chosen, we must develop alternatives because our current status quo is not acceptable. As we enter the new millennium, it is time for us to make hunger a thing of the past. We have the global capacity and knowledge to eliminate food insecurity; it's time for us to find the imagination and political will to find a solution. Women, who have always been central to food provisioning and have been the most victimized by the injustices of the current system, will play a crucial role in developing strategies and in leading collective efforts needed to transform the food system into one that's more equitable, sustainable and humane.

*Debbie (centre) and Mary Lou Morgan (far left) receive a truck
from Buzz Hargrove (third from right), President,
Canadian Autoworkers of Canada, Local 303, and
the CAW Social Justice Fund in June 1994.*

NOTES

This chapter also refers to ideas more fully discussed elsewhere in this volume. See Lauren Baker, "A Different Tomato"; Deborah Barndt, "Whose 'Choice'?"; Antonieta Barrón, "Mexican Women on the Move"; Harriet Friedmann, "Remaking 'Traditions'"; Egla Martinez-Salazar, "The Poisoning of Indigenous Migrant Women Workers And Children"; Deborah Moffett and Mary Lou Morgan, "Women as Organizers"; and Ester Reiter, "Serving the McCustomer."

1. Food security exists when people have access to adequate amounts of safe and nutritional foods that are both personally and culturally acceptable. The United Nations uses the term "food insecurity" to describe the absence of adequate amounts of food, or the condition of hunger. For the purposes of this chapter, I am using food insecurity in the narrowest sense, meaning the lack of access to adequate amounts of food. It is sometimes defined in a much broader way to include issues such as local sustainability, transportation and cultural acceptance.

2. Herman Daly and John Cobb, *For Our Common Good* (Boston: Beacon Press, 1989), 51–58.

3. Vandana Shiva, "Development, Ecology and Women," in Deane W. Curtin and Lisa M. Heldke, eds., *Cooking, Eating, Thinking: Transformative Philosophies of Food* (Bloomington: Indiana University Press, 1992), 337.

4. World Food Summit, *Food Security, Situations and Issues; A North American Perspective* (Ottawa: United Nations, 1996), 2.

5. Ken Battle, *Persistent Poverty* (Ottawa: Caledon Institute of Social Policy, 1977), 6.

6. Canadian Association of Food Banks, *Hunger Count 1997: A Report on Emergency Food Assistance in Canada* (Toronto: Canadian Association of Food Banks, 1997), 5.

7. See Carolyn Badum, Susan Evers, and Michelle Hooper, "Food Insecurity and Nutritional Concerns of Parents in An Economically Disadvantaged Communitiy," *Journal of the Canadian Dietetic Association* 56, no. 2 (1995), 75–80; Pat Evans, *Food Insecurity in Scarborough: A Study of Current Reality and A Report of Recommendations for Community Action* (Scarborough, ON: Scarborough Health Department, 1997); Cathy C. Campbell and Ellen Desjardins, "A Model and Research Approach for Studying the Management of Limited Food Resources by Low Income Families," *Journal of Nutrition Education* 21, no. 4 (1989), 162–171.

8. The US 1995 Census Bureau Current Population Survey (CPS) found that close to 12 percent of the population were food insecure, with 0.8 percent suffering from severe hunger. Advocacy groups report even higher numbers. The Community Childhood Hunger Identification Project (CCHIP) found 20 percent of the families interviewed with children under twelve years old were often hungry, with 50 percent being at risk of becoming hungry (Community Childhood Hunger Identification Project, *A Survey of Childhood Hunger in the United States* [Washington, DC: Food Research Action Committee, 1996], 342).

9. World Food Summit, *Food Security, Situations and Issues; A North American Perspective*, 14.

10. Brewster Kneen, *From Land to Mouth: Understanding the Food System,* 2d ed. (Toronto: NC Press, 1993).

11. Rod MacRae and the Toronto Food Policy Council, *If the Health Care System Believed "You Are What You Eat": Strategies to Integrate Our Food and Health Systems* (Toronto: Toronto Food Policy Council, 1996), 2.

12. Canadian Hunger Foundation, *Tough to Swallow: Canadian Perspective on Food Security* (Ottawa: Canadian Hunger Foundation, 1995), 3.

13. Mustafa Koc and Hulya Koc, "From Staples Stores to Supermarkets: The Story of TANSAS," (unpublished paper, Ryerson Polytechnic University, Toronto, 1998).

14. R. Krishnakumar, "A Successful System Under Threat," *Frontline: India's National Magazine* 14 (1997), 21.

15. Adilana de Oliveira, et al., *Public Policies: Innovating on the Supplies of Food in Belo Horizonte* (Belo Horizonte, Brazil: Department of Supplies, 1995).

16. Kathryn Scharf and Mary Lou Morgan, *The Good Food Box Guide* (Toronto: Food-Share Metro, 1997).

17. Debbie Field and Kathryn Scharf, *Food 2002 Proceedings* (Toronto: FoodShare Toronto, 1998.)

18. Sherri Torjman, *Women and Poverty* (Ottawa: Caledon Institute of Social Policy, 1996), 3–4.

19. See Valerie Tarasuk, George H. Beaton, Jennifer Geduld, and Shelley Hildtich, "Nutritional Vulnerability and Food Insecurity Among Women in Families Using Food Banks" (unpublished paper, Department of Nutritional Sciences, University of Toronto, 1998). Because they demonstrate a concern for the most vulnerable, food banks are seen as part of a progressive solution to hunger. They in fact play a different role. First, they are too ad hoc to be a universal safety net. Some communities have food banks, while others have none. Some people are comfortable using food banks, while others are uncomfortable for religious or cultural reasons. Some food banks provide an adequate basket of food on a regular basis; others restrict visits to once every three months. Second, food banks are very much the creatures of the marketplace, providing highly processed packaged food. They usually do not have refrigeration and rarely distribute fresh food. In Canada more than in the US, they are dependent on product donations provided by the food industry, saving them thousands in waste disposal fees and tax right-offs. Finally, food banks often reproduce some of the worst aspects of charity — often the recipients must justify their poverty to establish need. This pits food bank recipients against those handing out the food at food banks, in a situation too large and complex for charity to manage.

20. Tarasuk, Beaton, Geduld, and Hildtich, "Nutritional Vulnerability and Food Insecurity Among Women in Families Using Food Banks," 25.

21. World Food Summit, *Food Security, Situations and Issues; A North American Perspective*, 17.

22. See, for example, Arlene Voski Avakian, ed., *Through the Kitchen Window: Women Explore the Intimate Meanings of Food and Cooking* (Boston: Beacon Press, 1997).

23. In Lima, Peru, there are 100,000 women active in community kitchens which have been the backbone of the movement for subsidized food grains. In Canada, women make up the vast majority of participants in community kitchens as well, though we have yet to see a similar number of active community kitchens or as much political activity connected to community kitchens as in Latin America. A recent Ontario study of community kitchens, community meal and cooking with kids meal programs found that 100 percent of the adults were women and two-thirds of the children were female (Twylla Gayson and Frances Theodor, "An Evaluation of Healthy Families Together: 1996–1997 Groups, Executive Summary" [unpublished paper, Dellcrest Centre, Toronto, 1998], ii).

Chapter Eleven

GRASSROOTS RESPONSES
TO GLOBALIZATION:
MEXICAN RURAL AND URBAN
WOMEN'S COLLECTIVE ALTERNATIVES

*Asunción Amezquita, Reyes Márquez and Angeles Amezquita, members
of the women's group in Valencianita, Mexico, July 1996.*

GRASSROOTS RESPONSES TO GLOBALIZATION:

MEXICAN RURAL AND URBAN WOMEN'S COLLECTIVE ALTERNATIVES

Maria Dolores Villagomez

IN MEXICO, SINCE THE 1960S and increasingly in the 1980s, programs and policies that are proposed as solutions to the general economic crisis have been integrating women into productive activity. Within this difficult context, there has also been a multiplication of women's organizations that seek alternative ways to confront the crisis. It is important to recognize that women have, in fact, always been integrated into the economy through their domestic work — productive activity in the private sphere that is still devalued. Nonetheless, many women have moved outside the private space of the home, and, in addition to their domestic responsibilities, have entered the public sphere of work.

The economic changes and the globalization[1] process itself (the essence of which is economic — the internationalization of capital) at the same time limit the possibilities for women to find work and earn a stable income. Many women from diverse organizations are supporting one another in efforts to meet basic needs. Despite the pressures of globalization, collective efforts by women are multiplying and strengthening in the midst of an unequal and exclusionary economic development process imposed by the neoliberal economic model.[2] These increasing inequities and the economic crisis also explain the massive entrance of women into the informal economic sector, into commercial agriculture as well as subsistence agriculture, into micro enterprises, and into other areas of work. For example, official statistics show clearly the increasing participation of women within the Economically Active Population (Población Economicamente Activa, or PEA):

> The number of women who became members of the economically active population has doubled between 1970 and 1993 (from 24% to 44%). In 1993, women were primarily employed in selling (24%), in clerical work (14%), in manufacturing (13%), in domestic work (12%), and in agriculture (11%).[3]

In the state of Guanajuato, women officially make up 17 percent of the Economically Active Population. This number does not include those women who work in family businesses, whether they are agricultural, artisanal, industrial or commercial, which would increase the percentage considerably. At the same time it confirms the importance of women in the economy, particularly taking into account that one of Guanajuato's characteristics is the forced migration of the male labour force to the central provinces and, in even greater numbers, to the United States.

It is important to recognize that despite their greater participation in the labour market, women are not hired for the higher-paid jobs, nor do they receive social security; and combined with women's stronger presence, children's participation in the workforce is also steadily increasing. In Guanajuato, the context for the cases discussed here, it is common to find situations where child labour is indispensable. This is especially true in the so-called "industrial corridor" and the agro-industries — for example, in strawberry picking and in the shoe and textile industries.

The structural changes imposed by the neoliberal economic model have provoked not only greater gender inequities but also the mobilization of women in search of economic alternatives that would generate more income to meet their basic needs. In response to this situation, the civil society organization Proyectos Laubach de México (Laubach Projects of Mexico, or PLAMAC)[4] has promoted, within a popular education framework, educational and community development work with an emphasis on literacy and women's education. Since its founding in 1979, PLAMAC has expanded its work to over two hundred rural communities, primarily in the municipalities of Abasolo and Irapuato; currently they work in collaboration with the state Secretary of Education.

PLAMAC's educational thrust emphasizes training women for work and helping them form and develop small productive enterprises. PLAMAC trains women to be community leaders — to create and manage educational, economic and social projects. It also offers training in the areas of preventive health and health promotion. PLAMAC programs initially focused on *campesino* (peasant) women from the rural areas, and since 1996, the organization has been working with a group of urban women who have organized a community kitchen program in the city of Irapuato.

The great majority of women from rural areas work in agro-industries or in textile industries. Very few families have access to land to grow their own food, especially corn which is a staple crop for subsistence. Land is sometimes rented seasonally, and frequently families are unable to harvest all that they cultivate. Such conditions make women all the more vulnerable. This situation has led many of them to engage in collective projects such as making clothes, creating savings and loan collectives, and buying food in bulk.

Currently, PLAMAC is co-ordinating projects in twelve communities located in Abasolo and Irapuato, involving diverse groups[5] and benefiting over 6,000 people. These projects have taken many different directions and have different outcomes. I focus on two of these groups of women who have undertaken successful projects: the rural women in the community of Valencianita and the urban women in Irapuato.

THE RURAL WOMEN OF VALENCIANITA

The first group of women, in the rural community of Valencianita, have demonstrated tremendous organizational capability in seeking alternatives — forming savings clubs and bulk buying, credit and sewing co-operatives — in order to survive. These experiences have been for them a process of local empowerment, that is, it has been a process that has given them skills which enable them to participate more actively in the public sphere. This process has allowed them to become collective "subjects"; they are no longer "objects," but rather protagonists in their lives and interveners in their social context. It has also transformed their positions within the community, their relationships with other community members as well as with community authorities. Through this experience, the women of Valencianita are beginning to take part in the public sphere and to claim a political space.

URBAN WOMEN IN IRAPUATO

The women's group located in an urban neighbourhood of Irapuato has created a community kitchen, a project born to offer a food alternative in the face of the scarcity of food staples and in response to the increasing costs of the *canasta básica*, or basic subsistence diet. Collective cooking has reduced the costs of food; the food is of better quality and offers a more balanced diet. From their perspective, the women save not only money but also time. Now, through the collective project of the community kitchen, they might cook three or four hours a week, whereas it might take them four hours daily to do the same work on their own and in their own households. This has clearly benefited all the women, but especially salaried women workers who work outside the home.

PLAMAC initially hoped to implement the community kitchen program with women from popular (low-income) sectors. This didn't work, however, because these women and their families could not pay for their food, even though it was a minimal amount. It also failed because these women worked very long and exhausting days (averaging twelve hours a day), which left them with no time (or energy) to take on the tasks shared by the women in the community kitchen. Given the complexity of the situation of low-income women, then, PLAMAC did not seek other ways to respond to their basic needs of feeding their families daily and having the time to get their other housework done.

Thus, in 1996, PLAMAC formed a community kitchen collective in Irapuato, but the group was primarily made up of women with university education, working in full-time jobs and working full-time at their domestic duties in the home. Currently, the group actively involves about twenty women and the project of collective cooking benefits a total of around eighty people.

COMPARING THE RURAL AND URBAN
WOMEN'S GROUPS

In analyzing the organizing experiences of the rural group and the urban-based community kitchen group, we can see some commonalities, even as we keep in mind their cultural and environmental differences. The kinds of activities they have organized, in both cases, relate directly to activities they undertake at home for their families, which means they do the kind of gendered work that they have always done — producing clothes (sewing), domestic services (shared bulk buying, cooking) and household finances and credit (savings and loan collectives). In terms of the rural women's credit co-operatives, it is important to point out that most of the loans rural women access do not come from banks but rather from their own savings, and that such credit is used for developing small businesses in service activities, particularly in baking bread and making clothes.

The success of these groups has depended very much on the experience of women working together with other women to perform tasks that not only benefit them but also benefit their families. In fact, the programs try to emphasize the more personal benefits that the women gain from them: personal growth, an increase in knowledge, skills and self-worth, and above all the capacity to make decisions for themselves. Teresa, one of the women in the Valencianita group, recalls:

> At the beginning, I had to get permission from my husband to go to the group meetings; but now I see that I've had a very rich experience, and my husband, too, has changed his ways. Before, when I was just learning to sew, he wouldn't let me go to the sewing collective, he abused me (I never told the other women about this ... I wanted to keep going even with the suffering ...) But when my husband began to see the results of the project, for example, that I was asked to make people clothes and that they paid me for it, then he changed ... Now my husband helps me ... I'm working with a group of young girls, I'm teaching them to sew. Now I'm the teacher ... it's great to be able to learn and to teach.[6]

Through the experience of building these alternative organizations, the women have had to confront resistance in their families and, in the rural areas, also from their communities. There have been some who couldn't resist the pressure and have left the group, returning to the privacy of their homes. Clara explains, "Today women are fighting against the ways that men manipulate us. Before we were more long-suffering and self-denying, but not now; we ignore the criticisms and we keep moving ahead in our groups."[7] In fact, the women who successfully take on their families experience satisfaction not only at the personal level but also within their families, as they build relationships that are more vital, autonomous and independent.

An Economic Alternative for Women: *Empresa Social*

There is another positive result of these projects. Although the women first sought alternatives to meet concrete survival needs, once rooted in the organization process, they were introduced to new ways of understanding and working with the complexity of the issues in which they were involved. This is the case of the community group kitchen in Irapuato. From their beginning in 1996 and up until the first half of 1998, the group received a subsidy to cover the costs of rent, water and electricity in the locale where they cooked the food. But now that there is no more funding, they have found their own solution to the problem and have decided to incorporate as an *empresa social* (social business). *Empresas sociales* are economic units managed by poor people with the goal of maximizing the capital invested in order to generate some social value. To better understand this concept, see Table 1 for an outline of the characteristics of an *empresa social*.

Empresas sociales are understood more as forms of social commitment than as legal business entities. Of course, in the process of developing an *empresa social*, the women must find or create new legal forms that express their collective interests. It is important to note here that, unfortunately, in Mexico there is not yet very favourable legislation for the establishment of this kind of business.

Table 1: Characteristics of an *Empresa Social* (Social Business)[8]

Financial Aspects	Organizational Aspects	Social and Political Aspects
Production responds to felt and expressed needs	New legal forms need to be created that reflect the nature of social business	Social purposes that make it an alternative are made visible
It needs to be clear that the property is collective and not individual	Organized to involve workers in planning the productive process	Articulates locally and regionally its economic alternative in order to act more forcefully in the market and to facilitate its regional integration
Generates its own economic resources and is also capable of incorporating outside assets (private loans)	Promotes an enterprising culture (developing leaders, both entrepreneurial and managerial)	Strengthens local and regional social networks (if it is a strong social actor)
Based on a total cost accounting of a product: cultural, monetary, ecological, and political	Facilitates the learning and capacity-building of its members	Is able to balance business goals with social movement goals
Joins with other local actors to build local commerce	Adequately combines both individual and collective participation	Connects with public officials and entities, according to its own interests
Is able to integrate into the local market	Flexible and open to adapting new economic and political contexts	Builds the foundation for a model of alternative sustainable development
Has clear policies about the distribution of benefits (salaries, profits)		
Studies financial and market feasibility		

MULTIPLE OUTCOMES: FROM PERSONAL GROWTH
TO BROAD-BASED MOVEMENTS

An important effect of these experiences is that, even though the projects were initiated out of a personal necessity (and, implicitly, a collective one), these women have transcended their personal and family situations to create something broader, which is communal and social. After two years of operation, for example, the urban community kitchen group began to seek out other similar experiences and other women's groups. This led them to join the Movimiento Amplio de Mujeres de Guanajuato (the Broad-Based Women's Movement of Guanajuato). This movement brings together organizations working with women on a wide variety of issues: health, the economy, violence, human rights, the sex trade, promotion and development. The local coalition is also linked to organizations at the national and international level.

Another important dimension of these experiences for rural and urban women is that when they get together with other women to take common action, there are among them different levels of self-confidence. Women who do paid work outside the home as well as housework have greater self-esteem than women who are restricted to unpaid work within the home. In this new space for connecting with each other, women become more aware of their own potential and they learn to see themselves as other women see them, which makes them value themselves even more. As the process has unfolded, they have demonstrated how much they enjoy working with other women, to the point that they have invited their closest friends to join them so they can benefit from the same kind of experience. The projects have developed into support groups where the women can share many aspects of their lives, from their perspectives as women.

Through the experience of group work, the women have developed more democratic practices. As they construct and strengthen relationships that contribute to economic growth, they begin to see more ways that they can contribute to their communities. Through these projects, the women are gaining more recognition and respect from their families and within their communities. They no longer see themselves as objects but as women with a purpose. They realize that their own words and actions are valuable and can be heard, seen and used in building and strengthening their communities.

In a recent evaluation, the community kitchen group concluded that their project has helped them in many ways: they have lost their fear of cooking in large quantities, developed a greater consciousness of quality in preparing food, and have become more effective and efficient in working collectively. Their self-esteem, mutual co-operation, trust and respect for one another have grown, as have their tolerance for differences and their development of a kind of sisterhood among women in the group as well as outside the group. And, through all of this, they have discovered the importance of working as a team.

These women have had a social impact — they are now receiving public recognition for their work as a community organization. They offer advice and consultations to other groups of women interested in developing similar projects, while recognizing the problems that working women face. Finally, it is important to emphasize that the experience of sisterhood that these women have developed, for the most part, promotes among them creative thinking and alternative actions that benefit everyone and, in an integrated fashion, respect the environment, culture and different forms of social and political organizations around them.

Maria Dolores (left) with Dulce Maria Vargas during her women's radio program in Irapuato, Mexico, July 1996.

NOTES

This chapter was translated from the Spanish original by Deborah Barndt.

1. I am using the definition of globalization developed by Jean Claude Lavigne, who described it as "a mechanism of world creation made of interconnections, not only of exchanges, but also of finance, culture, information, and ways of life. This system leads to a consideration of the world as a single space in which decisions are taken to optimize the advantages, reflected in the search for low wages, for major fiscal advantages and for favourable exchange rates" ("Mundialización y Universalización," *Revista Christus* 702 [November–December 1997, Mexico City], 50). Editor's translation from the Spanish.

2. "Neoliberalism is expressed through economic policies of structural adjustment and commercial opening that make economic growth the raison d'etre of the economy. It restricts state intervention, eliminates social programs, privatizes businesses, opens the borders without barriers for business, capital and financial flows, leaves small producers unprotected and weak, subordinates the complexity of the public revenue to the adjustment of macroeconomic variables: balances fiscal budgets, reduces inflation and stabilizes the balance of payments" (Editorial, *Revista Christus* 689 [January–February 1997], 2). Editor's translation from the Spanish.

3. Fronteras Comunes, "Los Effectos de la Globalización" (unpublished document, Mexico City, 1997).

4. PLAMAC is a local member of an international literacy organization started in the early part of the century by Frank C. Laubach (1884–1915), in rural Pennsylvania. He developed an educational process that was technically simple and effective for teaching literacy. For Laubach, the starting point for the teaching of reading and writing is the concrete reality of the learners, in all its dimensions — social, economic, cultural, family. The horizons of the learners grow as does their capacity to identify and find solutions to personal or community problems and to create and develop both their personal and communal power.

5. The projects and the communities are: a savings club network in Penitas, Penuelas, Lo de Sierra, Valencianita, San Nicolas, Ojo de Agua (Irapuato), and Tinaja de Negrete (Abasolo); credit and savings clubs in San Nicolas, Valencianita, and Tinaja; and women's sewing collectives in Santa Rosa, Adjuntas, Lo del Lencino, Canada de la Muerta, Lo de Sierra, Ojo de Agua, Valencianita, Penitas, San Nicolas, Estancia, La Pena, and Tinaja de Negrete.

6. Teresa (pseudonym), interview with author and Deborah Barndt, Valencianita, Mexico, July 20, 1996.

7. Clara (pseudonym), interview with author and Deborah Barndt, Valencianita, Mexico, July 20, 1996.

8. These characteristics were drawn up by the Social Affairs Team of the Center for Ecumenical Studies (CEE), in Mexico City in 1998.

Chapter Twelve

WOMEN AS ORGANIZERS:
BUILDING CONFIDENCE AND COMMUNITY
THROUGH FOOD

Emily Chan (York University student) and Maeza Afwerki (Focus on Food participant)
offer food and stories at the Roots and Routes Festival, Toronto, 1998.

WOMEN AS ORGANIZERS:

BUILDING CONFIDENCE AND COMMUNITY

THROUGH FOOD

Deborah Moffett & Mary Lou Morgan

THIS CHAPTER FOCUSES on the women involved in two community food projects in Toronto, Canada: the Good Food Box and the Focus on Food training program. It highlights how these women use these and other community food projects as vehicles for small-scale resistance. We have been involved with the two programs in different capacities. Mary Lou, who has a passion for food, was co-founder of Metro Toronto FoodShare's Field to Table, the organization that gave birth to the two community programs that we focus on. She has been Field to Table's manager since its inception in 1992. Deborah has worked with the organization since 1994 as an organizational consultant, popular educator and, currently, as a volunteer co-ordinator and community outreach volunteer with the Good Food Box program. Both of us share strong interests in food, food issues and community development.

The Good Food Box and the Focus on Food training program bring to life examples of how women use food as a catalyst for personal and political change. Empowerment is an essential aspect of projects such as these, aiming to facilitate social change for women on personal and political levels. In this chapter, we describe how these two Toronto-based community food projects promote empowerment of women, discuss inevitable tensions that arise and share our renewed appreciation of how personal action can be inherently political even when it involves everyday activities.

The term empowerment has been criticized by many feminists as both overused and misused. Its meaning is often reduced to the personal level, without acknowledging the systemic barriers to change.[1] We use empowerment to mean "analyzing ideas about the causes of powerlessness, recognizing systemic oppressive forces, and acting both individually and collectively to change the conditions of our lives," as defined by Australian feminist Patti Lather.[2] No other word better describes these processes, so we have chosen it as an analytical frame, aware that it might spark some controversy. When examining the nature of and motivation for the participation of the women in these two community food programs, empowerment was an important concept for us to come to terms with; it helped us to better understand both the women's daily struggles as well as their activities geared towards longer-term change.

It has been useful for us to locate our use of the term empowerment within Janice Ristock and Joan Pennell's empowerment spectrum,[3] which ranges from the individual to the societal level. On an individual level, empowerment means "having the drive to take responsibility for one's own actions and assert oneself." Interpersonally it can mean "sharing resources for mutual benefit or working together co-operatively." On a professional level, empowerment can mean "facilitating and collaborating rather than prescribing and treating." Organizationally, it can mean "working democratically, participating equally, and sharing in decision-making and policy development in the work environment." In the broadest sense, empowerment on a "societal" level is "concentrated political activity aimed directly at changing the essence and distribution of power." We've added one more level: empowerment on a "collective" basis is political action by a group that challenges the dominant power structure. We've engaged this model as a way of examining the activities of the women in the community food projects we've chosen to highlight.

Food: Women's Joy or Women's Burden?

The responsibility of food preparation and, more generally, the struggle to provide families with access to healthy, reliable food sources have been, for the most part, the burden and struggle of women. The industrialized food system and corporate food processors have keyed into this with the development of a proliferation of highly processed "convenience" foods and fast foods, which dominate the choices within retail food stores and family restaurants. The preparation and sharing of food, which can be a joy and celebration for many, may become particularly stressful for those with difficult economic or social circumstances, who may not have enough food for their families.

The North American women's movement has had much to say about women and food. Three generations of North American feminists (primarily middle class) between the end of the American Civil War and the beginning of the Great Depression saw the preparation and serving of food as tasks that ghettoized women, trapped them in the home and kept their domestic work isolated and invisible. Some of the activities of this segment of the women's movement were targeted towards making domestic chores, including childcare and food preparation, more visible and socially organized. Reorganization of domestic work was seen as an essential prerequisite to the attainment of economic justice.[4] There is no doubt that, in this era, food preparation was one of the vehicles for social-change oriented activities.

There is another grassroots movement simmering here in Ontario today. Women are involved in a myriad of community food projects, including everything from community gardens and community kitchens to buying co-operatives and student nutrition programs, which all operate outside the dominant food system. Each food project demonstrates how women have, in one way or another, taken back some control over the food supply from the large corporate players and in the process have redefined who has access to healthy food and how it is accessed. These women have made the politics of food more visible to the members of their community. Each project is also rich with examples of women building personal confidence and social connections through their community actions. Before sharing stories of these projects, however, it is important to describe the social and political contexts which have fertilized the ground where food projects could blossom.

COMMUNITY FOOD PROJECTS: LOCAL
RESPONSES TO GLOBALIZATION

Community food projects have evolved in the midst of the restructuring of a globalized food system, which "distances"[5] the consumers from the growers of food, and also in the aftermath of social spending cuts brought in by Ontario right-wing Conservatives in 1995. Economic globalization, neoliberal trade policies and declining social welfare programs have resulted in large-scale socioeconomic disruptions and fewer public social resources, which, in turn, are making the historical roles of family food producer, purchaser and preparer more difficult for many women. This economic uncertainty leaves women feeling disempowered and marginalized.

Women, through community organizations, have been responding to the challenges of falling incomes and shrinking social services, using food for personal and political empowerment. They have found that organizing around food creates opportunities to exercise control over their lives and to strengthen communities, in a kind of "democratization of everyday life."[6]

The Good Food Box and the Focus on Food training program are both projects of a Toronto-based anti-hunger organization called Food-Share Metro Toronto. Since 1985, FoodShare has worked with low-income communities to advocate for an end to hunger and to educate around food issues. In 1992, the Toronto Food Policy Council commissioned a feasibility study to suggest practical solutions that would link low-income city people with farmers. The resulting community-based project, christened Field to Table, was adopted by FoodShare. Field to Table became the practical application of FoodShare's mission, "working with communities to improve access to affordable nutritious food." As we learned about the complexities of food security in a developed urban context, Field to Table responded by creating several outreach projects: a non-profit produce company with distribution through the Good Food Box system; a training program for women on social assistance called Focus on Food; a catering company to employ the graduates of the program; a licensed commercial kitchen available on an hourly rental basis to fledgling entrepreneurs; and a support system for urban and rural agriculture projects.

The Good Food Box

The Good Food Box is a community-based non-profit fresh-fruit-and-vegetable distribution system. It operates like a large buying club with centralized buying and co-ordination, and relies on the help of almost three hundred volunteers and a few staff to pack and distribute over 2,000 food boxes biweekly. Volunteer co-ordinators run the distribution system by neighbourhood and provide a host-site for neighbours to come pick up boxes of fresh produce. Launched in 1994 by Field to Table, the Good Food Box was a response to the needs and concerns voiced by women struggling to feed their families. Inspiration for this program came from listening to Toronto low-income women and examining other women-centred community food projects in Japan, Brazil and the United States.

From the perspective of the neighbourhood co-ordinators, the Good Food Box is much more than a produce-buying club. In addition to looking after the money and providing pickup locations, co-ordinators do community outreach, helping Field to Table and FoodShare understand the changing environment and the needs of women and their communities. Even more importantly, the program provides the opportunity for the co-ordinators themselves to link with other women in their communities. Community food projects modelled after aspects of the Good Food Box have sprung up all across Ontario.[7] These programs are part of the growing coalition of community and social organizations that support and strengthen each other and their communities, while strategizing around broader issues concerning social justice, community health and creation of healthy food systems.

In the Toronto Good Food Box program, co-ordinator drop-off sites include homes, churches, community centres, daycares, workplaces and agencies — any place in greater Toronto can serve as a pickup site for ten interested participants and a co-ordinator. Almost all (98 percent) co-ordinators are women, which is not surprising considering the central roles women have in both food provision and community organization. The women are from a mix of cultural backgrounds. All ages are represented, although the majority are between thirty and fifty-five. Many are mothers; some work at home and many are sole-support parents. Some are involved with and promote Field to Table through their church or through other religious organizations. While the program is targeted to low-income households, everyone is invited to participate. Co-ordinators come from all economic brackets and participate for a variety of reasons — for the social aspects, to support local farmers and to take an active role in building their communities.

We organized regional co-ordinator meetings and were quite surprised by the outcomes. Although co-ordinators had ideas for improving the program, they were more interested in sharing stories about their customers, the Good Food Box and the other community food projects they were involved in. Such sharing is clearly a demonstration of "interpersonal empowerment."

One of our hopes in bringing the co-ordinators together was to encourage them to mobilize on a collective basis by sharing with them the impressive social-change activities carried out by the Seikatsu Club. A twenty-five-year-old women-organized co-operative movement in Japan, the Seikatsu Club involves over 225 thousand members in everything from co-operative food buying and daycare to product development. The members have also worked together at a political level, mobilizing support to ban certain products, to eliminate pesticide usage on golf courses and to stop nuclear arms activity.[8] The efforts of the Japanese women are impressive and illustrate empowerment that moves beyond the local level to form a broad-based movement. The aim of these Japanese "housewives" has been no less than to change the nature and distribution of societal power. Their success has been partly due to the ability of the women to mobilize effectively in their own unique social context.[9]

We soon realized, however, that in our efforts to encourage a collective social-change agenda here in Toronto, we were not recognizing the importance of the women's knowledge and deep understanding of what is important in their own community contexts. We learned that many of the co-ordinators had been empowered community organizers on some level for years before they became involved with the Good Food Box. The reasons they have become co-ordinators are quite varied, but there are some central themes. The most common motivations for participation are social. For instance, Flo, a self-described "small-town Prairie girl," finds that the Good Food Box helps her connect with her roots and break through the isolation of the big city:

I find it hard to live in this big city. I love getting food directly from farmers — opening the box reconnects me with nature, my parents' farm and my roots. When my customers arrive, the kids head for the back yard while the parents socialize on the front porch.[10]

Many gain a connection to their communities through participation in this project as well as further their community outreach activities. These women have their own political and social agenda that is relevant for the community in which they live or work. Wendy was a former Good Food Box customer, but when she and her family moved to a new neighbourhood, she took on the role of co-ordinator "to meet the neighbours. And now that I am settling in, I use my free co-ordinator's box as a gift to introduce myself and welcome other people who move into our community. That way they get to know me and find out about the Good Food Box first hand."[11]

Others also use the Good Food Box to directly help people in their community. Joyce, an energetic senior, has the Field to Table driver load the boxes directly onto her cart so that she can hand deliver the box to each of her customers in her inner-city apartment building. What began for her as a curiosity about new fruits and vegetables became a way to care for others. Flo donates her box of food to the student nutrition program at her child's school and then uses the food to teach cooking to the students.

A surprising number of co-ordinators have family members who have allergies or other food-related health concerns. Many made a conscious decision to buck the processed food trend. Susan and Judith are both mothers of small children. The Good Food Box has provided an opportunity to obtain organic produce, go back to home cooking and take some small bit of control over their food supply. Susan told us: "My son has allergies and asthma. He can't eat processed foods with chemicals and preservatives. With the Good Food Box I can get a steady supply of organic produce. I find I am recapturing family cooking traditions rather than relying on the highly processed and chemical-laden foods I find on the supermarket shelves."[12]

Judith is a mother of four and is convinced that going back to basics is the only healthy alternative. She teaches a series of cooking classes in her neighbourhood to promote the simple cooking and shopping skills that we've lost with the advent of fast food and highly processed convenience foods. She told us, "I encourage my Good Food Box customers to use their box as a time-saving way to menu plan and prepare basic home-cooked meals."[13]

Other co-ordinators express satisfaction in circumventing the food manufacturing and retail industry's control of farmers and consumers. They represent, perhaps, a mounting public response against large supercentres based on importing food from all over the world. They like the fact that Field to Table is a community-based food project that supports local farmers whenever possible.

Despite being locally focused, the personal and community activities that the co-ordinators are involved in are undeniably political. They work to build alliances between agencies and other community resources, such as schools, shelters and service agencies. Their organizing work challenges the social frameworks and the food-system structures that determine how food is distributed and made accessible to people at a community level. In this sense, the program promotes organizational and societal empowerment.

FOCUS ON FOOD

The second FoodShare program, Focus on Food, illustrates how a group of marginalized women have been able to break out of their isolation, draw out inner knowledge, develop confidence, form friendships and build a support network. Like the Good Food Box, food is the vehicle, but the results have been more visible as personal empowerment. Despite this emphasis, empowerment on an interpersonal level, and even on a professional level, was also evident in the activities undertaken by the participants.

Focus on Food was created in 1995 by FoodShare as a year-long food training program for a small group of women on social assistance. The students in each of the 1995 and 1997 programs were among those hardest hit by the structural adjustments taking place in Ontario. Cuts to social assistance and other social safety-net programs affected these women, and they were struggling to keep their heads above water. Many of the women were isolated immigrants, most were single mothers, and many were underskilled for even basic jobs in a climate of high un-employment.[14] In their daily lives, food became the elastic band for all other pressures. They paid for shelter, utilities and emergencies first, and when it came to food, they often sacrificed their own needs to pro-vide for their children. The women were hungry, not only for food but also for social connections and for meaningful work. They felt isolated and were anxious "to get out there," as they expressed it. The program was designed to build their skills for entering the workforce and to open up a sense of options in their lives.

The training program offered so-called "life-skills" (English, math, computer, job search techniques) as well as opportunities to learn about food through gardening, food preparation, cooking and catering, and nutrition education. The learning environment was designed to nurture the self-assurance the women needed to begin to make personal changes while at the same time becoming connected to a community. Classroom work was balanced with practice: an apprenticeship in the catering company, participation in the packing of the Good Food Box and two placements in the workforce in food-related jobs. To comple-ment the practical skills taught, other workshops focused more on the development of critical thinking skills, through activities such as "de-coding" advertising messages with degrading and stereotypical portray-als of women, critically examining fast-food advertising and building an understanding of the globalized food system through viewing films and sharing stories of personal experiences in the food system.[15]

A popular education[16] approach was often used in the training pro-gram. One example was the preparation for and presentations at "Roots and Routes: Nourishing Connections from Land to Table," an Eco Art and Media Festival jointly sponsored by FoodShare and York Univer-sity's Faculties of Environmental Studies, Fine Arts and Education. Building on previous work linking graduate students and women in the program, a series of working sessions was organized to develop photo stories about the food that connected the women to their roots. To par-ticipate in the sessions, the women in the training program were asked to pick a recipe that represented something meaningful to them, to re-search its history, to cook it for one another, and to share stories around the food. The cooking process was to be photographed and each woman was to integrate the photos and her personal story into a "photo storyboard" for presentation and display at the festival.

At first the women were reluctant participants. They didn't really know what they were being asked to do or why. But one by one, each woman chose a recipe that reflected her personal and social "roots" (history and culture) and began making plans to prepare a meal for the staff and students. Once the women chose their recipes, they realized they needed to research the "roots" and "routes" of the ingredients, to check with parents and relatives (and even embassies) about cooking techniques and cultural practices, and to think about different ways to present their stories to others. A teacher in the program photographed the process of preparing, telling and eating. The women wrote out their recipes — many for the first time — and practised writing and computer skills in editing their stories. In this process, the students shared ideas and resources, demonstrating interpersonal empowerment. Their participation also stimulated the kind of deeper reflection on their cultural histories necessary for collective and societal empowerment.

Each meal created by the women over the two months leading up to the festival became an event, and they became the teachers. They planned, shopped and prepared the meal with the help of the other women. Before eating together, each woman presented the story of the meal's roots. Each of their meals was prepared in the big kitchen and it is significant that it was here — where the women made the food together, ate together and talked together — that their stories began to flow. For example, Maeza described how *teff*, the main grain in "Taita," an Ethiopian fermented bread, is too expensive in Canada, so she has adapted her recipe to use corn and barley. In her long journey to Canada through the Middle East, she had to constantly adapt this recipe to local ingredients. She also made the spicy beef curry that is served on the bread, and she demonstrated the customs of eating communally and of presenting the food to the mouth of a shy guest.

Joann's story told how her "Callalo Soup" would forever be linked to the war in Grenada, to her house arrest and to her mother who risked her life to find greens to feed her family. Tamara chose the Jamaican national dish, "Salt Cod and Akee." We learned that the salt cod originally came from Newfoundland in trade for rum and sugar, and that akee originated in Africa and is poisonous if not correctly harvested. Tamara hinted that there was a song about the dish, but she was too shy to sing it. Imagine our surprise when Beck, from St. Lucia, and one of the truck drivers for the Good Food Box, who was sitting in for the presentation, rose to the occasion!

Connections were made within and across cultures. Victoria made "Pastél de Chóclo" and reflected on how the casserole mixes Spanish and Native culture by using Spanish olives and Indian corn. She also remembered her father's farm labour and her mother's insistence on getting help in making this time-consuming dish; she laughed as she revealed that she herself had used a bag of frozen corn. Her story showed the family on her father's farm in Chile, the Andes in the background, and contained this poem that she wrote in English and translated back into Spanish to send home:

THE ROUTES OF MY ROOTS

Searching deep down into my roots
I find the sunny midday of my childhood;
the happy memories, the hard times,
the changing pace of my homeland.

My father coming from the corn field,
the harvest of his work upon his shoulders.
Many before him did carry the golden meal
many before him did sow the roots of my roots.

The Andes wind carries my mother's voice
she tells me to go searching further,
beyond the mountains and further more.
I'll discover the aromas I found in her hands,
I'll recognize the faces of those who came long ago.

I stop, I seize, I touch, I listen for the echoes,
of the first farmers of my land,
those who were forced to go,
those who went deep down into the forest;
at the beginning of the encounter of my two ancestors.

Melissa's story told of the role of food in her grandparents' English working-class family, her mother's food coping skills as a single parent, her own new respect for food and how she now looks forward to preparing a meal with her two-year-old. The serving of tea one day tapped a whole host of memories about racism, colonialism and the loss of mothers, themes that were shared among several women. The stories themselves were intensely personal, but the collective process of sharing them became profoundly political as the women's understanding of common historical roots and political aspects of their everyday lives deepened.

Another demonstration of their growing skills, deepening confidence and personal empowerment was illustrated after the women completed their first work-term placements. The women went to work for (arguably) Toronto's best professional catering company, where they performed well, received excellent work references and were offered follow-up work. In one sense, one of the training program's objectives was thus fulfilled: the women were skilled enough for jobs in the food industry. However, just as noteworthy as the women's success in "getting out there" was their sophisticated critique of the working environment they were exposed to in their placements. They described the nurturing environment the employers created to keep their employees happy. But the women said that this seemed to be a backhanded strategy to try to reduce employee dissatisfaction (and potential for labour organizing) even though the working conditions were exploitative: no breaks, long hours and low wages. They are able to articulate, more clearly now than ever, how exploitative the working conditions can be in the food industry.

Acting on this critical consciousness, all the women have elected to perform their final placement as food providers within community agencies, where they feel their understanding and skills can be helpful to other marginalized women. In some cases, they are returning to places such as women's shelters, where they have some previous experience themselves as clients. They want to share their experiences and knowledge about community resources and inspire hope among other women, both of which demonstrate empowerment on an interpersonal level as well as on an organizational one. From the small community they created within the program, they continue to build communities wherever they go.

The Focus on Food women have demonstrated the confidence that leads to personal change. Together they have formed a network of friends for support and sharing resources and are reaching out to others to locate themselves within the context of a broader community. They have developed a political awareness of oppression and resistance in societal structures and everyday activities. Where they have influence, they are starting to take action to make things better for themselves and others. These women have reminded us that individual and collective empowerment as well as personal and political action are intimately linked.

A GROWING MOVEMENT

The Good Food Box and Focus on Food are examples of the many interwoven activities that are part of a grassroots coalition — a coalition that is growing and linking the many community services that deal with women, food and shelter in the fight for social change. FoodShare promotes other activities that are also part of this growing movement — Baby Food Making workshops, peer training for community kitchens, support to community gardens and a youth training program called "Just Grow It." As well, FoodShare works with many community and farm groups to develop food policies that will ensure that healthy food is a right for all. These initiatives remind us that personal action in everyday activities is still inherently political. For community organizers, they affirm the importance of local programs that provide fertile grounds for personal, interpersonal and collective empowerment. As seeds for broader movements for social change, these programs and their participants offer us hope.

Deborah (far left) and Mary Lou (second to left) discuss their work at Field to Table with Zahra Parvinian, co-ordinator, Focus on Food program.

NOTES

This essay also refers to ideas more fully discussed elsewhere in this volume. See Debbie Field, "Putting Food First," and Harriet Friedmann, "Remaking 'Traditions.'" "The Routes of My Roots," by Victoria, reprinted with permission.

1. Janice Ristock and Joan Pennell, *Community Research as Empowerment: Feminist Links, Postmodern Interruptions* (Toronto: University of Oxford Press, 1996), 6.

2. Patti Lather, "Research as Praxis," *Harvard Education Review* 56, no. 3 (1986), 257–277.

3. Ristock and Pennell, *Community Research as Empowerment: Feminist Links, Postmodern Interruptions,* 12.

4. Delores Hayden, *The Grand Domestic Revolution* (Cambridge: The MIT Press, 1981), 36.

5. Brewster Kneen, *From Land to Mouth: Understanding the Food System,* 2d ed. (Toronto: NC Publications, 1993), 17, 37–53.

6. Vandana Shiva, Presentation at York University, August 1995.

7. Kathryn Scharf and Mary Lou Morgan, *The Good Food Box Guide: How to Start a Program in Your Community* (Toronto: FoodShare Metro Toronto, 1997), 61–85.

8. For more information about the Seikatsu Club, see the featured articles in *GEO* (Grassroots Economic Organizing Newsletter), no. 12 (March-April1994) and no. 13 (June-July 1994).

9. The social context was unique in that the Japanese women involved in the first years of the Seikatsu Club were largely from middle-class, middle-income households. Their husbands worked excessive hours and they felt isolated at home with children. The women had time to organize when their children were at school. They enjoyed the social benefits and became empowered through their active roles in the Seikatsu Club's activities.

10. Flo, Good Food Box co-ordinators' focus group meeting with authors, Toronto, Ontario, February 1999.

11. Wendy, Good Food Box co-ordinators' focus group meeting with authors, Toronto, Ontario, February 1999.

12. Susan, Good Food Box co-ordinators' focus group meeting with authors, Toronto, Ontario, February 1999.

13. Judith, Good Food Box co-ordinators' focus group meeting with authors, Toronto, Ontario, January 1999.

14. Immigrant women, in fact, come to Canada with many skills but they are often not recognized as transferrable, particularly in a context where work itself is being re-defined; and, as is the case for most women, the many skills they have developed through their work within the home, have been devalued and not even acknowledged as "skills."

15. A further elaboration of the approach used in these workshops can be found in Deborah Barndt, "Crafting a 'Glocal' Education: Focusing on Food, Women and Globalization," *Atlantis* 22, no. 1 (Fall/Winter 1997), 43–51.

16. Popular educator Deborah Barndt describes "popular education" as "a process in which people collectively develop the critical awareness of their social situation and strengthen their ability to change it" (Deborah Barndt, *To Change This House: Popular Education Under the Sandinistas* [Toronto: Between the Lines, 1991], 15–20).

Chapter Thirteen

A DAY IN THE LIFE OF MARIA: WOMEN, FOOD, ECOLOGY AND THE WILL TO LIVE

Women like Maria buy fresh food daily from small-town markets.
(Tlayacápan, Mexico, July 1996.)

A DAY IN THE LIFE OF MARIA:

WOMEN, FOOD, ECOLOGY AND

THE WILL TO LIVE

Ofelia Perez Peña

MARIA IS A MEXICAN WOMAN *and, like many women, she faces life alone, accompanied only by the wisdom that she has gathered from the experience of living. At the age of thirty, she became a widow, left with five children but without the money to take care of them, the owner of a piece of land that was infertile and useless. In a rapidly changing world, with so many economic uncertainties, her days filled with both joy and sorrow, Maria has managed to survive. Her knowledge, her abilities, her strength and her love of life have helped her to fight to keep her family afloat and moving ahead. Maria is not an "ideal woman," but we can learn a lot from her — her tenacious hold on life, her intimacy with nature, her struggle to resist, to be herself, to continue being Maria in a world that tries to homogenize individuals and subsume them within a global society. Maria's life is by no means a utopia, but it is blossoming in a world where people are resisting the aggressive waves of the unequal and unjust North American Free Trade Agreement (NAFTA), in which Mexico is the most disadvantaged partner. How does Maria survive day by day?*

Tick, tock, tick, tock. In the distance Maria can hear the clock striking four-thirty in the morning. She stirs, and not wanting to get out of bed, she opens her eyes and begins to stretch. She has to get up because soon the church bells will announce the first morning mass. It's only March 23, and in the coming months she will have to get up even earlier, perhaps at three-thirty a.m., since the government decided to move the clocks an hour ahead. She can't get used to this new schedule, and feels robbed of an hour of sleep. She wonders, What right do they have to do that? She'd like to stay in bed a little longer, but then she remembers that today her oldest son is arriving from Los Angeles, California, after being gone for ten long years; with this thought, she jumps out of bed, and dresses quickly. She has just enough time to find her cloth shopping bag and to wash out the pot which she will fill with the fresh milk she goes to fetch with her *co-madre*.[1]

She rushes off to the church, which is only five blocks from her house. Prayer is very important to Maria; it gives her strength and sustains her in her hard life. When she feels weak and vulnerable, she prays, asks for help, prays, asks for help, and keeps praying so that she gathers strength to carry on. Maria doesn't use psychotherapists or counsellors; praying is her way of tending her spirit.

She arrives at mass just as it is beginning. The priest, in his homily, talks about how the poor need our help. He asks that on the first day of every month, the Day of Divine Providence, the faithful bring offerings for the poor, like rice, beans, oil, soap, crackers, salt and sugar. As though this were sufficient to alleviate poverty! Maria feels that every day the number of poor people increases. Is it because there are more people? Is it because a small group of countries and people are left with everything?

In Mexico, during the six-year term of Salinas, thirty Mexican families controlled 25 percent of the Gross National Product (GNP) and eight Mexicans joined the club of the one hundred richest men in the world. Almost 40 percent of the national income belonged to 10 percent of the population. At the other end, co-existing with this extreme wealth, 10 percent of the poorest Mexicans had only 1.55 percent of the country's disposable resources. In the 1980s, given corruption in the public sector, the oil and banking crisis, and the rise of unemployment, the level of extreme poverty rose. In 1984 it reached 7 percent (compared to -1.3 percent in 1968 and 4.2 percent in 1981).[2] In the same decade, the government decided to promote a new model of accumulation based on a considerable opening up of the country to foreign investment; and so, the great neoliberal project, begun in Chicago in the 1970s, took off. At the beginning of the 1990s, after the signing of the North American Free Trade Agreement, it was proclaimed that Mexico had entered the First World. But the failures of the system were revealed again in 1994: the false security created by the massive presence of foreign capital collapsed in what was called the "tequila effect" and the Indigenous population launched a cry from the jungle, demanding that those who had been forgotten be remembered. Since then, poverty levels have remained high, encompassing more than 40 million people. Today most Mexicans continue to be profoundly concerned about their economic future.

For Maria, it is increasingly difficult to survive and move ahead. To pay off debts, she had to sell the small piece of land and the house that her husband left her. The money she receives from her work of teaching sewing doesn't cover the costs of all that she needs to buy. And food has become even more expensive. Her salary is small, about 836 pesos (or US$80) a month. But in comparison with others, this might be considered a good wage, since in Mexico now, over 36 million people only earn between US$8 and US$25 a month.[3]

Every time she goes to the store, Maria gets fewer goods for the same amount of money. When she complains, they say it's due to the crisis in Asia or in Russia. What do these events have to do with the price of the products that she buys? Recently, Maria proposed to the group of women in her sewing collective that as well as combining their resources to buy cloth more cheaply in bulk, they also buy among themselves other things they need for their homes; by buying wholesale, they can get things much cheaper. She recalls how much effort this has taken. Not everyone wants to participate or share the tasks involved. They've had to create rules for participation in the group doing bulk buying. It has also not always been easy to understand one another. Some want to drop out and work on their own; but the majority understand that they need this and that, if they are united, they can all benefit more. For Maria and her *compañeras* (friends), these strategies have helped them stretch the little money that they have. But not all are like them, there are many women who are in even worse situations.

From 1977 to 1982, the buying power of Mexican workers earning a minimum wage fell by almost 70 percent, while from 1983 to 1992, it fell another 57 percent.[4] From 1976 to 1996, the minimum wage itself dropped in real terms to 76.4 percent, and it's estimated that by the end of 1998, it will have dropped to 82 percent.[5] This loss of buying power is just the beginning of a cycle that becomes even worse over time: with more poverty, less food, less education and, consequently, less productivity, which diminishes the supply both for internal and external markets, inflation rises and peoples' buying power becomes even weaker.[6]

During the mass, Maria remembers Chencha, a woman in town that everyone knows. Chencha's situation is very desperate: she is a woman with disabilities, she had been sexually abused and had given birth to a son who was both epileptic and paralytic. She has no resources at all and sleeps under a small hut of branches, built on the edge of town, where the poorest people go (or rather where they are forced to go). She survives by selling *nopales* (cactus leaves) and plums that she gathers from the hillside, as well as ragdolls that she makes from pieces of fabric that people, like Maria, give her.

Now Chencha is eighty years old and can no longer work. She survives from pure charity, and her neighbours help out when they can. These networks of mutual support that develop among the poor are so difficult to explain, are hard for others (who aren't poor) to understand. Chencha also receives some minimal assistance from a government institution that for years has been distributing basic goods to poor families. Many poor people like Chencha would have rather been taught job skills and given jobs, but that wasn't the aim of this institution. Chencha used to do very well during elections because she would be given two or three more boxes of staple goods, but now that she can no longer walk, she can no longer vote for the party that gives out the boxes, so they have abandoned her.

The social programs and reserves, which today the Mexican government directs towards fighting poverty, have dropped in real terms to 40 percent of what they were in 1994. These cuts in social service spending have eliminated thirty-six of the forty-six social programs that the Secretary of Social Development initiated between 1988 and 1994; among the cancelled programs are Forestry Solidarity, the Mexican Institute for Social Solidarity Security, the Regularization of Urban Land, Nurses in Solidarity and Indigenous Community Development.[7] One common characteristic of these social programs implemented by the Mexican government is that they are often used primarily during the times of elections, negotiated with the hunger of the people.

The priest ringing his bell brings Maria back from her reverie. She realizes that she didn't even listen to the mass; her thoughts sometimes tend to wander and she forgets where she is. She hurries out of the church to be one of the first to buy milk, although it is no longer necessary to rush. Since they started to sell bottled milk, pure cow milk isn't sold as much. Maria doesn't understand why people prefer industrialized milk even though it is more expensive. She has bought the non-industrialized milk ever since there were public complaints during Carlos Salinas's government (1988–1993) that the National Commission of Popular Subsistence distributed milk contaminated by radioactivity from Chernobyl in Russia. This was never proven, but to be on the safe side, Maria prefers not to risk her own health or the health of her family.

Just like the industrialization of milk, many customs have changed in her village. Maria still remembers the big house she lived in with her husband. There they had a horse, a cow, chickens, rabbits, and even bee hives. As her husband would leave early every morning to work on the land, she got up to milk the cows. Using a kind of rope that was made out of a horse's mane, she would tie up the cow's back legs to avoid being kicked while she was milking. While the cow was tied up, she would put the calf beside her to get the milk flowing, then she tied the calf to the cow's horns and milked her. Finally, she left a little milk for the calf, which would later finish feeding in the pasture. All this was done with cows native to the area; today with hybrid cows, it's all done by machine. You'd think that perhaps this was an improvement, because now there's less work; however, before even poor people could have a creole cow, now only few people can afford a hybrid cow and the machinery to milk it.

Maria has learned how to get the most out of the little there is to eat. Hardly anything is wasted in her preparation of food. For example, the milk from the cow comes out very thick, with a cap of cream forming on the top; Maria boils this and her family eats it with bread. Then when she boils the milk, she saves the *nata*, or cream that forms from that to make butter. She collects all of the cream, and when it dries, she mixes it with water (previously by hand, but now in a blender), until it is well washed, and the water is very clear; from this she makes butter and bakes rich breads.

The remaining milk is left to curdle. It helps that there are now pills and drops to make the milk curdle, because before she had to prepare *rennet* from scratch.[8] The milk was used to make cheese, biscuits and *adoberas* (a hard cheese). She boiled the whey (the watery part of the milk) and extracted the cream, which is the richest part. The rest of it was fed to the pigs, to make them grow healthier. It's true that this work always left her exhausted and sometimes she got angry with her husband because he wouldn't help her; but he also worked hard all day and came home exhausted, so she came to realize that perhaps the problem wasn't completely his fault, but that there were other causes.

With the pail of milk on her arm, Maria walks to the market to buy fruit and vegetables that are in season. Even though it isn't any longer necessary to take a cloth shopping bag to the market, she continues to do it because now in the market they give you so many plastic bags, she doesn't know what to do with them. She doesn't like to throw them in the garbage, because it makes her think about the ugly garbage that ends up scattered along the side of the road and the piles of garbage that have accumulated in the ravines that today have become like waste dumps. She knows that all this business of plastic bags, food in cans and instant soups in package has to do with the kind of activities that people are involved in now, but she thinks that with a little bit of effort people could find other alternatives that would create less garbage. For her part, even though she imagines that this phenomenon of so much waste has something to do with the large companies that produce waste these days, following only the interests of many other groups and countries, she also feels that it also has to do with the lack of consciousness and responsibility among people in the village. Although she doesn't quite understand the whole complex picture, she at least makes an effort to do something. For example, even though she prefers to get food in its more natural state, when she has to buy it in bottles or cans, after emptying the contents, she washes the containers and saves them in her cupboard. She always saves cans, flasks, empty cartons, paper, all the things that she thinks some day she will be able to use again.

Maria's cupboards are like treasures to explore, since she doesn't only save empty containers there, but there are also many jars filled with canned fruits, rich syrup and jams of mango, cherry, pitaya and strawberry; jars with tomatoes, chiles and vegetables in vinegar; old tuna and sardine cans now filled with delicious breads; boxes filled with dry meat and rolls of sausage hanging from nails. An entire banquet could be made with everything that is found in Maria's cupboards. Besides, it's very economical, because she prepares these foods with seasonal fruits and vegetables. This is the way that Maria has learned to save money and to provide nutritious food for her family; still one has to ask about how much work this means for Maria, preparing all these products, and how much time is left for herself.

Maria still enjoys giving away some of the foods that she makes. The exchange among family members, friends and neighbours, of these home-made foods — such as Maria's jams, marmalades and cheeses, and of the produce from the fields such as corn, squash, potatoes and cucumbers — continues, even though the practice has diminished. Maria thinks this began to change when people started to leave the countryside. Before they gave more, now they don't share as much, because people don't have as much now. They used to cultivate more, but not now, now they go to the United States because there they can survive better. They send money to the family and some even build their own homes, even though it doesn't necessarily go so well for all of them. From what Maria understands, the food that they grew before was enough to feed the people in the village, and now they have to bring it from other places. When she hears on the news that in other countries there are droughts, floods and rising temperatures, she wonders what's going to happen when in those places there also isn't enough food to eat.

It makes Maria very angry to see peasants and cattle farmers let their food rot on their land or throw their milk into the river. She does not understand why they do this and each time she sees someone do this, she quarrels with them. Now she understands better, because she has also had this experience, even though she still is not in total agreement with this kind of response. What's happening now is that every day products are brought into the country from other places, mainly the United States, and they are cheaper, so they lower the price of the foods that Mexican peasants and cattle ranchers produce. Since they can't even recover the costs that they invested by selling it, they sometimes prefer that it be wasted. Suddenly Maria recalls her visit to the city last year, seeing meat being sold at a very low price. It was because there was a lot of frozen meat being imported. Sure, it was cheaper, but who knows how long it had been refrigerated?

Returning home from the mass and the market, Maria hurries up a bit, because it's gotten a little late. She has to get her children ready for school, and get herself ready for work. Since she lost her husband, she has had to work to sustain the family. Her older son had to leave when he was only fifteen years old to find work elsewhere, but he hasn't been able to send home very much money, because he only finds seasonal work. So Maria hasn't had any other choice but to work outside of the home. Luckily, she was able to find a job.

Learning to make clothes gave her skills that got her the job as a sewing teacher, when she was left without a husband and became the sole support of her family. Maria learned to sew even before she was married, when she went to visit an aunt in the city. There, during two different seasons, she learned to sew. In those days, what she earned sewing she spent on personal expenses, clothes, going out, having meals with friends, going to fiestas and buying what she wanted. After she married, she continued sewing, but instead she used her income to buy clothes that her children needed, or she saved small amounts of it, because she knew that big debts are paid from small savings. She didn't spend much on herself. What more was there to buy now that she had already "bought" a husband, and now had someone to take care of her?

As she was heading towards work she remembered that she had forgotten to mix scraps of left-over tortillas with water to feed the chickens. She had bought the chickens just in time, so they would be ready now that her son was coming for a visit. And besides, she liked free range chickens that tasted good and maintained their nutritive qualities. There was just enough time for them to grow being fed tortillas, alfalfa and corn, without putting them out to pasture. Maria wasn't interested in raising chickens quickly so they could be quickly sold; she preferred that they grew naturally. Besides, her sons and daughters liked these chickens better. They were raised in the small patio in the centre of the house, where Maria also grew medicinal and decorative plants.

Maria pauses to think about how much life has taught her. She's usually been happy; in spite of the difficulties of her life, she has learned to value what she can do and what she has. The juggling that she has to do to survive doesn't leave her with much time to feel bad, nor to get depressed, much less to get sick. This doesn't mean that she doesn't have any problems, she does and it has been very hard for her to raise five kids on her own; nonetheless, she faces her life with a sense of hope. She is as strong as an oak and as beautiful as a flower. This optimism and strength with which she encounters her daily life, she transmits to others.

When she finishes work, she returns home and, in a kind of ritual, she begins to prepare dinner for her son. She has decided to welcome him home with *tamales*, the dish that he has missed the most and mentions in every letter he writes. It makes Maria angry to remember what the US custom officials did to her sister five years ago. Her sister, Susanna, was going to visit her kids in the US. Knowing the pleasure and joy they felt when they ate certain typical Mexican dishes, she got the idea of taking them a big surprise — some rich tamales. So with a lot of love and anticipating the happiness on the faces of her beloved family members, she had prepared some delicious tamales. But it was her luck to arrive at the US border and have the customs agents open the tamales, one by one, getting their dogs to sniff them, and then throwing them into the garbage, one after the other; and with each one, her smile disappeared, and with it the pleasure she had experienced in preparing them for her family.

First, she goes to the patio to select the biggest and fattest chicken, and tells him what she's going to do with him, as if he understands. Then she prepares the chicken with a rich sauce of tomatoes, fried crackers, chocolate, oregano, garlic, cinnamon, cloves, vinegar, sugar and a pinch of salt. She stuffs the tamales with this mixture and then places the tamales in a big pressure cooker to steam them. Finally she prepares the *atole* (corn drink) to serve with the tamales.

Then Maria cleans the house. Even though it is very humble, she likes to keep it clean and decorated with flower pots in the hallway. She sets the table with a pretty white table cloth that she herself has embroidered. She runs to the patio to cut some fresh roses and puts them in a vase. She quickly changes her clothes and combs her hair. And, just in time, because her son will be there any minute now. Her precious son!

Maria wonders what he will be like, how much he has grown. An immense joy penetrates every pore of her skin, as she offers the finishing touches to the table, setting it with the plates, cutlery, glasses. Everything is finally ready.

Maria rushes through life, extending her days to the limit to accomplish all the work she must do. But within the dynamism and complexity in which she lives, Maria tries to grab some moments for laughter and fun. Such brief instants are for Maria a kind of oasis in the middle of the demanding life that she leads. Even though she appears to have a very close relationship with the natural environment, in reality she moves constantly between both a distancing and a narrowing of her links with nature. Because she wasn't able to keep the land that her husband left her, she was forced to sell her labour and her son had to migrate to the US to do the same. At the same time, she tries to enjoy the few natural resources that she does have access to.

Maria walks through her day and struggles through her life primarily alone. She hasn't had the opportunity to learn and understand that, like her, there are many other women in the world living in similar circumstances. Maria has pursued her own survival strategies and her own form of development, a development that is different from the "ideal model" that has been imposed and that thousands of Latin Americans have internalized as the only valid model. But can people like Maria continue resisting this model on their own? Can these individual forms of resistance serve to build and strengthen an alternative model of development? Or is it both necessary and urgent to combine different strategies to face globalization with greater collective strength?

Ofelia makes sopes *at home in Guadalajara, Mexico, December 1997.*

NOTES

This chapter was translated from the Spanish original by Deborah Barndt.

1. *Co-madre* in Spanish refers to a very close friend, often a godmother to one of the woman's children.
2. Vania Salles and Rodolfo Tuirán, "Familia, Genéro, y Pobreza," *Cotidiano* (México, 1995).
3. Alberto Arroyo, *La Política Salarial en el Modelo Neoliberal* (México: Universidad Autonoma Metropolitana, 1992).
4. Julio Boltvinik, "La Pobreza en México," *Salud Pública* 37, no. 4 (July-August 1995).
5. Mario Alberto Santillana, *Pobreza y distribución del ingreso en México* (México City: ITESM, 1996).
6. ASIC, "Caen Partidas Federales para Combatir la Pobreza," *Público* (March 25, 1998), 20.
7. Enrique Quintana, "Hechos y Cifras en México," *Reforma*, 10 January 1994, 19A.
8. When a cow is killed, part of its stomach is laid out to dry with a lot of salt — this is called the *rennet*. Once dry, the *rennet* is cut into pieces and soaked with water or whey. This mixture makes the milk curdle and thicken, and it is from that substance that cheese is made.

Chapter Fourteen

A DIFFERENT TOMATO:

CREATING VERNACULAR FOODSCAPES

Lauren (left) shows her seedlings at Annex Organics to co-author Harriet Friedmann.

A DIFFERENT TOMATO:

CREATING VERNACULAR FOODSCAPES

Lauren Baker

THE MOST POIGNANT MOMENTS I experienced in Mexico, while researching a tomato's exhausting journey from field to table, were conversations with Mexican activists about community-based resistance
strategies that challenge the global food system and globalization itself,
and conversations about the omnipresent "web of oppression" in which
we are entangled. As an academic and activist, I used my involvement
with the Tomasita Project as a profound way to learn about the path
our food takes from "land to mouth" in a food system that has shifted
from relative self-reliance and seasonality to one where food is brought
from the far reaches of the globe to fill our supermarket shelves on a
year-round basis.[1]

The Tomasita Project provided an opportunity to engage in "pas-
sionate scholarship"[2] and in a cross-border research process that combines personal and political interests. The research moved between the
local and the global, playing with the dialectical nature of this relationship. It began by acknowledging the importance of women's daily lived
experiences (material realities) and then linked these experiences to
global issues. Women are central to both the dominant food system as
well as to alternative food systems. As the primary workers in the agricultural, processing, retail and service sectors of the globalized food system, women bare the brunt of the system's exploitation and injustice;
they are also catalysts for creating community-based alternatives. The
Tomasita Project was concerned with the relationships of power that
shape women's daily experiences. As the dichotomy between the local
and the global is reinforced, community identity and cultural diversity
are threatened. At the same time, new cultural fusions emerge and new

opportunities for resistance across borders are created. As such, the Tomasita Project is an example of a transformative research process.

In my research, I discovered the path that Tomasita the tomato takes from Mexican fields to Canadian tables. I also discovered the path a more local tomato takes from field to table. Therefore, I was simultaneously engaged in and critical of the dominant food system, while also discovering opportunities to challenge it. Historically, we as humans have shaped the food we eat in cultural, economic, social and political terms. Consequently, our relationship to our food is reflected in who we are as individuals and as a society, and the processes that bring our food from field to table tell us a lot about the nature of this relationship.[3] J. Baird Callicot, an environmental philosopher who writes extensively about food systems, suggests that "how people go about producing food both reveals and reflects their world view. Indeed, because food production is one among several absolutely fundamental and universal human activities, it affords a particularly clear window into the ambient cultural mind."[4]

THE GLOBAL FOOD SYSTEM

While wandering through food terminals and tomato fields, and exploring the food system with women workers, community activists, popular educators and academics, both here in Canada and in Mexico, I picked up pieces of the Tomasita story: the journey of one commodity from field to table. This story sheds light on the dominant global food system.[5] It begins with seeds, imported from Israel or California, that are planted in greenhouses in the north of Mexico and also sent by truck to other production sites, depending on the season. For example, when I visited Mexico in December, seedlings had been planted near Sayula, Jalisco, in central Mexico. The seedlings and mature tomatoes are cared for and picked by nearby peasants and Indigenous migrant workers from other states. These workers come annually to work on tomato plantations during peak harvest season. Earning around US$4 per day, they can barely afford to buy the beans and tortillas that form their traditional diet. Year-round, these workers migrate from one region to the next to harvest whatever crop is in season.

Once the tomatoes are picked, they are loaded on a truck and brought to the nearby packinghouse, where, en masse, they are disinfected by chlorine, waxed, and sorted by quality, colour and size. The most perfect tomatoes are packed for export, while the blemished ones are destined for the domestic market. In the packinghouse, the workers are primarily young Mestizo women who also follow the tomato harvest around the country and earn more money than their Indigenous counterparts in the field — up to US$15 per day. This system of labour illustrates the gendered and racialized nature of export tomato production. The system of growing crops where it best suits the corporation illustrates the highly exploitative nature of the production cycle. For example, Santa Anita Packers, the largest Mexican tomato producer, has been nicknamed "grasshopper" by the local residents. They farm the land intensively through monocrop production for several years until it lays fallow and *ya no se da* (no longer produces), at which point the company "hops" to the next fertile field, which could be in another region of the country. In the process, they leave behind a degraded environment and a community that has come to depend on the economic activity.

When harvested, the tomatoes are refrigerated until they are needed. When an order comes in, the tomatoes are gassed so they ripen quickly and the order can be filled. This is known as just-in-time production. Once ripened, the tomatoes are ready for the second, more lengthy stage of their journey: they are transported by refrigerated truck to their destinations. For example, some travel 3,000 kilometres to Toronto.[6] Distributors in Toronto or in Nogales, Arizona, or San Diego, California, sell the tomatoes to wholesalers and retailers who buy them and take them to their various destinations, which include fast-food restaurants, food manufacturers and supermarkets. These outlets vie for consumer dollars by launching multimillion dollar marketing campaigns and creating their own product lines. For example, consumers often buy tomatoes that are already processed in the form of President's Choice lasagna or Del Monte ketchup.

Local Alternative Food Systems

Since my involvement with the Tomasita Project, I have begun to work with Annex Organics, a socially and environmentally responsible organization that is involved in a variety of urban agriculture projects in Toronto. My experience with Annex Organics has unravelled a different tomato story and has provided the basis for a more democratic way of growing food.

Operating out of FoodShare's dynamic Field to Table warehouse, Annex Organics produces certified organic sprouts, tomatoes, peppers and eggplants. Consulting services and educational workshops around issues and practices of urban agriculture are an important part of Annex Organics' activities. At the warehouse, Annex Organics has a rooftop garden and greenhouse, a sprouting operation and several small-scale aquaculture experiments. Much of the food grown at the warehouse is sold to Field to Table's Good Food Box project and to the Field to Table Catering Company. This creates a self-sustaining food cycle turning the warehouse into an urban farm and a vibrant alternative food system. Even the waste is composted into valuable fertilizer, which is fed back into the garden and greenhouse. Overall, this system reclaims and preserves traditional farming practices in an urban setting. Urban agriculture starts at home. Annex Organics also works with indoor, backyard and community gardeners to teach them the concepts of nutrient recycling, composting, food plant biodiversity and urban sustainability.

Annex Organics is part of a mosaic of diverse, yet complimentary food-related projects that converge in the Field to Table warehouse. The warehouse itself is a living illustration of an alternative food system that forces us to think about food differently. A tour of the warehouse makes it apparent that food is not only a human right, essential for our body's nutritional requirements, but also that food production and distribution can address social problems, build cultural awareness, create economic opportunity, generate environmental awareness and integrate political issues. For example, the projects at Field to Table recognize that women are the key actors in creating alternative food systems. Women on social assistance participate in the Focus on Food Training Program, the program graduates work for the Field to Table Catering

Company, and women in neighbourhoods co-ordinate the distribution of the Good Food Box. Combining these distinct, yet interrelated projects in one building strengthens our knowledge about the necessity and potential of food systems alternatives. In fact, projects such as Annex Organics plant the seeds for many new community-based initiatives. Through my involvement with the Tomasita Project, Field to Table and Annex Organics over the past five years, I have come to realize that when we understand the history of the food we eat, we better understand the social and environmental processes that bring it to us. We are, indeed, what we eat.

Our understanding is drawn from analysis that integrates social, ecological, political and economic issues. Knowing the many paths that our food travels from field to table enables us to be more critical of what we eat and to make more conscientious choices. The dominant global industrial food system, which I have briefly described through the Tomasita story, centralizes power in the hands of multinational food corporations and urban consumers, ignoring sustainable agricultural practices and rural communities.[7] A critical analysis helps us to identify the key components of corporate food production — large-scale production and processing, its transportation and distribution systems, and the marketing and advertising that promote ready-made food products.[8] Alternative food systems such as Annex Organics and Field to Table identify different components — small-scale food production, traditional preparation and preservation of foods, maintaining diverse cultural values and practices and ecologically sensitive recycling and waste disposal. Above all, alternatives decrease corporate concentration and control of our food.[9] Harriet Friedmann describes the social basis for democratic food policy and outlines the democratic principles that correspond with such alternatives — proximity, seasonality and a sensitivity to time and place.[10] Democratic food production is rooted in local economies and reconstructs the diversity (biological and cultural) that has been destroyed by the global food system.

Choosing to eat locally produced foods, connecting oneself with the source of production and participating in alternative food distribution networks transforms what we learn from eating. This profound knowledge is an integral part of what I call our "foodscapes." A foodscape includes the many paths our food travels from field to table as well as the intrinsic relationship we have with the food we eat. As consumers, we shape the food we eat through supporting its production, distribution and preparation and, at the same time, we are shaped by these processes when we eat the food. Instead of perpetuating the exploitation and degradation that are part of my foodscape when I eat a tomato imported from Mexico, I learn about the ecology and community of a vibrant, local alternative food system when I eat a tomato grown on the roof of the Field to Table warehouse.

The journey of a tomato grown on the roof of Field to Table is not as long as Tomasita's journey. To begin with, the seeds are collected from the rooftop garden after each harvest, acquired at a community seed exchange or purchased from seed companies that promote open pollinated, non-treated seeds. Once germinated, the small plants are taken into the rooftop greenhouse, where they are watered twice a day and carefully observed for signs of disease or pests. Because of the organic soil mixture used and the diversity of plants grown in the greenhouse, disease and pest problems are minimal. The tomato seedlings, once large enough, are sold to gardeners across Toronto who are interested in unusual heritage vegetable varieties or they are transplanted into the rooftop garden. This intensive method of growing food is certified organic, and Annex Organics is the only commercial urban rooftop food grower in Canada. Once mature, the tomatoes are sold to the Field to Table Good Food Box project downstairs, to small health food stores and to restaurants interested in organic vegetables.

The story of Tomasita's journey is a story of environmental degradation and human exploitation. The social and environmental costs of the food system that produces the imported Mexican tomato are hidden by long distances and complicated transactions from field to table. The story of the Annex Organics' tomato is a story of urban regeneration, co-operation, biodiversity and strengthening of local economies. By simultaneously producing food for commercial purposes and educating urban dwellers about organic food production, the route this local tomato takes from field to table is more clearly understood. Consumers who shift from eating imported tomatoes to eating locally grown organic tomatoes gain a profound understanding of the way our local economy works, and they are more likely to support a more sustainable vernacular foodscape.

Vernacular Foodscapes Within
Imagined Communities

If we internalize the social and environmental practices of particular foodscapes, we reflect these practices in the way we live as human beings.[11] Presently, those of us who are fed from the global food system do not acknowledge (or even understand) the processes that bring our food from the field to our table. We do not understand that our foodscape is based on processes that others control: processes of domination, exploitation and degradation. These, in turn, perpetuate a web of oppression formed of "distinct parts which can and must be focused upon separately as well as together."[12] Ecofeminist Val Plumwood suggests that in "dealing with such a web, it is essential to take account of both its connectedness and the capacity for independent movement among the parts ... The strategies for dealing with such a web require cooperation."[13]

In our efforts to create socially just and equitable food systems, we must challenge domination and acknowledge difference and diversity. Chandra Mohanty writes about the difficulty of making connections across distinct material realities such as race, class, sex, colonialism and imperialism. She suggests using the notion of an "imagined community." "Imagined" not because it is not "real," but because it suggests potential alliances and collaborations across divisive boundaries, and "community" because, in spite of internal hierarchies within Third World contexts, it nevertheless suggests a significant, deep commitment to "horizontal comradeship ... imagined communities of women with divergent histories and social locations, woven together by the political threads of opposition to forms of domination that are not only pervasive but also systemic."[14]

The global food system in its current form perpetuates a web of oppression, but cross-border efforts such as the Tomasita Project enable us to form imagined communities and explore women's stories, to follow the path of one commodity and develop successful resistance strategies. Working together within our own communities as well as across borders, we can begin to understand the complexity of globalization and create alternatives to it. Alternative food systems, for example, challenge globalization by posing questions about the food we eat and how it is grown. These alternatives expose how globalization's foodscape ignores the ecological processes that it disrupts or destroys and how it ignores the human exploitation and inequities it perpetuates.

Alternative vernacular foodscapes need to be rooted in the local context. The sociocultural practices of any one community will make the alternative food system(s) distinct. There may, of course, be conflicting interests in our increasingly multicultural urban environments. The ecology (natural processes) of a particular community will also partly determine what kinds of alternatives are possible. Vernacular foodscapes will be based on bioregional activity that is both culturally and environmentally defined. Annex Organics and the other projects operating out of the Field to Table warehouse are examples of how we can create vernacular foodscapes. These projects are expressions of the distinct communities we live in and are particular to specific locations and social realities. They are transforming the way we think about food and are based on the principles of social justice and equity and ecological economics.[15]

Ecological economics deals not only with sustainable food production, but also with social issues such as food access, cultural diversity and the unpaid labour of women. The economics of our dominant food system, however, is driven by values of maximum productivity and efficiency, ignoring diverse material realities that define our access to healthy, nutritious and culturally appropriate food. Vernacular foodscapes acknowledge diversity within the broader community, and, instead of dictating what can and cannot be consumed, enable us to develop culturally and socially appropriate ecological criteria for making food choices. At the Field to Table warehouse, these issues are grappled with everyday. What will be put in the Good Food Box this week? How can the food choices serve a culturally diverse population? How can a particular farmer be supported? What will be planted on the rooftop garden that meets both ecologically appropriate and commercially viable considerations? These are not easy questions to answer, but the process of grappling with them is a struggle well worth it.

Linking Northern Consumers
with Southern Producers

Leonardo Llamas, a health promoter I met in Sayula, Mexico, advocates on behalf of Indigenous tomato workers to improve their living conditions. He calls the globally produced tomatoes "fruits of injustice." I had a long conversation with his partner, Maria Isabel Muñiz, also a health promoter, about possibilities for change and what Northern consumers and activists could do to support their work. She told me, "Look, what would really help us, in so many ways ... is if in the North there were a consciousness among people about all the pesticides that are put on tomatoes, so that consumers would say, 'We don't want these tomatoes, we want organic tomatoes.'"[16]

Maria Isabel's statement is a powerful directive to me as a Northern consumer and community food activist. Through engaging in dialogue with people in the South, I can begin to make food choices that break down the web of oppression and create foodscapes that are based on the principles of proximity, seasonality and a sensitivity to time and place. I begin by choosing local produce, and when that is not available, I demand imported food that is grown in an ecologically appropriate, non-exploitative way. One of the complexities surrounding food choice is that not all of us can access or afford organic produce. Choosing organic is often a middle-class luxury and can cloud the overriding importance of eating locally produced, seasonal foods. Through the construction of vernacular foodscapes, "imagined communities" of people challenging the global food system will emerge across borders. These communities will increasingly recognize the diversity and complexity of our food system and exchange ideas about how to eat food that does not perpetuate human exploitation and inequality.

As consumers we need to become critical participants in the food system. Where is our food produced? Under what social and environmental circumstances? How has its quality been affected by the route it took to get from field to table? How are women's lives shaped by their involvement in the food system? How do women, who predominate as both workers in the global food system and as catalysts for food systems alternatives, shape the food system? My involvement in the Tomasita

Project, and more recently in Annex Organics, has been a profound experience, teaching me how the web of oppression can be transformed into a web of imaginary communities that link daily lived experience to global issues. Learning about the path most of our food travels from field to table inspires me to make different food choices and to work with others to create alternatives to the global food system.

Lauren shares the table with Maria Isabel Muñiz in Sayula, Mexico, during a research trip in July 1997.

NOTES

This chapter refers to ideas more fully discussed elsewhere in this volume. See Deborah Barndt, "Introduction"; Deborah Moffett and Mary Lou Morgan, "Women as Organizers."

1. William H. Friedland, "The Global Fresh Food and Vegetable System: An Industrial Organization Analysis," in Philip McMichael, ed., *The Global Restructuring of Agro-Food Systems* (Ithaca: Cornell University Press, 1994), 173–295.

2. Maria Mies, "Liberating Women, Liberating Knowledge: Reflections on Two Decades of Feminist Action Research," *Atlantis* 21, no.1 (1996), 10–22.

3. Martha Crouch elaborates on this idea in a playful way in her article "Eating Our Teachers: Local Food, Local Knowledge," *Raise the Stakes* 22 (1993), 5–6.

4. J. Baird Callicot, "Agroecology in Context," *Journal of Agricultural Ethics* (1988), 3–9.

5. The elaborated story and analysis of the tomato story appears in Deborah Barndt, *Tamasita's Trail: Women, Work, and the World Through the Tomato* (forthcoming).

6. In fact, only about 10 percent of the tomatoes produced by Santa Anita Packers are destined for the Canadian market. The majority are sold to the United States, which is closer and maintains a higher demand.

7. Harriet Friedmann, "The International Political Economy of Food: A Global Crisis," *International Journal of Health Services* 25 (1995), 511–538.

8. This definition of what a food system analysis includes was developed in Lauren Baker, Jane Hayes, and Deborah Moffett, "Mapping Food Systems: Participatory Food Systems Education," paper presented at the Sustainable Urban Food Systems Conference, Toronto, Ontario, May 1997.

9. CIAS, "Regional Food Systems Research: Needs, Priorities, and Recommendations" (Madison, Wisconsin: College of Agricultural and Life Sciences Research Division, University of Wisconsin-Madison, 1995).

10. Friedmann, "The International Political Economy of Food," 511–538.

11. Vandana Shiva also discusses how humans internalize "monoculture" in her book *Monocultures of the Mind: Perspectives on Biodiversity and Biotechnology* (London: Zed Books, 1993).

12. Val Plumwood, "Ecosocial Feminism as a General Theory of Oppression," in Carolyn Merchant, ed., *Ecology* (Atlantic Highlands, NJ: Humanities Press, 1994), 215.

13. Ibid.

14. Chandra Talpade Mohanty, "Introduction: Cartographies of Struggle: Third World Women and the Politics of Feminism," in Chandra Talpade Mohanty, Ann Russo, and Lourdes Torres, eds., *Third World Women and the Politics of Feminism* (Bloomington: Indiana University Press, 1991), 6.

15. Ellie Perkins, "Introduction: Women, Ecology, and Economics: New Models and Theories," Special Issue on Women, Ecology and Economics, *Ecological Economics* 22, no. 2 (February 1997), 105–106.

16. Maria Isabela Muñiz, interview with author, Sayula, Mexico, December 8, 1996.

GLOSSARY

Agribusiness: Usually referring to large-scale industrial farm production, agribusiness is used to describe the food system from farm inputs to the end product.

Agromaquila: An agribusiness which is structured like a maquiladora, and which depends on a deregulated industry that is free of tariff barriers and characterized by subcontracting and part-time flexible (and primarily female) labour. See *Maquiladora* and *Maquilization*.

Aquaculture: A water-based agricultural system in which both plants and sea animals (fish) are grown. In urban areas, plant aquaculture often filters wastewater while producing food.

Austerity measures: The conditions imposed on indebted national governments by the International Monetary Fund as part of debt payment negotiations, often limiting public sector expenditures. See *Conditionalities, International Monetary Fund* and *Structural Adjustment*.

Biodiversity: The variety and variability of life forms in an area, which together sustain an ecosystem and can be threatened by monocultural agricultural production processes.

Cold War: The period of hostile diplomatic, political and economic relationships between the two superpowers, the United States and the Soviet Union, from the early 1950s until 1989. The Cold War ended with the fall of the Berlin Wall, the collapse of the union of Soviet states and a reassertion of US hegemony.

Commensality: The human habit of sitting down to eat together as a group, emphasizing the social and cultural values of eating practices.

Commodification: The process of transforming goods into items to be bought and sold, often obscuring or denying their social, cultural or ecological values and focusing on their exchange value solely in economic terms.

Community garden: The combination of urban food production with community development and urban greening. Community groups create gardens to increase their food security, enjoy the recreational benefits of gardening, share their cultural knowledge and heritage, and improve their neighbourhoods.

Community kitchen: The sharing of space, resources and labour among members of a community (usually women) in order to prepare meals that are shared amongst themselves and their families.

Community shared (or supported) agriculture (CSA): An arrangement that connects food consumers directly to farmers. In a typical arrangement, consumers pay for food in advance of planting time (buying shares), helping to finance the farmers' seeds and equipment and allowing farmers to do mixed organic farming. Besides buying shares of the farm produce, consumers often help out on the farms.

Composting: The process of decomposing plant material and transforming it into a rich garden fertilizer. Composting can reduce the amount of garbage in the mainstream disposal system by recycling household, restaurant and business organic waste (food scraps, garden waste).

CONASUPO: The Mexican food agency established in the 1970s to help create small shops in neighbourhoods too poor to support private businesses. Creation of the agency completed the government-organized national food system, which already protected small farmers (through the *ejido* and managed prices) and which processed basic food, such as sugar, in factories.

Concession bargaining: A negotiated union settlement that results in "take-backs" or losses with respect to wages, benefits, seniority provisions and any other entitlements won by a union through collective bargaining.

Conditionalities: Conditions required by the International Monetary Fund in return for extending deadlines or lending money for interest payments to indebted governments. During the 1980s and 1990s, conditionalities involved devaluing currency, removing subsidies to consumers and farmers, reducing government and other public sector employment and privatizing public enterprises. These conditions are also labelled "austerity measures" or "structural adjustment."

Core labour force: A stable labour force employed on a full-time, full-year permanent basis, usually assigned to perform the basic production requirements of a firm.

Deflationary pricing: A decrease in the price of goods as a result of increased competition from lower-cost industry competitors.

Deregulation: The downgrading or elimination of national regulations for private firms, allowing capital to compete freely. Deregulation is a process initiated by multinational corporations which usually results in higher profits and lower quality services and wages.

Development: Though rooted in a long history of colonial practices, the word was first applied by US President Truman in 1947 to describe the goal of improving economic performance and welfare in other countries. In the 1990s, social and environmental critics have called into question whether "development" really means improving people's lives.

Ecofeminism: An analysis that links the historical domination of women with the human domination of non-human nature; also a growing social movement with diverse streams and debates within it.

Ecological economics: The synthesis of two disciplines, ecology and economics, ecological economics is concerned with the relationship between the economic system and the resources upon which it is dependent. It promotes "full cost" accounting, which takes into account the social and environmental externalities associated with development.

Ejido: A Mexican form of collective ownership by self-governing communities, which has been eroded since NAFTA. It is understood as a way of recreating Indigenous ways of life in conjunction with modern forms of collective ownership of property.

Employee buyouts: A cash payment offer made by an employer to an employee, or group of employees, in lieu of full retirement benefits, as severance for a job termination or for some other change in employment status that reduces an employee's income (for example, a shift from full-time to part-time status).

Empowerment: The process of acting both individually and collectively to change the conditions of our lives. Empowerment ranges from individual and interpersonal levels to collective and societal levels.

Export monoculture: Land and labour devoted to a single crop to sell to customers abroad. This form of farming is often included among IMF conditionalities. It transforms agricultural practices from more ecologically sound mixed farming to a monoculture that harms the environment and decreases the sustainability of the farming community.

Family wage: A wage paid to a male worker that is sufficient to support a dependent wife and children. The idea of a family wage is problematic as it has been used to legitimize discrimination against women in the workplace.

Farm-gate marketing: A marketing strategy used by local farmers who want to sell their produce directly to the consumer, eliminating distributors and retailers. Farmers markets are a popular farm-gate marketing strategy.

Flexibilization: The "flexbilization of labour" strategy being applied by corporations in the restructured global economy. Flexibilization favours a part-time, contingent labour force that allows companies to respond to just-in-time production needs, and at the same time lower wages, limit benefits and erode unionization.

Food insecurity: A term used by the United Nations to describe the absence of adequate amounts of food, or the condition of hunger.

Food security: This is achieved when people have access to adequate amounts of safe and nutritional foods that are both personally and culturally acceptable.

Foodscape: The path our food travels from land to mouth and the relationship we have with the food we eat. Our personal foodscapes include the ways we obtain food, our cultural eating practices and the seasonal availability of food products.

Fordism: Sustained assembly line mass production combining technology with a bureaucratic organization that resembles a military hierarchy. Fordism reflects a set of institutional arrangements that existed in the post–Second World War era in which earnings of workers increased with increases in productivity. See also *Post-Fordism*.

Free trade zone: Industrial areas created to attract foreign investment in industry. Corporations that set up in these areas import components for assembly and export the finished or semi-finished goods to the buying country. Free trade zones are also referred to as export processing zones. Regulations governing these zones give tax breaks to multinational corporations and weaken environmental restrictions and labour rights.

Globalization: With increasing ease of movement of money, technology, information and goods across national borders, globalization is shifting production practices around the world. It is now a common practice to make parts of a product in one or more countries, assemble the final product in another, and then market it worldwide. In political terms, globalization has reduced the ability of governments to manage their national economies. There is a growing counter-movement now being referred to as the "other globalization," which refers to links among non-governmental organizations and social movements that cross national boundaries to challenge the policies of corporate globalization.

Green Revolution: The transformation of agriculture in Third World countries based on a model inspired by US agricultural practices. Countries participating in this project use hybrid seeds (from international research laboratories) to produce monocultural crops and are dependent on imported chemical fertilizers and mechanical inputs. This agricultural practice usually increases crop yields but also contributes to ecological degradation and the loss of smaller, more independent farms.

Imagined community: A concept that brings people together across potentially divisive realities (race, class, sex, colonialism, imperialism) to collaborate in a way that acknowledges difference.

Indigenous peoples: A general term that refers to the heterogeneous First Peoples in the Americas and other parts of the world. Indigenous peoples use this term to negotiate and communicate with dominant cultures.

International Monetary Fund (IMF): Created by the Bretton Woods Agreement in 1944 along with the World Bank, its sister organization, the IMF was designed to help countries cover short-term balance of payments deficits. In the 1980s and 1990s it became an agent of structural adjustment. See *Structural Adjustment Programs.*

Just-in-time production: A management system fashioned after Japanese manufacturing models, in which a small core group of employees are maintained for full-time work. Production needs determine the size of the part-time, temporary and contingent workforce, whose shifts and work weeks are tailored to meet the demands of production.

Lean production: An approach to production which is supposed to produce more with less. It combines new management techniques, such as a multi-skilled workforces organized into various teams (Total Quality Management, Continuous Quality Improvement), with sophisticated machinery and reduced inventory to produce more and a greater variety of products with fewer resources and less labour. Proponents maintain that increased productivity is achieved by intensifying workers' labour.

Levelling down: The effect of governments competing to attract corporate investment or buyers of government bonds, by offering low wages and few labour or environmental regulations. Also called "race to the bottom."

Machismo: The dominant attitudes and behaviour of men, characterized by aggressive and possessive behaviours. These behaviours reinforce patriarchal attitudes in men's relationships with women and children. Machismo also refers to institutionalized sexism that permeates social practices.

Maquiladora or Maquila: An assembly plant in Mexico, originally situated along the US border, that finishes products for another company. These plants are unregulated, exploit a primarily female workforce and are set up in free trade zones. See *Agromaquila.*

Maquilization: Originating in the maquila free trade zones of northern Mexico, maquilization now refers to a more generalized work process characterized by the feminization of the labour force, extreme segmentation of skill categories, the lowering of real wages and a non-union orientation.

McDonaldization: A model the fast-food restaurant has offered as a way to organize work in all sectors. The model is based on efficiency, predicability, calculability or quantifiability, substitution of non-human technology, control and the irrationality of rationality.

Mestizaje: A system that officially recognizes the racial, ethnic and cultural Indigenous and Spanish mixed backgrounds in Latin America. In practice, however, it usually privileges European heritage.

Modernization: A sociopolitical and economic theory and strategy for western development based on notions of progress versus backwardness. It was assumed to be the model for Third World countries to aspire to and achieve. In agriculture, modernization opposes subsistence economies and has introduced macro policies of modernization that include export-oriented cash crops, cattle ranching, massive irrigation and intensive use of pesticides.

Monoculture: See *Export monoculture*.

Multilateral Agreement on Investment (MAI): A proposed treaty that would severely restrict and shape the action of states in relation to foreign investment within their boundaries. The MAI was being negotiated at the Organization for Economic Cooperation and Development (OECD) but is currently on hold, due to lack of support from member governments, such as France, and to international resistance organized by non-governmental organizations, with strong participation of Canadian groups.

Multiskilling: The current demand in the marketplace, largely due to technological innovations, for employees with significant variety of work skills, both "hard" (technology) and "soft" (behavioural).

Multitasking: This occurs when separate, often unrelated tasks, are combined into one job position, eliminating or significantly changing traditional jobs. Multitasking also requires employees to move among various duties within the workplace.

Multitiered wage structure: A wage structure in which newly hired employees are paid at lower rates of pay relative to senior employees.

Naturalize: The process through which systems of domination and oppression are seen as normal and natural. For example, women are seen as emotional and weak, Black people are seen as inherently aggressive and Indigenous peoples as primitive, drunk and lazy. These entrenched prejudices among the dominant group make it easier to implement discriminating policies at social, economic and political levels.

Neoliberal: Current political-economic practices based on notions of an unregulated capitalist market economy, which represent the dominant ideology in the Americas shaping the economic restructuring of the 1990s. These practices are sometimes referred to as "neoconservatism," as they were encouraged by Tory regimes in Britain, Canada and the United States beginning in the 1980s. The association of these practices with the classical liberalism of Adam Smith makes the term neoliberal appropriate.

North American Free Trade Agreement (NAFTA): A trinational economic arrangement among the United States, Mexico and Canada. NAFTA was promoted as a policy to lower trade barriers between the three countries during the administrations of George Bush, Carlos Salinas de Gortari and Brian Mulroney. It went into force on January 1, 1994.

Nutrient cycles: The interdependence of nutrients and waste in a food system. Nutrient cycles are closed when they use organic wastes as inputs to the agricultural system. In the global food system, nutrient cycles are not closed. For example, petroleum-based inputs are added into the agricultural system through chemical fertilizers.

Peripheral labour force: The part-time, temporary or seasonal labour force who work in response to the variable or fluctuating production or service needs of a firm. Many young people and women are in this position. They are also called contingent workers.

Post-Fordism: A stage of capitalist development, typically identified as occurring after the early 1970s, in which Fordist production arrangements broke down and were replaced by flexible forms of work such as just-in-time production and use of part-time workers. As a result, the rate of productivity declined and production practices were decentralized and became more fluid and global in nature. See also *Fordism*.

Product Look Up (PLU) Code: The number on the stickers now appearing on most fresh fruit and vegetables sold in grocery stores and supermarkets. The PLU replaces the barcode of other consumer items. When punched into the computerized cash register, it identifies the type of produce and gives the current price as well as other information.

Racialize: The process of justifying exclusion, inferiorization, subordination and exploitation of certain groups based on physical or social differences that supposedly are related to innate characteristics of members of the group. Racial hierarchies are transferred to all activities, benefiting those who belong to the dominant race/ethnicity and culture. In North America, white people are at the top of the hierarchy, and Indigenous people and people of colour are at the bottom. In most Latin American countries, the majority of Indigenous peoples and Afro-Latin Americans constitute the poorest sectors of the social hierarchy.

Racism: The belief that one's race, culture and ethnicity is superior to all others. In most contexts, white and Euro-North American cultures are seen as naturally superior. This belief is reflected in personal and social attitudes and in ideologies, institutions and practices.

Rooftop garden: The use of roof structures to grow plants. Rooftop gardens are planted to produce food, to create additional greenspace and to buffer buildings from the exterior environment, acting as another insulating layer.

Self-provisioning communities: For most of human history, people lived in villages where they worked together to provide their own food, clothing, shelter, tools and cultural life. These villages divided the labour and distributed the goods among themselves.

Seniority: The length of time an employee has worked for an employer. Seniority is used to establish employee benefits and rights relative to other co-workers.

Sprouting: Many seeds, when germinated, increase in nutritional value as the plant begins the growing process. Seed sprouts can be grown by first soaking seeds in water, draining the water and keeping them in a cool, dark place for several days. It is important to rinse the seeds daily to keep them moist. Sprouting is a quick and easy way to increase food value in common seeds, nuts and beans.

Structural Adjustment Programs (SAPs): A series of measures and conditions set in place by international financial institutions, such as the International Monetary Fund. SAPs require indebted nations to reorganize their economies so that debts can be paid. See *Conditionalities*.

Third World: A term that usually refers to the nations of Africa, Asia and Latin America, which were former colonies of Western Europe and the United States. Originally, the "First World" referred to the advanced capitalist nations and the "Second World" to socialist countries. A Third World country is often considered synonymous with a "developing" or "underdeveloped" country.

Trade liberalization: The process of opening up borders and lifting tariffs that limit foreign investment and trade between nations. This process is integral to neoliberal policies and practices, such as NAFTA.

Transnational corporation (TNC): A corporation that operates in more than one country. TNCs have come to dominate the world economy, and some are richer and more powerful than Third World governments.

World Trade Organization (WTO): An international institution headquartered in Geneva, Switzerland. It was created through a multilateral agreement on trade and investment that emerged from the Uruguay Round of negotiations of the General Agreement on Tariffs and Trade (GATT). Like NAFTA, the WTO can enact into law the basic tenets of the neoliberal model of economic development and political governance in participating countries.

ORGANIZATIONS ALONG AND AROUND THE NAFTA FOOD CHAIN

The key organizations referred to in the chapters of this book are listed here as well as other organizations relevant for academics and activists interested in issues of food security, women's work and globalization.

CANADA

CENTRE FOR STUDIES IN FOOD SECURITY
Ryerson Polytechnic University
350 Victoria Street
Toronto, Ontario M5B 2K3
Phone: 416-979-5000 ext. 6210 or 6931
Fax: 416-979-5204
E-mail: mkoc@acs.ryerson.ca or jwelsh@acs.ryerson.ca
Contacts: Mustafa Koc and Jennifer Welsh

COMMON FRONTIERS
15 Gervais Drive
Don Mills, Ontario M3C 1Y8
Phone: 416-443-9244
Fax: 416-441-4073
E-mail: comfront@web.net
Contact: Patty Barrera

FIELD TO TABLE
GOOD FOOD BOX
ANNEX ORGANICS
200 Eastern Avenue
Toronto, Ontario M5A 1J1
Phone: 416-363-6441
Fax: 416-363-0474
E-mail: ftt@web.apc.org
Contacts: Mary Lou Morgan and Lauren Baker

FOODSHARE METRO TORONTO
238 Queen Street West, Lower Level
Toronto, Ontario M5V 1Z7
Phone: 416-392-6653
Fax: 416-392-6650
E-mail: fdshare@web.apc.org
Contact: Debbie Field

MAQUILA SUPPORT NETWORK
606 Shaw Street
Toronto, Ontario M6G 3L6
Phone: 416-532-8584
Fax: 416-532-7688
E-mail: perg@web.net
Contact: Lynda Yanz, Bob Jeffcott

THE RAM'S HORN
S-12, C-11, R.R. #1
Sorrento, British Columbia V0E 2W0
Phone/fax: 250-835-8561
E-mail: ramshorn@jetstream.net
Contact: Brewster Kneen

THE TOMASITA PROJECT
Faculty of Environmental Studies
York University
4700 Keele Street
Toronto, Ontario M3J 1P3
Phone: 416-736-2100, ext. 40365
Fax: 416-736-5679
E-mail: dbarndt@yorku.ca
Contact: Deborah Barndt

TORONTO FOOD POLICY COUNCIL
277 Victoria Street, Suite 203
Toronto, Ontario M5B 1W1
Phone: 416-392-1107

Fax: 416-392-1357
E-mail: lmarks@city.toronto.on.ca

WOMEN'S NETWORK ON HEALTH AND THE ENVIRONMENT
736 Bathurst Street
Toronto, Ontario M5S 2R4
Phone: 416-516-2600
Fax: 416-531-6214

WORLD FOOD DAY
OXFAM Canada
Suite 300-294 Albert Street
Ottawa, Ontario K1P 6E6
Phone: 613-237-5236
Fax: 613-237-0524
E-mail: www@oxfam.ca
Contact: Linda Ross

UNITED STATES

CENTER OF CONCERN
1225 Otis Street NE
Washington, DC 20017-1194
Contacts: Maria Riley, OP and Marina Durano, visiting Filipina economist

COALITION FOR JUSTICE IN THE MAQUILADORAS
3120 W. Ashby
San Antonio, Texas 78228
Phone: 210-732-8957
E-mail: cjm@igc.org
Website: http://www.alamo.digiweb.com/cjm

COMMUNITY FOOD SECURITY COALITION
P.O. Box 209
Venice, California 90294
Phone: 310-822-5410
Contact: Andy Fisher
Website: http://www.foodsecurity.org

HIGHLANDER RESEARCH AND EDUCATION CENTER
1959 Highlander Way
New Market, Tennessee 37829
Phone: 615-933-3443
Fax: 615-033-3424
E-mail: hrec@igc.apc.org
Contact: Susan Williams

INSTITUTE FOR FOOD AND DEVELOPMENT POLICY/FOOD FIRST
398 60th Street
Oakland, California 94618
Phone: 510-654-4400
Fax: 510-654-4551
E-mail: foodfirst@foodfirst.org
Contact: Peter Rosset

RURAL ADVANCEMENT FOUNDATION INTERNATIONAL — USA
P.O. Box 655
Pittsboro, North Carolina 27312
Phone: 919-542-1396

TENNESSEE INDUSTRIAL RENEWAL NETWORK (TIRN)
1515 E. Magnolia Ave.
Suite 403
Knoxville, Tennessee 37917
Phone: 423-637-1576

TENNESSEE INDUSTRIAL RENEWAL NETWORK (TIRN))
2001 Elm Hill Pike
Nashville, Tennessee 37210
Phone: 615-874-3559

MEXICO

AMIGOS DE LA NATURALEZA
EL GRUPO DE SALUD NUEVA VIDA
Calle Francisco Villa #1
Colonia Tepayac
49300 Sayula, Jalisco, Mexico
Phone: 011-52-342-2-17-60
Contacts: Leonardo Lamas and Maria Isabel Muñiz

CAMPO (peasant women's organization)
Hidalgo 871
Interior #1
Guadalajara, Jalisco, Mexico
Phone: 011-52-3-825-22-86
Contact: Lourdes Angulo

FRENTE POR EL DERECHO A LA ALIMENTACION
Peten 204
Col. Navarte
Mexico, D.F.
Phone: 011-52-5-543-28-17

INSTITUTO MEXICANO PARA EL DESARROLLO COMUNITARIO, A.C.
Pino 2237, Colonia del Fresno
C.P. 44800
Guadalajara, Jalisco, Mexico
Phone: 011-52-3-811-09-44, 011-52-3-610-45-36
Fax: 011-52-3-811-07-14
E-mail: imdec@laneta.apc.org

RED MEXICANA DE ACCIÓN FRENTE AL LIBRE COMERCIO (RMALC)
Godard 20
Colonia Guadalupe Victoria
Mexico 07790 D.F.
Phone: 011-52-5-556-93-75/14
Fax: 011-52-5-556-93-16
E-mail: rmalc@igc.apc.org.
Website: http://www.laneta.apc.org/rmalc/rmalcing.htm

CONTRIBUTORS' NOTes

FRAN ANSLEY is an associate professor of law at the University of Tennessee College of Law in Knoxville, Tennessee. She has been active in continental coalitions responding to NAFTA, and has worked with the Tennessee Industrial Renewal Network and the Highlander Research and Education Center to link women workers affected by global restructuring on both sides of the US/Mexican border.

KIRSTIN APPENDINI is an economist and former professor in the Colegio de México in Mexico City. She is currently working with the Food and Agricultural Organization in Rome, co-ordinating research on food security issues at an international level.

LAUREN BAKER is a graduate of the Master's Program in Environmental Studies at York University. She is an educator and food security activist currently working with Annex Organics, a food alternative organization based at the Field to Table warehouse of FoodShare in Toronto, Ontario.

DEBORAH BARNDT teaches in the Faculty of Environmental Studies of York University, in the areas of critical education for social change, cultural production and women and development. She is a mother, popular educator, photographer, and author of several books, and has many years of experience working with migrant and immigrant women in Canada and in Central America.

ANTONIETA BARRÓN is a professor of Economics at the National University of Mexico (UNAM) in Mexico City. Specializing in rural employment, she has undertaken extensive survey research on internal and international migration over the past two decades, and has pioneered in studies of gender in the rural sector. Most recently, she has conducted research on the Mexican migrant workers brought to Ontario every summer through the FARMS program.

ANN EYERMAN completed the Master's Program in Environmental Studies at York University, where she studied women and work issues. Her major paper, "Doing What I Have to Do: Women and Work in Transition," is the basis for her book about women office workers, which she is now researching and writing for Second Story Press (forthcoming Fall 2000). She currently serves on the Board of Directors of Times Change Women's Employment Service and on the Executive Committee of the Clerical Workers Centre. She has spent most of her working career as a secretary.

DEBBIE FIELD is the executive director of FoodShare Metro Toronto, a grassroots organization whose mission is to "work with communities to improve access to affordable, nutritious food." For close to thirty years, Debbie has been an activist in the women's, union, environmental and social justice movements.

HARRIET FRIEDMANN is a professor of Sociology at the University of Toronto, with many years of experience in studying and writing about global food regimes. She has also been active in local food intiatives, serving as co-chair of the Toronto Food Policy Council.

JAN KAINER recently completed her PhD in Sociology at York University. Her dissertation analyzed pay equity negotiations in the supermarket sector in Ontario.

EGLA MARTINEZ-SALAZAR is completing the Master's Program in Environmental Studies at York University in Toronto. Guatemalan Mestiza by birth, she has experience in human rights, popular education, and peer counselling with abused women in Canada, Mexico and Guatemala. Her current research is on Indigenous peoples.

DEBORAH MOFFETT is a community food issues educator, a volunteer co-ordinator and a newsletter editor for a community food access program. She is taking a sabbatical from her graduate work in Environmental Studies to enjoy time with her young daughter.

MARY LOU MORGAN is director of the Field to Table program of Food-Share in Toronto. A founder of the Big Carrot Health Food Store, she has also co-authored *The Farm and City Cookbook* (Second Story Press).

OFELIA PEREZ PEÑA co-ordinates the Master's Program in Environmental Education at the University of Guadalajara in Mexico, and is also the Mexican co-ordinator for the Consortium on Community Sustainable Development and Planning. She did her master's degree on "popular environmental education," and is currently completing a doctorate at the Centro de Investigaciones y Estudios Superiores en Antropología Social (CIESAS) in Guadalajara.

ESTER REITER teaches in Social Sciences and co-ordinates the Women's Studies Program of Atkinson College at York University in Toronto. Her doctoral research on Burger King in the 1980s led to the publication of *Making Fast Food: From the Frying Pan into the Fryer* (McGill-Queen's University Press).

MARIA DOLORES VILLAGOMEZ currently works with the Center for Ecumenical Studies (CEE) in Mexico City. She previously taught at the University of Quetzalcoatl in Irapuato, Mexico, teaching political theory, research methodologies and communications. She has also worked as a journalist, as a correspondent for *Nueva Vida* and and as an editor for *Ciencia y Desarrollo*.

ROYALTIES DEDICATION

*The authors have agreed to donate all royalties of this book to the work of
two groups in Sayula, Jalisco, Mexico, who are advocating for the health of
the tomato fieldworkers as well as for the health of the land
itself. These groups, Grupo de Salud Nueva Vida (New Life Health Group)
and Amigos de la Naturaleza (Friends of Nature), have
collaborated with the Tomasita Project since 1996 and will make
good use of the book as well as the funds raised from its sale.*

PHOTO CREDITS

All photographs by Deborah Barndt, with the exception of
page 76, Maria Dolores Villagomez; page 141, Al Levenson;
and page 205, Janice Gillespie.